The University System and
Economic Development in
Mexico Since 1929

DAVID E. LOREY

The University System and Economic Development in Mexico Since 1929

Stanford University Press

Stanford, California

1993

Stanford University Press, Stanford, California
© 1993 by the Board of Trustees of the
Leland Stanford Junior University
Printed in the United States of America

CIP data appear at the end of the book

To Laura Meyer
for the first ten years

Acknowledgments

This study has benefited from the support and criticism of many people. My largest debt is to James W. Wilkie, who introduced me to life and work in Mexico and has been the main critic of the study from the outset. Three good friends and part-time critics of my research stand out for special thanks. Enrique Ochoa has followed the themes and problems of the project from its early beginnings in graduate seminars at UCLA and has provided many insights on Mexican history and historiography during travel in Mexico. Aída Mostkoff served as an insightful critic of general and conceptual aspects of the study as it developed. Laura Meyer, to whom I dedicate the book, has been a stimulating traveling companion in the Mexico beyond the paved road and has provided a refreshing, non-Mexicanist viewpoint.

Many scholars contributed helpful comments at different points during the preparation of the book. Manuscript drafts or selected chapters were read by Roderic Camp, Enrique Cárdenas, Stephen Haber, Raúl Hinojosa, James Lockhart, José Moya, Silvia Ortega Salazar, Sergio de la Peña, José Angel Pescador, Jesús Reyes Heroles, Carlos Alberto Torres, and Sergio Zermeño. The comments of these scholars helped me avoid numerous errors of fact and broadened the scope of both questions and interpretations. A special thanks is due John Coatsworth who, in a series of readings of different versions of the manuscript, raised many significant questions and suggested important modifications. I also want to acknowledge the moral support of Norris Hundley of UCLA and Clint Smith of Stanford University and the Hewlett Foundation. The usual disclaimers apply.

I am grateful for research support in Mexico and in Los Angeles. Licenciada Ader and her staff at the ANUIES library in Guadalupe Inn were generous with their time, copying machine, and coffee. Doctor Juan Casillas, Ing. Ermilo Marroquín, and Lic. Jesús Barrón of ANUIES helped me out in several pinches. Ing. J. Alberto González I. of the Dirección General de Profesiones gave me access to DGP archives and invaluable informal information in a long series of short conversations. The University Research Library at UCLA proved an inexhaustible resource, containing more material on my topic than many Mexican libraries devoted to higher education issues. Two research assistants at the UCLA Program on Mexico—Christof Weber and Martín Valadez—devoted significant portions of their time to the manuscript during various revisions.

Several sources of financial support helped the study along. Grants from UCLA's Program on Mexico and Latin American Center provided support for early research trips to Mexico. A UC-MEXUS Grant provided funds for research and writing during the final stages of the project. The Universidad de las Américas in Puebla, Mexico, provided me a stimulating academic setting and interested students, as well as numerous financial benefits, during the academic year 1987–88. Special thanks are due Enrique Cárdenas, rector of the UDLA, for his support during my stay in Cholula and his continued interest in the project through its completion.

Finally, I would like to thank Grant Barnes, Peter Kahn, and Julie Carlson of Stanford University Press for their support and editorial labors.

Contents

Preface

Since at least the late 1950s, Mexican leaders and scholars as well as outside observers have spoken of a Mexican university system in crisis. Policymakers have expressed concern over student political activism and violence, apparently declining quality, and crowded campuses. When the student movement of 1966–68 turned violent in 1968, world attention focused on the Mexican university and its crisis.

During the severe economic slump of the 1980s, the fundamental weaknesses of the Mexican economy—its inefficiency and inability to compete in the world marketplace—were sometimes attributed to failings of the university system. The intense discussion that took place after 1982 about how to restructure the Mexican economy often drew the university system to its center. Many believed that the university was out of touch with the policy priorities of Mexican leaders, did not fulfill the economy's needs for professionals, or did not provide significant social mobility.

The original aim of this study was to examine the university crisis and how it had affected the university system's ability to provide the professionals needed for economic development. My initial hypothesis was that the higher-education system had been constrained in this effort by attempts to educate large and steadily increasing numbers of Mexicans to the university level. I intended to measure need for professionals in certain career areas and assess Mexico's historical success in meeting those needs.

I have expanded greatly on these original goals to include a new understanding of the "crisis" and how the need for professionals can be measured. Two important factors made this broader analysis necessary. First, it seemed to me that the dominant characteristics of the perceived crisis could not have solely intra-university causes, but rather must reflect the nature of economic growth and social mobility in Mexico. Second, the characteristics of the crisis, far from showing a university system on the verge of collapse, could be construed as indicating a long-term adaptation of the university to the reality of Mexican development. Rather than look solely at the university's troubles, I have studied the university system in the context of the outside forces that have shaped its various roles.

There are three reasons why I have not made the measurement of success or failure to educate "enough" professionals, or the "right" kinds of professionals, the principal aim of the study. First, there is no universal standard that allows assessment of the "critical mass" of experts necessary in a particular country for achieving economic development goals. Any use of "manpower" ratios in the developed countries as a standard fails to take into account the widely divergent development paths of wealthier and poorer countries. Second, since the late 1950s the Mexican system has been producing large numbers of graduates who are unable to find employment at the professional level. Employment trends are closely related to university output and must be carefully considered in any discussion of "needs" for professionally skilled persons. And third, professional-level skills are not the only product of Mexican university training. The relationship between the university system and social mobility greatly affects the demand for places at the university and the supply of professionally skilled persons. I came to see that the history of the Mexican university must be analyzed along with its essential counterpart—the history of employment opportunities for professionals.

To carry out my research, I developed original time-series data to reexamine the historical roles of the university and the aspects of the university system that were thought to be in crisis. I used quantitative data to explore three basic questions: How has the university responded historically to government policy for economic development? How has the university responded to the economy's demand for professionals in specific areas of expertise and at different levels of expertise? And how has the university responded to demands for upward social mobility through higher education?

The explicit quantification of these questions in the following chapters contributes to the existing literature on the Mexican university system in several important ways. Previously, essentially quantitative assumptions about the university and its role went untested; no one had ever considered long-term trends in the number of university graduates and their fields of study in the context of economic and social change. In addition, as I began my work I uncovered a reservoir of quantitative data never before developed for purposes of scholarly inquiry. The quantitative basis of the study thus stems from a major gap in research on the Mexican university rather than from any belief that a quantitative approach yields a more objective view. Throughout the study I stress not the numbers for any given year but rather the long-term trends revealed in time-series data. Trends are reinforced by the comparison of overlapping data sets and secondary materials.

I chose to focus on the period from 1929 to 1989 because these sixty years represent a key period in Mexican political and economic history. Bracketed within these dates are the progressive institutionalization of political change under a series of three official parties and a full cycle of state-led economic development. The goals of development were first articulated by Mexican presidents in the 1930s and reached their fullest expression (and greatest degree of internal contradiction) in the late 1970s. The rapid dismantling of the state's role in the economy after 1985 and the political crisis brought about by a serious opposition threat in the elections of 1988 marked the period's close.

Analysis of quantitative data for the period from 1929 to 1989 reveals that, on the one hand, Mexican universities may not now be producing the sorts of expertise which policymakers and scholars think is necessary for development in a period of an open economy and Free Trade with the United States, quality may have declined gradually over time, and the university may not advance social mobility much. Yet, on the other hand, the university system and its students have responded pragmatically, perhaps inevitably, to a difficult set of demands by the government, the economy, and society, suggesting a substantial degree of "success" for the university system as a whole. The evidence of the university's response, detailed in the following chapters, suggests that the crisis is not fundamentally a *university* crisis but rather lies in the economy and society at large.

Because I found that the development of the university system and professional employment had both economic and social implications, this study is by necessity an exercise in both economic and social history. I hope the book will further our understanding of the relationship between economic and social change in twentieth-century Mexico.

D.E.L.

Figures and Tables

Figures

Statistical Appendix Tables

xviii / *Figures and Tables*

The University System and
Economic Development in
Mexico Since 1929

CHAPTER I

Introduction

The Revolution of 1910 shook Mexico to its foundations. Ten years of civil war and intense political infighting reshaped the social and political map of the country and changed the way Mexicans thought of themselves and their future. The diverse forces that had brought about the upheaval united behind the Constitution of 1917, a document that synthesized the myriad desires for change unleashed during the Revolution. The loose coalition of victors that emerged from the ruins of the violent decade oversaw the rise of an increasingly active state during the 1920s. Focusing on political stabilization and economic reconstruction, these leaders set Mexico on the path of rapid economic and social change.

By 1929, with economic growth restarted and significant political challenges to the ruling group successfully repelled, Mexican leaders took the first major step toward "institutionalizing" the Revolution by consolidating competing political factions into the first official party of the Revolution—the Partido Nacional Revolucionario (PNR). The PNR united Mexico's diverse regional interests and cleared the way for the energetic pursuit of economic and social goals. Institutionalization had two essential objectives: to forestall the rebellions of regional strongmen, which had fueled a decade of fighting after 1910, and to channel the economic and social aspirations released by the Revolution.

As part of its 1929 initiative to institutionalize the Revolution, the government formally incorporated the university system into its development plans. Policymakers saw the university system as central to the process of institutionalization—necessary for political stabilization, economic development, and social change. The university system and Mexican development were to evolve in a symbiotic fashion, closely linked in both public policy and popular imagination.

Since 1929 the Mexican university system has been shaped by three principal challenges: the policy priorities of Mexico's leaders, the demand of a changing economy for professionals in specific areas and at specific levels of expertise, and the broad-based demand for social mobility by way of professional education.[1] Government goals for the university system, laid out in a general fashion in the Constitution of 1917, focused on making university education a spur to the two main components of development policy: rapid economic growth and government-sponsored social reform. Together, these two components constituted a major challenge to the university—a demand that the university be responsive to government plans for economic and social transformation.

The government's challenge to the university immediately called into question the university's form and its relation to the state. How could the university meet the government's needs and at the same time achieve the status of an independent critical body? President Emilio Portes Gil (1928–30) attempted to solve the problem by granting the National University of Mexico its autonomy—freedom from direct government intervention—in 1929.[2] The university would henceforth "freely determine its programs of study, methods of teaching, and the application of funds and resources."

Despite the granting of autonomy, a strong connection between the state and the university system remained. The organic law of the National Autonomous University of Mexico (UNAM) of 1929 illustrates how the university and the government were linked from that time on. The first article stated that the role of the university was to educate those professionals that are "useful to society." The university was to be a "national" institution that would contribute to the achievement of state goals, and the university's autonomy would remain subject to "the vigilance of public opinion and the representative organs of the government."[3] University autonomy was thus made conditional on the university's support of the government program. In particular, the UNAM was expected to educate the professionals needed for the development strategies of the government.

In return for the cooperation of universities, the government would not limit enrollment, force universities to increase fees, influence the fields of study of students, raise achievement standards, or in any other way attempt to control internal university policy. Yet the government would retain a significant measure of control by determining the total level of university financial support. Because Mexico's leaders and intellectuals were committed to universal and free education, the university never charged more than nominal fees for its services—the large gap between fees and costs was made up by a large government subsidy. Such an exchange of benefits and cooperation was standard operating procedure in Mexico from early in the revolutionary period. Because in 1929 UNAM was the sole national university, both written and unwritten agreements would serve as a model for the entire university system.

After 1929 universities also responded to the demands of the Mexican economy for professional expertise. The careers that university students chose and the sorts of jobs they found were intimately related to Mexico's economic development. It is generally agreed that the development of professional skills through formal education is crucial to "modernization" or "development," and there is a large body of literature on this relationship. But the structure and function of a university system are also shaped by economic realities—most importantly, employment opportunities for professionals. Economic development influences professional employment; professional employment in turn affects the evolution of a university system.

For a half century between 1929 and 1982, the economic

environment in which the university system evolved was characterized by the active protection and guidance of the state.[4] Policymakers saw the government's task as overseeing the relationship between economic growth and social change, balancing the interests of the private sector with a strong public presence.[5] A large political center supported these aims, hoping that state management of development would lead to a rate of economic growth greater than the rate of population increase, to price and financial stability, to enlarged social-welfare services, and to an increase in labor's share of productivity.[6] By establishing the mechanisms to accomplish these goals, the active state would "institutionalize" the changes promised by the Revolution.[7]

Economic policy went through several distinct phases between 1929 and 1982, all of which witnessed the growing presence of the state in the economy. The 1930s were a decade of frantic economic reorganization. President Lázaro Cárdenas (1935–40) stressed social restructuring and is best remembered for his agrarian reform, which distributed land to peasant communities.[8] Cárdenas also set the stage for economic growth based on the expansion of industry by nationalizing or extending state control over basic industrial inputs such as rail transport, electricity, and oil. Under Cárdenas, the government subsidized a wide range of goods and services, including food and education for urban workers.

The 1940s and 1950s saw an emphasis on economic development through rapid industrialization. Implicit protection provided by restrictions on U.S. exports during World War II touched off three decades of dramatic manufacturing expansion oriented toward a rapidly growing domestic market. During the administration of Manuel Avila Camacho (1941–46), the implicit protection provided by the war was joined by U.S. investment, an increased demand for Mexico's agricultural exports, and policy to stimulate "new and necessary" industries. After the war, protection from competing exports and implicit supports for industry became explicit economic policy (import-substituting industrialization) under presidents Miguel Alemán (1947–52) and Adolfo Ruiz Cortines (1953–58). The 1940s and 1950s were also characterized by stepped-up government investment in infrastructure projects to enhance industrialization—dams, irrigation networks, roads, and hydroelectric works.

In the 1960s and 1970s the state's presence in the economy continued to expand. Under presidents Adolfo López Mateos (1959–64), Gustavo Díaz Ordaz (1965–70), Luis Echeverría (1971–76), and José López Portillo (1977–82), the share of GNP claimed by central-government expenditure climbed steadily, from 11.1 percent under López Mateos to 12.2 percent under Díaz Ordaz, to 15.9 percent under Echeverría, and finally to 26.5 percent under López Portillo. After outbreaks of social unrest in the late 1950s, López Mateos and Díaz Ordaz refocused government policy on balancing economic and social priorities and reemphasized the social role of the state for the first time since the 1930s. The pace of state expansion into both economic and social spheres increased during the period, culminating in the explicitly statist administrations of Echeverría and López Portillo. Total government expenditure (including central government and the decentralized parastatals) reached 52.2 percent of GDP in 1982; employment in the public sector grew to 20 percent of all employment in 1983.

The state-led strategy that had lasted more than fifty years collapsed with the Mexican economic crisis of the 1980s. In 1982, international prices for oil plummeted and the burden of debt raised against oil reserves in the 1970s grew unmanageable, especially with the peaking of interest rates. Mexico's declaration of bankruptcy shook the world's financial markets. As Mexican leaders began searching for ways out of the immediate crisis after 1982, they found that the country's industrial base was inefficient and uncompetitive. As a consequence, Mexico would be unable to follow the new world model of using exports of manufactured goods to pull the economy out of its slump and to restart growth. Raising the efficiency and competitiveness of industry became the first priority of the governments of Miguel de la Madrid (1983–88) and Carlos Salinas de Gortari (1989–94). De la Madrid and Salinas began dismantling the state-led model through privatization of state enterprises, increased foreign investment, and the opening of the economy to foreign trade. Under Salinas, policymakers came to see a free trade agreement with the United States as the primary way to solve the underlying problems of the Mexican economy.

The breakdown of state-led economic development during the 1980s had a major impact on the Mexican university system. The university system had been viewed in the state-led model as one of the key institutions in advancing government policy priorities. But the university system was supposed to have contributed to the efficiency, technological sophistication, and competitiveness of the Mexican economy. If it had not played its assigned role, why not? Could it play that role in the future? While the university system came to be seen as a scapegoat after 1982, it was also looked to as a possible savior.

The Mexican university system was also shaped by social demands after 1929. Mexicans came to see university education as a way to derive individual benefit from the economic development promised by leaders. Higher education would lead to increased income and to a better standard of living. Pablo González Casanova, the Mexican sociologist and former rector of UNAM, expressed these hopes in 1962: "In today's Mexico, which is being industrialized and urbanized, there is permanent social mobility. The peasants of yesterday are today's workers, and the workers' children can be professionals."[9] Because these hopes were widespread among intellectuals, policymakers, and Mexicans at large, university education became one of the most important symbols of upward mobility and social status in Mexico.

Three sets of questions about the nature of these interrelated demands—the demands exerted by policymakers, by the economy, and by society—and the university's response to them are explored in the following chapters. First, how have changing policy priorities of the Mexican government affected the university's production of professionals? Has the Mexican university trained professionals in numbers and in fields of expertise consistent with government plans for development? Second, how has the economy's changing need for professionals and technicians shaped the functioning of the university system? What does the evolution of the university imply about the nature of economic development in Mexico since 1929? And third, has the university been able to advance social mobility? What has been the social function of the university over time?

Because of its central role in the mythology of the Institutionalized Revolution, its relationship to political power, and its importance in the process of development, university education has drawn attention from many disciplines.[10] Historical writing on the Mexican university system has tended to treat the university as a hermetic institution, one that has an evolutionary dynamic independent of outside economic and social evolution. Such a focus, relying heavily on traditional, institutional sources and perspectives, has left unexplored the question of why different forms and functions of the university developed over time. The most important immediate products of universities—professional-level graduates—have seldom figured in such institutional histories.

A great number of analysts have focused on sociological aspects of university education and have considerably expanded our knowledge of how the Mexican university reinforces the power of elites. These observers are concerned with elite political actors, and they address university education principally as a defining characteristic of elites. But the principal historical role of the Mexican university has not been to produce elites, and university-trained elites are not representative of Mexican university students in general. Elites do not study the same professional fields as do the majority of Mexican students, and the majority of university graduates do not become important actors on the national political stage. As one observer of Latin American higher education noted, "Universities are not simply political institutions . . . [but] continuously graduate scientists, professionals, and intellectuals who [contribute] to the development and functioning of their nations."[11]

The eventful political history of the Mexican university has also been covered well by scholars. The granting of university autonomy in 1929 set the stage for a long series of political contests between university students and the state; these conflicts have been the focus of much study. The student movement of 1968 in particular has had many chroniclers. Political scientists have also contributed important works that detail the modus vivendi undergirding the relationship between students and government leaders and that describe the internal political culture of universities.

Only rarely have economic aspects of university education

made their way into the dominant currents of writing on Mexican universities, the one key exception being the work of the human-capital school. The concept of human capital was developed in the 1950s to describe the role of education in making labor more productive in the developed world. The theory posited that expenditure for education should be seen as investment in human capital (rather than as consumption) and argued that education was a key ingredient in increasing productivity, spurring economic growth, and creating an egalitarian distribution of wealth.[12] The assumed implications of the human-capital model for the poorer countries of the world were summed up by Harbison and Myers in their *Manpower and Education: Country Studies in Economic Development* (1965): "In the final analysis, the wealth of a country is based upon its power to develop and to effectively utilize the innate capacities of its people. If a country is unable to develop its human resources, it cannot build anything else, whether it be a modern political system, a sense of national unity, or a prosperous economy."[13]

The notion of developing human capital through education was not a new one in Mexico; it was enshrined early on in the rhetoric of the Revolution. It is found, for example, in the work of Mexico's most famous twentieth-century muralist, Diego Rivera. On the walls of the Ministry of Public Education, Rivera painted pictures of peasants and workers being given books while a revolutionary guard watches over them. The artist asserted pictorially that investment in basic education, actively supported by the state, would be one of the social and political cornerstones of the new Mexico.

The hope that investment in human capital would lead to both increased national productivity and individual well-being had a direct impact on public policy as well as on rhetoric in Mexico. During the 1960s and 1970s, policymakers sought to stimulate economic development through quantitative expansion at all levels of education, but particularly at the university level.[14] Application of human-capital ideas in Mexico spawned a literature on higher education and "manpower" in Mexico in the 1960s.[15]

The 1970s saw the questioning of several major tenets of

human-capital theory. In the most penetrating criticism, scholars suggested that the productivity of workers in developing economies is not as closely related to skills gained through education as it is to the productivity inherent in jobs created by an economy. The education process, rather than providing a worker with specific skills necessary for raising productivity, makes job applicants "trainable" by shaping their attitudes and their aptitude, providing a "fit" among workers, jobs, and firms. Worker "trainability" is determined by employers only partly on the basis of specific technical qualifications gained through education, since bringing a worker up to the level of productivity of a job is in large part a function of the personal characteristics of the worker. Desirable characteristics of workers, frequently attitudinal rather than manual or cognitive in nature, reduce the cost of training and turnover to employers and principally in this manner lead to higher profits.[16]

Many of the studies that followed the work of the early human-capital theorists showed that higher education does not cause economic development. Rather, the structure and function of higher educational systems are shaped by the process of economic development itself. A new literature on higher education in Mexico emerged in the 1970s to relate this fundamental change in perspective to Mexican experience.[17] I take this perspective as my point of departure in the present study. I am concerned primarily with examining how the functioning of the Mexican university system was shaped by the pattern of economic development after 1929.

The present study proceeds by quantifying and analyzing questions raised many times in the existing literature but left unanswered. How many professionals have Mexican universities educated? Has Mexico trained "enough" professionals? What do we mean by "enough"? In which fields have professionals been trained? Have they been trained in the "right" fields? How do we determine which fields are the "right" ones?

My analysis of these fundamental questions, and the economic and social roles of the university that they imply, is based on original quantitative data for graduates of all Mexican universities in ten major professional fields since 1929. To date historians have not developed long-term series of statistical data on university graduates or considered the few data that exist in useful form. The sources for data on the Mexican university system are scattered physically, many are unpublished, and some have been published in forms that seem to defy historians' efforts to use them. It takes a great deal of work to assemble unorganized data sets into consistent time series for in-depth analysis of historical change. Reliable data on numbers of professionals educated at Mexican universities and on their fields of study do exist, but they have never been systematically, comprehensively studied.

The data make it possible to analyze the function of the university system in Mexico as the result of thousands of discrete decisions about economic and social opportunity—in essence, the job market for professionals and technicians. Because neither the government nor universities have intervened to guide students in their choice of career (at least until late in the period examined here), students' decisions are the prime indicator of policy, economic, and social environments. Students' decisions are our key to assessing whether demands by government, the economy, and society have been met over time. The data make it possible to see the evolution of the university system as a reflection of deep economic and social change.

The comparison of original data sets forms the basic methodology of the work. I set data on university graduates and egresados (students who have completed the coursework but not the required thesis project for the licentiate degree) in the context of trends in a wide variety of economic and social phenomena, ranging from federal expenditure and occupational structure to social mobility. I have not in general performed complex statistical manipulations of the data. The idea of making sophisticated statistical tests is attractive at first glance, but because of the nature of the data tests will not yield conclusive findings; historical meaning cannot be derived mechanically from such tests. For detailed series and discussion, the reader is advised to consult my companion volume, *The Rise of the Professions in Twentieth-Century Mexico: University Graduates and Occupa-*

tional Change. A sample of the original statistical series is presented here in a statistical appendix. The most important time-series and cross-sectional data have been presented in graphic form in each chapter in order to make the approach more accessible and to make clear the quantitative basis of my arguments.

My approach leads us beyond the political aspects of the university that have been featured so prominently in the work of past writers on the Mexican university. The reader will not find detailed descriptions of the university crises of 1929 and the mid-1930s, of the university and social crisis of 1966–68, or of the university reform conflict of 1986–87. Yet the analysis offered here can be used to place those events, and other political aspects of the role of the university in Mexican society, in the context of economic and social change since 1929.

My findings suggest that the political crises that have attracted so much attention from observers of the Mexican university are related ultimately to the development of the Mexican economy and the university's integration into that development. The paradox of the Mexican university crisis is that the crisis is not only, not perhaps even primarily, a crisis in the university but rather a reflection of stresses outside the university. Expected to lead development, the university system has followed development. This paradox provides insight to many questions about the development of the Mexican university system.

The study is organized around the three historical demands on the Mexican university outlined above: policy demand, economic demand, and social demand. Each chapter examines issues related to one of the demands and to the central paradox of university crisis in Mexico. Chapter Two describes how the three demands developed during the colonial period and nineteenth century and how they took their present form after 1929. After the Revolution of 1910, debate over the purposes of the university in Mexican society took two basic forms: one group of policymakers championed a socially active institution with a socialist orientation, another upheld the university system's importance to economic growth. Underneath the currents of policy debate a relatively stable policy toward the university system prevailed.

Chapter Three assesses the impact of government policy priorities on the university system's functioning. This difficult and complex task is carried out in two steps. First, the basic dimensions of the development of professional fields are outlined; second, trends in this development are compared to the evolution of government expenditure. The story of the relationship between the university system and the government is revealed to be one of subtle responsiveness rather than of crisis.

Chapters Four and Five examine the need of a changing economy for professionals and the impact of this need on the university system. Chapter Four gauges the economy's demand for specific areas of professional expertise and for different levels of expertise over time. This demand and the university's response reveal a Mexican economy increasingly unable to create new professional opportunities after the 1950s. The university system responded to changing economic demands by modifying, both quantitatively and qualitatively, the education of professionals. In the process Mexican universities—public and private, metropolitan and provincial—worked together as a system. While many writers have assumed that the lack of organization among Mexican universities gainsays systematic coordination, lack of comparable curricula and admissions criteria do not rule out coordinated response to economic and social demands. Chapter Five discusses the functioning of the university system by examining quality at Mexican universities, differences in employment opportunities for private- and public-university graduates, and the historical deconcentration of the system.

The social role of the university system, analyzed in Chapter Six, has in large part determined the university response to the demands of policy and economy. The Revolution promised upward mobility and the attainment of professional status, and the university had to comply in order to contain social and political pressures arising from the stresses of development. I explore trends in historical social mobility, the social profile of public-university students, and the careers of women professionals to illuminate this role of the university system. Chapter Seven concludes the volume by summarizing findings and returning to the central paradox of university crisis in Mexico—a contradiction that helps us answer many questions while raising new issues and suggesting policy dilemmas for the future.

CHAPTER 2

Three Historical Demands on the University

The dialectic of challenge and response that links the university system to economy and society in Mexico did not begin in 1929. While the policy challenge was fully expressed with the incorporation of the university in government plans during that year, the demand of the Mexican economy for professional skills and the widespread demand for social mobility and status through professional careers were present from the colonial period.

The Colonial Period

During the first century of European settlement in Mexico, the society of sixteenth-century Europe was transplanted to Mexico in all its essentials, including the professions, with their formal and informal professional hierarchies and mechanisms for controlling access to the practice of professional careers. The lawyer and the doctor were members of the first waves of immigrants; lesser professionals—notaries, barber-surgeons, and teachers—were also present from the beginning. The progressive professionalization taking place in Europe developed apace in the New World.[1]

Formal study in professional fields and the granting of official permission to practice professions were established early in Mexico. The Royal and Pontifical University of Mexico (the precursor of the UNAM) opened its doors in 1552, and with its successors would dominate Mexico's professional life until the late 1950s. This university was both an autonomous organization and an institution that received its funding from Spain's royal treasury, an arrangement that survived into the twentieth century and remains a source of conflict between the public university and the state in Mexico.

Theology, law, and medicine were the main subjects of study at the university until the early twentieth century. Medicine, because of its ties to a past of barber-surgeons and witchcraft, ranked lower in prestige than either theology or law.[2] Professionals such as teachers and notaries were trained outside the university, in the Church, or through an apprenticeship. From the beginning, different levels of professional skills were ranked according to the prestige attached to them by society.

Economic and social demands on the structure of professional education were present from the beginning. Both demands were shaped by local conditions and processes, rather than by imperial law or institutions, and the two were closely related. In the early period, however, the social demand had the greatest influence over the nature of professional training.

In colonial times, the principal social demand on the university was that it provide professional status to members of families with property and standing, although not necessarily to the families of the highest echelon. Children of the topmost elite generally did not seek professions because they already had "careers" in family businesses and because no appreciable extra prestige would result from their acquiring a professional career. "A lawyer of elite background gave more prestige to the profession than it gave to him."[3]

The professional hierarchy was dominated by lawyers, who practiced both canon and civil law. Lawyers were always in great demand in Mexico because of Mexico's economic and political importance in the Spanish overseas empire, and the demand for lawyers grew over time as colonial society became increasingly complex. The government bureaucracy, characterized by many competing branches and departments with overlapping responsibilities, generated an ever-increasing demand for lawyers to manage its affairs. Every economic pursuit, then as now, had its legal aspect, and as colonial society became more and more complicated, its demand for lawyers increased.

The elite status of lawyers within the professions is clear from their family backgrounds. Almost all lawyers came from families that had agricultural holdings, ran commercial establishments, had a history of professional or government employment, or some combination of the three. To the sponsoring family, a lawyer certified respectability, provided legal advice, and served as a contact with influential persons in business and government.[4] Lawyers themselves were prominent in estate ownership, commerce, mining, and, to a lesser extent, money lending.

The second major social function of the professions was to provide social mobility for non-elites. The university offered an opportunity for the ambitious and talented to join the ranks of the privileged, and for this reason a considerable number of university students were poor.[5] The lower professions, and particularly medicine, became gradually filled by *mestizos* (people of mixed ethnicity) and other persons of humble social background. This was particularly noticeable in the case of barber-surgeons, who were perceived to be of a much lower status than doctors (*médicos*).

Some persons of humble background even made it into the higher professions. All the laws about the purity of blood lines necessary for practicing law or theology could not keep mestizos and mulattoes from rising in some cases to the top of the professional hierarchy. As they achieved wealth and position, they came to be considered "Spaniards," in accordance with dominant attitudes toward race and class in early Mexico.[6] In low-level professions such as medicine, the pressure from mestizos, mulattoes, and humble Spaniards grew greater over the course of the colonial period as persons of mixed ancestry made up an ever-larger percentage of the Mexican population. By the end of the period, the pressure from below found social and political expression as many lower-level professionals participated in the struggles for independence from Spain. Lower-level professionals were clearly more dissatisfied with their limited opportunities for mobility than with an imperial system that had less of a direct effect on their daily lives.[7]

From early on, then, the system of professional education provided and maintained the social status of the relatively well-off while giving opportunities to humbler persons working their way up the social ladder. To some extent, the professions were divided between those that fulfilled the former function—law and theology—and those that catered to the second group of aspirants—medicine, notarial work, and teaching. The humble persons who found their way into the most prestigious professional niches were exceptions to the rule. Two related social developments characterized professional training. First, the offspring of professionals tended to themselves become professionals, causing the development of professional families. And second, members of professional families would generally follow different careers—one the law, another theology—creating within families a diversity of professional careers with similar levels of prestige.

The development of the professions was closely linked to the structure and growth of the Mexican economy, and this link would grow stronger and more important over time. Because the main motor of economic development throughout the colonial period was silver mining, an increasing number of professionals were affiliated, directly and indirectly, to the mining, transport, and trade of silver. Whenever a dispute arose involving a mine, for example, lawyers would be needed to straighten out claims, and accountants as well as mining inspectors would be required to evaluate the venture in question.

In addition, the development of increasingly sophisticated silver-mining technology required a growing corps of mining technicians. For most of the colonial period, mining know-how was empirical and mining professionals were trained by experience. Yet mining expertise was nonetheless sophisticated,[8] and each further refinement of mining techniques required more highly trained mining technicians. By the middle of the sixteenth century, for example, when surface ores had been depleted, the mercury amalgamation process for recovering silver from poorer ores was developed. This innovation led to a boom in output that lasted to the end of the century and increased the demand for professional masters of the technique.[9] Later technical introductions, such as blasting and the cyanide process, brought similar demands for professionals skilled in associated techniques, and as the colonial period progressed, the tendency toward ever-larger mining operations, as veins exploited early on became exhausted and mines were sunk ever deeper, created a need for basic architectural and hydraulic knowledge. Mining expertise became more specialized, and mine owners came to rely increasingly on trained experts rather than directing mining operations themselves.

Mining expertise combined European technology and Mexican technique. Iron tools, gunpowder, and draft animals were early European introductions to New World mining, and Europeans knowledgeable in mining techniques contributed greatly to the development of New World techniques. Spaniards from the mining regions of the Iberian peninsula long dominated silver mining in the New World and in Mexico.[10] Yet even though foreigners and foreign equipment were important, Mexican miners developed very specialized and area-specific mining techniques over the course of the colonial period. At the turn of the nineteenth century, Mexican mining techniques were among the most advanced in the world, and were also uniquely suited to Mexico's geography and economy.

Although mining is the most obvious case, the professional fields clearly responded to other sectors of the changing colonial economy. The cotton and wool textile industries became highly developed in Orizaba, Puebla, and Querétaro, and their more sophisticated techniques and larger operations required more knowledgeable experts. The development of early industrial forms as well as the expansion of national and international commerce led to a great demand for accountants at all levels of the public and private economic hierarchies, anywhere that bookkeeping required more than rudimentary mathematics. Although there was no formal training in accounting until the nineteenth century, many students enrolled in mathematics and engineering courses in order to be able to work in commercial and administrative offices as accountants.[11] As the government bureaucracy expanded, government too began to need the services of trained professionals in many fields.[12]

In the early colonial period, most of the professionals who fulfilled the economy's demand for expertise were informally trained. Training in mining and accounting techniques, unlike preparations in law or medicine, generally did not take place at the university. For this reason, both mining and accounting professions were considered to have relatively low prestige. Formal training in such fields as commerce and money lending would only become important as Mexico's regional economies became increasingly integrated in the course of the nineteenth century.[13]

The non-institutional character of training in fields essential to the economy began to change toward the end of the colonial period, reflecting the increasing complexity of the colonial economy. In the last half of the eighteenth century, attempts were made to improve the quality of training in surgery, pharmaceutical studies, architecture, and mining. New, lay institutions were created for study in these fields. Only in the late eighteenth century did the training of mining experts, for example, become institutionalized on the scale of legal or medical studies, with the establishment in 1792 of the Mining College in Mexico City.

The Nineteenth Century

In the first half of the nineteenth century, newly independent Mexico experienced a period of economic decline and political instability. Public policy was seriously hampered by chronic fiscal crisis, and particularly by the lack of, or inability to exploit, a domestic tax base. All facets of Mexican society were affected by the severe depression in the mining industry, which lasted until at least mid-century. Adding to the economic and psychological shocks of the early independence period was the loss of half of the national territory to the United States in 1848.[14] University faculties devoted to professional training suffered from all these various stresses, especially from the depressed economy and the instability of political life. The university came to play an important role in economic and social change only with the establishment of relative political peace and the emergence of national programs for economic development after 1867.

Mexican Liberals of the nineteenth century saw the existing university in a very negative light, calling it "useless, pernicious, and irreformable."[15] This attitude was not shaped simply by the anticlericalism of the Liberals (the university was both "pontifical" and "royal") or by the fact that the university was a bastion of Conservative political strength. The university also seemed to Liberals a backwater of "unmodern" professional knowledge and learning.[16]

When they came to power in the last third of the century, Liberals brought with them the idea that the educational system should produce professionals for the rationalization of the Mexican economy, a role in line with their distinctly Mexican Positivism.[17] Liberals closed the university in 1865 and focused their attention on primary and preparatory education; higher education became the preserve of the professional schools formerly organized into the university. The aims of Liberals, summed up in the Law of Public Instruction of 1867, increasingly found expression in public policy after relative political calm was established under Porfirio Díaz, who ruled Mexico from 1876 to 1911. The Positivist slogan "Order and Progress," adopted by Díaz and his advisors, dominated public policy and the pursuit of economic development until the Revolution.

From 1867 on, and particularly under President Díaz, both the rhetorical and practical focus of higher-education policy settled on the economic utility of professional expertise, a view that led the Liberals to close the university from 1865 to 1910. Professionals were seen as especially important in the creation and maintenance of economic infrastructure: roads, railroads, ports, and other public works. Attitudes toward professional education were conditioned by the widely held conviction that rapid economic growth would lead Mexico into the modern world. And with the emphasis on the economic value of professional expertise came increased expenditure on higher education: spending on higher education grew under Díaz to seventeen times the amount spent for primary education.[18]

Díaz and his advisors believed that economic development depended on foreign technology and techniques as well as on foreign investment. As a result, European and U.S. professional expertise came to dominate the higher level of Mexico's economic development effort, both in policy and practice. The influence of foreign professional experts, particularly from the United States, is seen clearly in the development of economic infrastructure during the Porfiriato.[19] By the late Porfiriato, 61.8 percent of investment in railroads, 87.2 percent in electricity, 100 percent in petroleum, and 97.5 percent in mining were controlled by foreigners.[20] Foreign investment brought foreign experts. The early development of oil into Mexico's most important industry was accomplished almost entirely with U.S. capital and professional expertise. Companies contracted to survey Mexico's public lands were also often operated by foreign experts. In all four key economic areas—railroads, mining, oil, and real estate—professionals from Europe and the United States were prominent, reducing the immediate need for domestic education of professionals. Foreign experts were commonly employed in manufacturing as well; professionals were imported to help start up both textile and glassmaking operations in the late nineteenth century.[21]

Imported capital goods had an equally important effect on professional training. Mexico did not develop independent capital-goods, machine-tool, or specialty-metals industries during the late nineteenth century. The growth of the railroad, mining, and oil sectors was based on foreign machinery and therefore on foreign professional expertise. As a result of the lack of local employment in the production of capital goods, Mexico's leaders did not give priority to domestic professional education. Technical innovation occurred instead in more developed parts of the world and was transferred to Mexico by way of imported machinery and processes. Once innovation in the economy was dominated by foreigners, it would prove difficult to reverse.

During the course of the Porfiriato, some Mexicans expressed dissatisfaction with the prominence of foreigners in professional-level jobs. The late nineteenth century saw increasing complaints, for example, that Mexico imported foreign engineers when Mexican engineers were just as good.[22] One of the salient grievances in labor strikes of the first decade of twentieth century, including the famous mining strike at Cananea, Sonora, was that Mexicans were not being hired at the technician and professional levels. Although some companies did make a point of employing Mexican engineers and mechanics and employed U.S. workers only at the very highest levels of professional expertise, they were in the minority.[23]

Despite concern about the presence of foreign professionals and technical expertise, foreigners and their technologies did stimulate a measure of domestic technical innovation in the late nineteenth century, particularly in mining. Foreign capital and expertise made possible the exploration for and more efficient exploitation of mineral deposits. Both mechanical and chemical expertise came to play more important roles in the mining industry, stimulated by foreign experience in these areas, which were still relatively undeveloped in Mexico. Perhaps the most important late-nineteenth-century innovation in mining was the adoption of the cyanide process, which made recovery of silver from lean ores more efficient. The process accelerated the development of domestic professional expertise in fields relating to mining, construction, and hydraulics as water was harnessed for power and other inputs were developed for the new fine-crushing mills.

Even if the Mexican economy did rely heavily on foreign expertise for its late-nineteenth-century economic spurt, the economic recovery during the last third of the century greatly stimulated domestic training of professionals, particularly engineers. In 1867 the military and mining colleges were reorganized into the National Engineering School. The establishment of this school marks the beginning of concern with creating a national base for professional training. In fact, the influence of U.S. know-how was itself important in this development. In 1901, for example, the American Institute of Mining Engineers held its annual convention in Mexico City; the U.S. engineers toured the country's mining regions and were feted by their Mexican counterparts at every stop.[24] The influence was to continue: especially talented Mexican students at the National Engineering School were given grants to study at advanced levels in Europe and the United States.[25]

The development of domestic professional expertise in mining, agriculture, and allied fields reflected the development of the Porfirian economy. Mining dominated the economy of the Porfiriato as it had the period before independence. It was directly and indirectly linked to most other areas of the economy, stimulating the construction of railroads and the development of commercial agriculture. Development in the primary and secondary economic sectors was particularly pronounced in northern Mexico, where mining, railroad lines, and commercial agriculture were closely linked. In Sonora, Coahuila, and Chihuahua, the railroads, generally introduced to export minerals, would lead to the orientation of agricultural techniques and crops toward production for external markets. The development of both railroads and commercial agriculture, like that of mining, depended to a great extent on foreign capital and foreign professional expertise, and this reliance was particularly marked in the North.[26]

While mining dominated the Mexican economy during the Porfiriato, the last third of the nineteenth century was also a time of expansion in business, finance, and commerce not directly related to mining. As a result, formal training in business-related skills became increasingly common. Business training had been available from the beginning of the nineteenth century with some courses leading to professional degrees. But business-oriented programs were generally short technical courses and did not cover traditional university-level subjects such as Latin and philosophy, emphasizing instead writing and bookkeeping. The Higher School of Commerce and Administration was founded in 1868, reflecting the general economic expansion and the specific demands of banks and commercial establishments for more advanced business expertise. Business professionals were not accepted as the professional equals of lawyers, mining experts, or doctors in the late nineteenth century, but this would change in the twentieth.

The government itself played an important part in creating demand for professionally skilled persons. As it expanded the scope of its involvement in the economy, the government created many new positions at the professional level. State-sponsored public works such as railroads, irrigation, and other infrastructure projects greatly expanded the need for professionals, particularly engineers.[27] Even though the Liberal creed emphasized a passive role for government, and although the Porfiriato represented the height of Liberal power in Mexico, the government bureaucracy grew more rapidly than in any previous period. The bureaucracy that managed Porfirian development provided a large number of positions for lawyers, accountants, notaries, and doctors.

An explicit policy demand on the professional education system resulted in the late nineteenth century from the conscious planning of economic development by Díaz and his advisors. This planning affected the way educational theorists thought, stirred debate over the ideal role of the university in society, and greatly stimulated the consolidation of separate professional schools into a newly constituted national university in 1910. Although only a loosely defined plan in the late nineteenth century, the Díaz model for development constituted the first explicit expression of the idea that the university should respond to the policy priorities of the government.[28] The government's aims for development shaped the demand for professionals, directly and indirectly, and the growing state apparatus increased opportunities for professionals.

At the heart of the Porfirian planning effort was the group of professional men, advisors and associates of President Díaz, who were known as the "científicos" because of their faith in the scientific method and in the scientific planning of the economic development process in Mexico. Recent scholarship has shown the científicos to have been far less concerned with the creed of Positivism and its application in Mexico than they were with the practicalities of political management of Díaz's order and progress.[29]

Although the científicos were once portrayed as traitors because they supported foreign investment and took active personal interest in that investment, this negative view has recently undergone significant revision. The científicos are no longer seen as opportunists masquerading as Positivists, but rather as men who had a "genuine vision of a dynamic, developing Mexico."[30] While they may have shared the blind faith of the times in, for example, the profitable and lucrative capacity of railroads as the most important requisite of "progress,"[31] they were sincerely interested in bringing about the national development of Mexico. The notion that the científicos had an unreasonable faith in the power of economic growth to modernize Mexico, which has made them the scapegoats of champions of social revolution in Mexico, has also been challenged by recent scholarship. It is now acknowledged that "both científico thinking and government policy recognized that development also depended on factors which were 'non-economic.'"[32]

The científicos, in fact, were the first Mexican leaders to champion educational reform, preventive medicine, and urban sanitation as key components of progress.[33] And the ideas of the científicos were not eclipsed by Díaz's fall from power in 1910. Although the development strategies of the científicos were frequently ridiculed rhetorically by Mexico's postrevolutionary leaders, they were often adopted in practice.[34] The essence of their goals for the university, for example, were adopted, with rather minor modifications, by revolutionary and post-revolutionary regimes after 1910. Perhaps the most lasting legacy of the late-nineteenth-century científicos in the realm of university education is the debate over the purposes of universities and professional education. The debate over education took on much of its twentieth-century shape in the late nineteenth century with the writings of such intellectuals as Justo Sierra, a member of the científico clique, and would take center stage in education policy disputes after the Revolution of 1910.

Thus the científicos constitute a link between the development policies of the late nineteenth century and those of the period after 1910 with their idea that the university should answer the demands of policy.[35] The National University established by Justo Sierra in 1910 was given the responsibility of meeting the needs of the nation as defined by the nation's leaders, but the specific forms of that responsibility remained undefined until the 1920s. The internal goals established for the National University when it opened just before the Revolution broke out were limited to strictly professional and academic concerns—making available advanced training in law, medicine, engineering, and the arts; providing research facilities; and training secondary

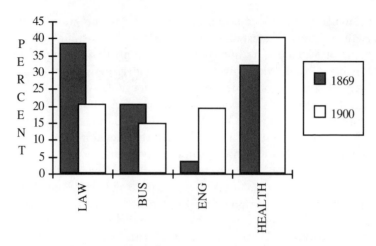

Figure 2–1. Mexican Professionals in Four Fields, 1869 and 1900. SOURCE: Calculated from Mílada Bazant, "La república restaurada y el porfiriato," in *Historia de las profesiones en México*, pp. 208, 214–215, 218–219.

teachers and university professors to educate more Mexicans.[36]

While there is very little quantitative data on professionals for the colonial period, particularly for the early centuries,[37] data for the late nineteenth century are more plentiful, if not very broad or consistent in coverage.[38] The distribution of professionals by field in late-nineteenth-century Mexico illustrates the effects of the three demands outlined above (Fig. 2–1). Data for 1869 and 1900 allow us to gauge change between the mid-nineteenth and the early twentieth centuries.

The growing importance of engineers as a percentage of all professionals shows the stimulation of the late-nineteenth-century process of economic development and reveals its basis. Business professionals, whose share of all professionals declined due to the rapid rise of engineering, grew rapidly in absolute terms. The high percentage share held by lawyers illustrates the functioning of professional education to meet social demand for status. Clearly this profession, dominated by the upper and middle classes, remained very important in the late nineteenth century. The social mobility function of professional careers is also apparent in the prominence of the medical profession, which allowed for more social climbing opportunities than law.

The professional backgrounds of the científicos reveal an interesting pattern. An exhaustive study of men associated with the científico group shows that fully 71.4 percent were lawyers, 11.9 percent engineers or surveyors. The economic and social functions of professional education, as well as the relationship between científico planning and professional expertise, are apparent in this sample of the elite that directed Mexico's late-nineteenth-century economic development.[39]

The Twentieth Century

In the twentieth century, and particularly after 1929, state-sponsored plans for economic development grew in scope and influence and came to constitute a major demand on the university. Higher-education policy, rooted in the aims of the Constitution of 1917, formed a rhetorical cornerstone of government plans for both economic and social change, and debate over the role of university education came to the fore in national policy disputes. The lines of debate would force policymakers to alternate between, or combine, two conflicting objectives: the need to provide professionals for economic development and the need to establish opportunities for social mobility.

The contemporary debate over the purposes of the university can be traced to José Vasconcelos, rector of the National University (1920–21) and the first secretary of Public Education (1920–25). Beginning in the 1920s, Vasconcelos championed education for Mexico's masses as the means to free Mexico from "barbarism and misery." Reacting against the Mexican Positivism of the late nineteenth century, the elitist educational system that developed under Díaz, his teacher Justo Sierra, and the National University Sierra had created in 1910, Vasconcelos emphasized the spiritual and cultural over the utilitarian functions of education. In Vasconcelos's view, education should serve to inculcate nationalism and democracy.[40] Most participants who have entered into the ideological fray since the 1920s have shared Vasconcelos's conviction that the higher-education system should serve all Mexicans and should bring Mexico into the modern world on Mexican terms. But there has been little agreement on the appropriate means to this end.

Since the heyday in the 1920s of Vasconcelos's educational crusade, higher-education policy has been dominated by a conflict between two major ideological currents represented here by the two men who articulated them most fully: Vicente Lombardo Toledano (Mexico's premier labor leader in the 1930s) and Antonio Caso (philosopher and renowned litterateur).[41] These important cultural personalities defined the terms of debate for years after their active involvement in it had ended.

Lombardo Toledano urged, beginning in the 1930s, that the university should adopt Marxism as an official university philosophy. Marxism would dominate teaching, study, research, and cultural diffusion. Followers of Lombardo conceived of the university's proper role as helping the state to further the social goals of the Revolution of 1910. The professional expertise produced by the university was seen by proponents of this view as a way of linking academia with the working classes—the opening of technical careers would provide social mobility.

In contrast to Lombardo, Antonio Caso championed academic freedom (particularly the freedom of professors to teach what they wished). Espousing a multitude of independent views over a single ideological approach or an overarching state-university bond, Caso saw the university's role as conditioned by the needs of the Mexican economy. Supporters of Caso saw the development of professional expertise by the university as essentially reflexive, that is, the higher education system should adjust itself to the demands of economic development.[42]

Lombardo and Caso debated their views before the university's academic congress in 1933, and Lombardo was declared the winner by a vote of 22 to 7 among members of the audience.[43] But the vote was hardly the end of the affair: from 1944 to 1945 Caso served as rector of the UNAM and wrote the university code (1944; effective 1945) that has guided the UNAM ever since.

Mexican presidents have alternated between the two ideological stances represented by Lombardo and Caso in their official pronouncements and educational plans.[44] President Lázaro Cárdenas (1935-40) tried to impose Lombardo's socialist ideals on the higher education system in the mid-1930s. In 1946, under President Manuel Avila Camacho (1941-46), and while Caso was reworking the UNAM code, the thrust of Lombardo's and Cárdenas's work for all levels of education was undone by a rewriting of the constitutional article on education. These two ways of seeing the social and economic purposes of university education, humanitarian and utilitarian, were summed up in an anecdote by John Gunther, who visited Mexico in 1940. Gunther asked several eminent Mexicans of different professions what the country needed most. A musician answered "education and public health," seeing education as a social good. An ex-president of the republic answered "capital, technicians, education, and hard work," seeing education primarily as an economic good. These two responses show that tension still existed between the two goals long after the the most heated phase of the debate was over.[45] The debate continues in much current discussion of the university crisis.

Behind the debate over the proper role of the university, the Mexican government pursued relatively stable policy goals for the university system. The greatest element of policy continuity has been the emphasis on the production of professional expertise to meet the demands of the country's changing productive structure. The second element of policy continuity has been a linking of professional expertise with the goal of social mobility— professional careers, and thus university education, have been championed as a medium of social ascension. This linkage has provided a way to relate government aims to rhetoric emphasizing the university's role in offering upward social mobility for the children of workers and peasants. Just as in the prerevolutionary period the university provided status and mobility, the university system was widely seen after 1929 as controlling access to the most prestigious and high-paying jobs. The presidents generally considered most concerned with social change— Cárdenas and Echeverría—overtly attempted to facilitate the upward rise of working-class Mexicans through the higher-education system. Both presidents encouraged the development of lower-level technical programs that were shorter in duration and thus lower in opportunity cost for students from working-class backgrounds.[46]

These two continuities have framed the higher education policies of presidential administrations from 1929 to the present. The Cárdenas administration of the 1930s has often been noted for its drive to "socialize" the impact of the education system at all levels, in line with Lombardo Toledano's urging. Yet it is clear that Cárdenas saw the university as primarily "responsible for providing the technical skills and professional services that would support national production." The six-year plan for the Cárdenas administration gave higher technical education (which "readies man to utilize and transform nature") preference over training in the liberal professions. The ultimate purpose of technical training was to better "the material conditions of life of the Mexican people."[47]

Cárdenas's aims, then, were a curious blend of the humanistic and the utilitarian focuses of Lombardo and Caso. Cárdenas's desire to advance both economic and social aims of the Revolution is clear in his sponsorship of the National Polytechnic Institute (IPN), established in 1936. The IPN was to accept more students from the lower classes than the UNAM, thus serving both to produce needed professionals and to open up professional careers to less-favored Mexicans. The IPN was seen also as a counterweight to the "reactionary" UNAM, which emphasized liberal professions and opposed Cárdenas's program of socialist education.

Some of Cárdenas's economic policies presented major challenges for university policy. The crisis surrounding expropriation of the foreign-owned oil industry in 1938, for example, provided a dramatic stimulus to development of technical expertise in the late 1930s and 1940s. The difficulties of technical adjustment following the expropriation startled Mexicans and underlined for policymakers the importance of the university's utilitarian function. Mexicans realized the enormity of their dependence on foreign expertise and the historical inability of Mexico's higher-education system to produce professionals capable of managing the exploitation of the country's resources. At the time of the expropriation, the country's sole politechnical institute had been functioning for only two years, and Mexico was barely able to muster the domestic expertise necessary to keep the oil industry running. Mexican technicians, hurriedly rounded up after the expropriation, reestablished typical daily activities in the oil fields from worker recollections and proceeded to reconstruct Mexico's most important industry.

During Mexico's economic boom in the 1940s and early 1950s, presidents Avila Camacho, Alemán, and Ruiz Cortines managed a period in which development aims and higher-education policy were integrated. The programs of these administrations, particularly those of Alemán and Ruiz Cortines, created new opportunities for professionals, especially technical and administrative personnel for the public sector. Both public- and private-sector demand were stimulated by state projects for economic development in the Alemán and Ruiz Cortines periods: roads, dams, airfields, bridges, highways, ports, public buildings, and electrical and irrigation works. Agricultural policies favoring medium and large producers stimulated the need for professionals to mechanize production; diversify crops; introduce fertilizers, insecticides, better seed, and crop-rotation techniques; as well as manage rural credit and investment. The presidents responded to the greatly increased demand for professionals to plan and manage these projects by building UNAM's new campus (the University City) in the southern part of the capital, by supporting the development of regional universities, and by sending promising students and civil servants abroad to acquire advanced training.[48]

This era integrating university and development policy has been called the "Long Peace," because political conflicts between the university and the state reached all-time lows in quantity and intensity. "Rather than a bastion of conservatism and reaction out of which came guerrilla-like attacks on cherished government programs, UNAM . . . became a partner in the Revolution."[49] It was not that the attitude of students, professors, and administrators at the UNAM had not changed; rather the policy priorities of presidents had come to explicitly emphasize rapid economic change rather than thorough social transformation.

Two aspects of the integration of government priorities and higher education policy are especially noteworthy. First, the

UNAM was reorganized under Caso's Organic Law of 1944 (the law took effect in 1945) as a decentralized state agency. In return for increased financial support, the university community allowed new restrictions on the university autonomy granted in 1929, an encroachment that indicates a basic coincidence in university and government interests. Second, university graduates were brought into the government in large numbers, especially during the administration of Alemán. Alemán's support for the construction of University City also helped win over the students to the government's aims.

Adolfo López Mateos entered the presidency in 1958 with a call for university reform and stepped-up social programs. From the beginning of the López Mateos administration into the 1980s, the main theme of government higher-education policy has been "reform." The end of the period of relative peace between the university and the state was caused by many factors. University students did not adopt monolithic positions, and student political agitation became a problem for the government, for example, "sometimes because of its pro-Communist, pro-Castro, anti-American appeals, other times because of its anti-Communist, pro-Catholic Church, and anti-'atheistic' education appeals."[50] The confused nature of student pressure on the system is important because, as I suggest in the following chapters, it is due in good part to the changing nature of employment opportunities provided by the Mexican economy after 1929. The ideological orientations of students and leaders are perhaps not as central to university-state tensions as commonly thought.

Each six-year presidential administration following that of López Mateos has emphasized reform of a university system that policymakers have seen increasingly as beyond the control of government policy and out of touch with economic and social needs. But the rhetoric of reform has not led to a fundamental restructuring of the higher-education system. The main problem affecting the university's role in development has been seen by Mexican leaders since the late 1950s as the "masification," or crowding of campuses, caused by rapid growth of university enrollment.[51] By 1958, the demand for higher education, created during the period of "Long Peace," had outstripped university capacity. A successful, thirty-year-long policy of rapid expansion of the number of places in the university system had produced complications. The crowding that grew during the 1960s, and came to world attention with the violent clashes between Mexican students and soldiers in 1968, had its roots in the rapid expansion of university places during the era of overt university-government cooperation.

As demand for university education grew, students claimed that the university should allow all applicants a place. Demanding an "open door" to higher studies, students condemned the use of academic records or test scores to exclude them on the basis of their secondary-school preparations and aptitude for university-level study. Critics of an open-door policy contended that it would damage the quality of the university's product. The open door won out by the 1960s with the institutionalization of open enrollment procedures, flexible admission standards, and low fees.[52]

Increasing university-state conflicts and debate about masification provided the main stimuli for programs of reform under López Mateos in the 1960s.[53] López Mateos, who entered office during a period of student strikes and violence, introduced an eleven-year plan for education system reform soon after taking office. The eleven-year plan, which was to mesh with the president's economic development plan for "stabilizing development," emphasized strategies for satisfying social demand for primary education and was Mexico's first attempt to institute planning in the education system. López Mateos increased expenditure on all levels of education to its highest level since the 1930s (from 10.6 percent under Cárdenas to an average of 11.5 percent during the López Mateos administration).

President Díaz Ordaz, who entered office in 1964, further emphasized planning as the route to reform. More so than López Mateos, Díaz Ordaz supported the economic importance of university education, speaking of Mexico's need to "achieve high rates of intellectual investment in the formation of technicians, researchers, experts in administration . . . to foment . . . education for economic development."[54] The 1960s were a high point for the manpower approach to educational planning in Mexico; attempts to mold the education system to fit projections of economic growth in specific sectors of the Mexican economy reached a climax under Díaz Ordaz. With the government repression of student protests in 1968, however, most of the positive attitudes produced by the reform efforts of López Mateos and Díaz Ordaz quickly disappeared; the repression of students was widely viewed as an attack on the university.

Luis Echeverría, who as interior minister had played a key role in the 1968 repression of student-led demonstrations, tried to resolve tensions between the university and the government in two main ways when he became president in 1970. First, Echeverría promised a political opening for university-educated intellectuals and professionals—and he did give some posts to highly educated friends and important intellectuals.[55] He also stepped up the grants program of CONACYT (Consejo Nacional de Ciencia y Tecnología) to allow advanced Mexican students to study in the United States, Europe, and Japan. Expanding state employment by 62.3 percent between 1970 and 1976, Echeverría attempted to resolve social tensions by creating employment for university graduates in the public sector.[56] Second, Echeverría supported the creation of new public institutions of higher education in an attempt to counterbalance the political power of the UNAM and IPN. The creation in Mexico City of the three-campus Universidad Autónoma Metropolitana (UAM) system in 1974 considerably reduced overcrowding of the the two public-university giants in the capital city during the 1970s; by focusing on technical professional fields, the UAM was to make up for a perceived deficiency in UNAM's production of graduates and encourage the IPN to bring its production in line with government policy priorities.

Echeverría did not seek to change the basic structure of the higher-education system. Although his creation of political opportunities for intellectuals and professionals dissipated the tension remaining from 1968, Echeverría supported the open-door enrollment policy, increasing pressure on an already strained physical plant. His basic higher-education policy, in fact, was to greatly increase public expenditure in the hopes of creating enough jobs for the many new aspirants to professional positions.[57] Echeverría continued the twin historical emphases on training for economic advancement and university education as a form of social mobility, stating: "The contribution of education to development is obvious. It shows itself in the formation of qualified individuals, in the ability of a people to absorb and produce technological innovation and raise the level of productivity on the job. . . . Education also has direct effects on socioeconomic mobility."[58]

Under Echeverría, technical schooling was given a boost in order to provide social mobility and to reduce pressure at the higher technician level. In 1970, when Echeverría took office, there were 70 technical junior secondary schools in Mexico; by 1975 there were 581.[59] But the increase in opportunities at the secondary level would in fact lead to increased pressure on the universities: graduates of secondary programs were not content to be technicians. Echeverría's attempts in various fields to lay the basis for a "university of the masses" expanded the system to massive proportions.

Presiding over the oil boom of the late 1970s and early 1980s, President López Portillo did not feel the same need to use the university as a major policy tool to solve social and political problems. Whereas Echeverría had used educational reforms to patch up holes in the political fabric after the events of 1968, López Portillo strengthened political alliances by forging agreements with the private sector through his Alliance for Production. Further, López Portillo oversaw a short period of austerity to counteract the bad image of Echeverría's spendthrift final years. Major oil finds came on line by 1978 and flooded the treasury with new revenue. The consequent hiring boom in both public and private sectors suspended concern about the mismatch between the university system and society. Faith in a seemingly inexhaustible oil resource (and unconstrained world prices for oil) led Mexican leaders to base their sexenial plan—the Global Development Plan—squarely on oil financing.

The theme of university reform returned with the economic crisis of the early 1980s. The universities began an unprecedented process of self-criticism, with the major public universities releasing such documents as "The Strengths and Weaknesses of the UNAM," "Programs and Goals of the IPN, 1986–88," and the "Plan for Institutional Development" of the Universidad Autónoma Metropolitana (UAM). In 1986, ANUIES, the national university association, introduced its ideas of necessary reforms in an "Integral Plan for the Development of Higher Education" (known by its Spanish acronym PROIDES).

Shortly after taking office, President de la Madrid introduced a policy to modernize higher education that had as its centerpiece the geographical decentralization of university opportunities, with costs shifted to the states. The university would be streamlined to match the new, "modernized" Mexican economy that would emerge with privatization and freer trade. The de la Madrid administration claimed that decentralization of opportunities would benefit both the professionals and the regional economies of the provinces, which had suffered historically from a lack of opportunities for higher education. But the aim to decentralize higher educational costs ignored the fact that the states did not have the monies to fund these new opportunities.[60]

As he attempted to reshape industrial production to make Mexico competitive in the world economy, de la Madrid reinforced the idea of the economic utility of university education. The universities were to be reformed because Mexico would need a great number of highly qualified professionals to be competitive in the world market. This reform was developed in part by de la Madrid's Secretary of Planning Carlos Salinas de Gortari, the architect of the legal basis for dismantling the state's involvement in the economy.

Salinas, who succeeded de la Madrid as president in 1988, carried forward the privatization and internationalization of the Mexican economy in his efforts to restart sustained economic growth in Mexico and to open the traditionally closed economy. As he moved to free the economy from the state, from corruption, and from inefficiency, he took the same actions for the university system. Salinas stimulated private universities by various measures, including by bringing large numbers of privately educated professionals into his administration. For the public universities, he established an informal system of incentives and penalties. Universities that supported government initiatives by tailoring their programs to government needs and orientations were rewarded with budgetary allocations that kept up with inflation; universities that encouraged advanced research in fields the government approved of were granted special salary supports for active researchers.

Under Salinas, ideas for dramatic changes at the public universities, never before openly discussed, emerged into the policy arena. These ideas, many of which resulted from close consultations with foreign education experts, included limiting the size of the student body, raising fees, seeking non-government sources of funding, and establishing closer ties with the business community. In a potentially far-reaching move, Salinas's team suggested changes to Article 3 of the Constitution of 1917, which had guided education policy for over seventy years, to provide a legal framework for reform of the entire educational system.

Underlying these shifts in debate and policy in the period after 1929 was a growing disparity between the goals of the government and those of the public universities. A low point in the relationship was reached in the 1930s with the battle over socialized education fought by the rectorship of the UNAM of Manuel Gómez Morín (a well-known conservative intellectual and statesman who would found the PAN in 1939). One of the government's major problems during the 1930s, according to administration policymakers and sympathetic observers, was a "scarcity of capable technicians loyal to the revolutionary program of the government."[61] The government attempted to force UNAM's subservience by cutting off its subsidy, granting it a severance endowment of only 10 million pesos in 1933. The IPN was established in 1937 in good part to balance the power of the UNAM.[62] During the late 1930s, there was some discussion in high government circles of taking over the UNAM and making it an institution under the direct control of the state,[63] but relations improved from 1940 through the 1950s.

Differences became particularly troublesome for both sides after 1958. Public-university goals were increasingly shaped by student demands rather than those of the university administration or national government. While government policy emphasized the university's role in producing expertise for economic development, students agitated for universal education and social mobility, continually pressuring for broader access to the university and lower standards for achieving professional degrees. The government's historical respect for autonomy had come to restrict its ability to initiate significant reforms such as caps on enrollment, changes in career-area concentrations, increased fees, and achievement standards.[64]

Further deterioration in relations between the government and public universities in the 1980s, as the government made plain its dissatisfaction with the functioning of the public system, led in good part to the popularization of the idea of a university crisis. The conflict between government and the public universities had the dual effect of making the public-university system less useful for government plans for economic development and of making the government less supportive of the public university system. Unable to force changes at the public universities through direct means, the government actively supported efforts to decentralize the higher-education system, encouraged the development of private universities, and attempted to wrest control over national university policy from the public university giants. The government became the champion of higher educational quality; during the 1986–87 student strikes at UNAM, the government sided with drastic university reform measures introduced by the rector.

Summary and Conclusions

Three essential demands for professional education were present in Mexico from early in the colonial period and were strengthened by economic and social changes in the nineteenth century. The first demand was the desire of individuals and families for social mobility and social status; the second was the economy's need for specific areas of professional expertise, most notably in mining, commerce, and agriculture. During the late nineteenth century, a third demand developed as national economic development was planned under Porfirio Díaz and policy priorities shaped attitudes toward university education. Statistical data on university graduates in the late nineteenth century reflect the impact of multiple demands on the professional-education system.

With the rise to power of a new group after the Revolution of 1910, the challenge to the structure and function of the Mexican university posed by government policy priorities took a more definite shape. After 1929, the university was incorporated explicitly into strategies for development. Policy priorities molded the expression of both economic and social demands, converting them rhetorically into challenges for revolutionary economic and social change. In the following chapters, each of the three challenges to the university system, and the university's response, are examined in detail.

CHAPTER 3

Government Policy Priorities
and the Development of the
Professional Fields

Looking beyond the debate over the proper role of the university system in Mexican society, and beyond the plans and pronouncements of Mexico's leaders, this chapter examines what really happened as universities were incorporated into the government's drive for development after 1929. Did universities respond to government strategies for economic development? Or did they become increasingly independent of government control, as many analysts of university "crisis" believe? To answer these questions, historical changes in the number of professionals trained in Mexican universities and shifts in their fields of study are compared with trends in government policy. Changing field concentrations of professionals produced by Mexican universities give insight to the university system's response to national policy; the evolution of federal budgets since 1929 provides a guide to the shifting priorities of Mexican presidents.

Basic Trends in University Graduates and
Their Fields of Study

Three basic data series on the professional output of Mexican universities are introduced in this chapter and will be used throughout the study. The university system's production of professional expertise is measured by the number of persons who have (1) received a licentiate degree,[1] (2) completed course work for a licentiate degree but left the university without completing the required thesis or project for the degree (egresados), or (3) registered a licentiate degree with the Mexican government.[2]

Statistical series on these three categories of university-trained persons are used here as indicators of overall production of professional-level skills by Mexican universities. Each provides a different view of how the university system functions; together they permit an evaluation of change over time. The three series overlap for a few years, making cross-checking possible and providing a way to assess the character of each indicator. Because there is a lag between the time a student makes a career choice and his or her appearance as a statistic, a six-year time lag is incorporated in parts of the following analysis.[3]

First and most basically, the series reveal the number of professionals produced in a given year in specific areas of expertise. In the 1960s and 1970s, data such as these were employed in other Latin American countries by analysts of the human-capital school to judge the level of preparation of these societies for economic development.[4] Development planners used the data to forecast "manpower" needs based on roughly calculated estimates for future economic development. But development did not take place as predicted, and manpower needs were frequently found to be overly optimistic. Many Latin American countries showed signs of overproducing university graduates in relation to the number of professional jobs available.

Second and more significantly, the data on university graduates and egresados represent evidence of career decisions made by students—decisions based on government rhetoric and spending as well as on actual employment opportunities. Because the data reflect real and perceived strengths and weaknesses of the market for professionals in specific specialties and at specific skill levels, they are useful gauges of trends in employment and thus of trends in the economy in general.

Data on the degrees granted by Mexican universities allow us to analyze the period from 1900 to 1971. From 1900 to 1927, data are aggregate, thus making it impossible to discern year-to-year changes among career fields. Beginning in 1928, annual figures are available, and from 1940 the data are more detailed, allowing for more accurate analysis of shifts among fields. Although the year 1940 is a key date in the traditional historiography of Mexico's development in the twentieth century and is the major breaking point in this first set of data as well, I have modified the series to allow for consideration of long-term trends that span this important date. Historians have tended to see a sharp break in 1940 between the social reform of the 1930s and the focus on economic growth of the 1940s and 1950s. As organized here, the data shed new light on the nature and dimensions of shifts in economic development at this juncture.

Aggregate data for the first series on the 1901–27 period, along with data on the late nineteenth century presented in Chapter Two, provide a benchmark for comparison with later periods (Fig. 3–1). The professional makeup of Mexican society during the first decade of the twentieth century and the violent phase of the Revolution was dominated by lawyers (37.2 percent), doctors (37.0 percent), and engineers (17.3 percent). These three professional groups had grown substantially during the colonial period and nineteenth century, providing both prestige to professionals and necessary services for the increasingly complex Mexican economy, as noted in Chapter Two. The large share of doctors reflects their rise in utility and social status as medicine became increasingly less primitive.

The absolute number of professionals educated between 1901 and 1927 was not striking—on average, approximately 300 graduates per year. This number does not seem significantly higher than that in the late nineteenth century. It is even possible that the rate of graduation during the violent phase of the Revolution was lower than it had been prior to 1910.[5] As in many other spheres of Mexican life, the Revolution in its violent phase may have acted as a disincentive to the development of professional expertise. On the personal level, potential university students probably did not find the early revolutionary period the most propitious time to begin or complete university careers.

The pace of graduation from universities picked up noticeably

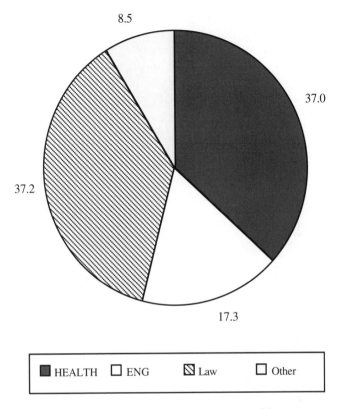

Figure 3–1. Professional Degrees Granted, Three Fields, 1901–27. Note: Upper-case letters indicate career area comprising several degree fields; lower-case letters indicate single-degree career area. For example, HEALTH includes degrees in medicine, dentistry, and optometry. See Statistical Appendix for career-area details. SOURCE: Calculated from Dirección General de Estadística, *Anuario estadístico*, 1930.

after 1928 (Fig. 3–2). By 1940, the number of graduating university students had grown to more than three times the average for the years between 1901 and 1927. Thus, with the consolidation of political peace and the rebuilding of the economy in the late 1920s, the professional fields had expanded quantitatively at a rapid rate. The quickened pace of graduation was closely related to the consolidation and expansion of institutions of higher

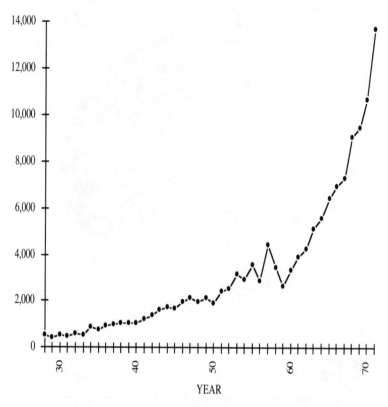

Figure 3–2. Total Professional Degrees Granted, 1928–71
SOURCE: Lorey, *Rise of the Professions*, Table 1; sample data are given in Statistical Appendix, Table 1.

learning in the 1930s. The political consolidation of 1929, revived economic growth after the mid-1930s, and government policy to control the orientation of the public university system all stimulated university enrollment. The proliferation of new public universities, and growth by the late 1930s of private universities, followed expansion at the major public institutions.

Between 1928 and 1940, the basic pattern of field concentrations continued without radical change, as shown by degrees granted. Health, law, and engineering continued to account for almost nine-tenths of all university graduates. The only notable change in the period was seen in degrees for secondary-school and university teaching, which grew from a low average of 1.3 percent between 1930 and 1934 to an average of 8.1 percent between 1935 and 1939. The increasing relative importance of teaching was reflected in the slight decline in the percent shares of the three most important fields—health, law, and engineering—during the 1930s. Yet the similarity in field concentrations to earlier patterns implies that little structural or sectoral change in the Mexican economy occurred during the late 1920s or early 1930s.

Both the pace of growth in the number of professionals educated at Mexican universities and the relationship among professional fields changed dramatically just before 1940. From an average of 570 between 1928 and 1934, the number of degrees granted yearly to graduating students climbed to 977 under Cárdenas, to 1,599 under Avila Camacho, to 2,176 under Alemán, to 3,405 under Ruiz Cortines, to 4,143 under López Mateos, and to 8,326 under Díaz Ordaz. The highest rates of growth in the number of degrees granted came in the 1960s during the sexenios of López Mateos (109.1 percent) and Díaz Ordaz (65.7 percent), the lowest under Alemán (18.2 percent) and Ruiz Cortines (9.3 percent). The rapid quantitative expansion in degrees granted by Mexican universities under Cárdenas (33.8 percent) suggests that the universities responded to a sharply increased demand for professionals to accommodate emerging industrialization and rapid urbanization. High growth rates through the end of World War II (59.8 percent under Avila Camacho) indicate that the numbers of graduating students increased rapidly as the Mexican economy expanded from the late 1930s through the mid-1940s.

Quantitative growth was not experienced equally by all professional career fields in the period after 1940, as shown in the distribution of graduates by field (Figs. 3-3 and 3-4). The traditionally dominant professions declined markedly in importance, while other professions rose to prominence. Health fell steadily from a high of almost 60 percent of all degrees in 1929 to a low of 21.4 percent in 1971. Law, which maintained a high average of almost 30 percent until 1940, saw its share decrease to less than

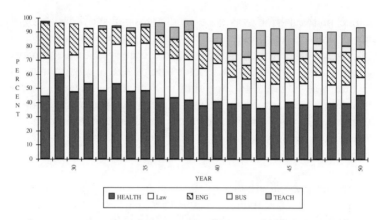

Figure 3–3. Professional Degrees Granted, Five Major Fields, 1928–50. SOURCE: Lorey, *Rise of the Professions*, Table 1; sample data are given in Statistical Appendix, Table 1.

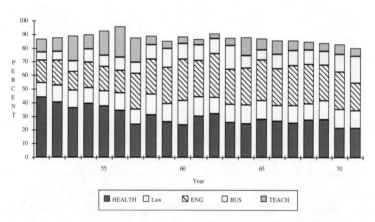

Figure 3–4. Professional Degrees Granted, Five Major Fields, 1951–71. SOURCE: Lorey, *Rise of the Professions*, Table 1; sample data are given in Statistical Appendix, Table 1.

half that share thereafter. While it is commonly thought that the legal profession remains the dominant profession in Mexico, it is clear from these data that law was never as important as health, and that as early as the 1950s law had fallen behind both health and engineering in importance. By 1971, business too overtook law in importance. Lawyers may have been very important in Mexican politics historically, but among the general population of university graduates, they have formed a distinct minority.

In the three decades after 1940, business, engineering, and teaching grew to take the place of fields in decline. Of particular interest is the sudden quantitative increase in degrees granted in the business field after 1940. This degree-area leapt to prominence in the early 1940s, attained a high plateau in the 1950s, and then grew rapidly again in the late 1950s and early 1960s. The yearly rate of growth for the business degree-area was 13.0 percent for the period between 1940 and 1971, significantly higher than the 8.4 percent annual growth in all other fields. From under 6 percent of all degrees in 1941, business grew to 20.0 percent in 1971. This rapid growth of the business field implies that the universities stepped up production of those professionally skilled persons necessary for creating infrastructure and managing industrial change and economic growth.

Engineering experienced the same sort of rapid and prolonged growth. Although important before 1940, engineering experienced its most rapid growth in the late 1950s, moving from 13.5 percent of all degrees in 1950 to a high point of 31.9 percent in 1962. Teaching increased its ranks quickly in the 1940s and 1950s to a high of 22.3 percent of all degrees in 1956, then fell to less than half that during the 1960s. In the late 1950s and early 1960s, both engineering and business saw large increases in their relative importance, while the secondary-school teaching and health fields declined. Trends in the percent shares of numerically less-important professional fields—architecture, economics, and science—are also noteworthy. Architecture experienced dramatic increases after the late 1950s, and economics saw strong growth by the mid-1960s. Sciences, relatively strong during the 1940s, increased a bit in the 1950s and then in the 1960s to lows not experienced since the late 1920s and early 1930s.

In summary, the predominance of the historically most important professional groups was sharply curtailed by the rise of business and the increasing importance of engineering after 1940. The data on degrees granted suggest that the process of economic development in Mexico underwent a major shift in orientation in the years just before 1940, and in response, professional career fields shifted dramatically from the pattern established in the late nineteenth century. The mid-1960s saw the beginning of a second very rapid quantitative expansion in the number of degrees granted overall, accompanied by significant shifts among professional career fields.

Because the series on degrees granted ends in 1971, I turn to data on egresados of university professional programs to examine the period from the late 1960s to the late 1980s. (An egresado is a person who has finished course requirements for the licentiate degree but still has to finish a thesis or similar project in order to be granted the degree.) Egresados pursue their professional training to a relatively advanced level of competence. Most, however, never achieve the final degree, and many of those who do not achieve the degree eventually find employment in technician-level positions. Other egresados will go on to achieve the degree, and most of these graduates will take jobs at the professional level in the private or public sectors.

Between 1967 and 1989, there was a dramatic quantitative expansion in the number of egresados, as large numbers of students completed all coursework and left Mexican universities. The total number of egresados of all professional fields increased nine times during the period. Comparing the growth rate of egresados with that of degrees granted shows that the number of egresados grew at a much faster rate in the sexenio from 1971 and 1976 (105.3 percent) than did the number of degrees granted in the previous sexenio, between 1964 and 1970. This difference in growth rates between the two series indicates a large gap between the number of students who were finishing coursework and the number of students who went on to achieve the licentiate degree.[6]

Rapid growth in the numbers of business, engineering, health, and teaching egresados occurred during the twenty-year period. The number of egresados in business in 1989 was 11 times what it had been in 1967, 9 times what it had been in engineering, 5 times in health, and 22 times in secondary teaching. Minor

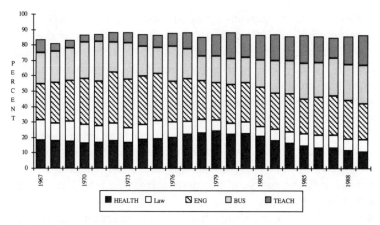

Figure 3–5. University Egresados, Five Major Fields, 1967–89. SOURCE: Lorey, *Rise of the Professions*, Table 3; sample data are given in Statistical Appendix, Table 2.

fields also displayed strong growth in absolute terms. The combined psychology/social-work area led the smaller fields, increasing in absolute terms 29 times, with dramatic leaps after the mid-1970s. There were 8 times as many egresados in social sciences in 1989 as there had been in 1967, while there were 10 times as many in the sciences. Architecture and law increased nearly 5 times each and economics almost 4 times over the period.

While absolute growth of egresados occurred at a rapid rate in the 1970s, the relative importance of career fields remained stable for most of the period under consideration (Fig. 3–5). Engineering increased its share slightly to a high of 33.0 percent in 1972 and then fell gradually back down to make up about one-quarter of all egresados in the decade 1976–86. Health fields moved up from an average of 17 percent during the period 1967–73 to a high of an average of 22.3 percent between 1977 and 1982. Business held steady at about one-fifth of all egresados throughout the period. Law continued its historical decline in relative importance, sliding from a high of 12.2 percent of all egresados of professional fields between 1967 and 1972, to a low average of 7.7 percent between 1980 and 1989; this decline represented a dramatic decrease from law's position as the second most important field (after health) in the 1928–44 period. The only field that experienced impressive growth in relative terms was secondary teaching, which grew from a low of 6.6 percent (1967–76) to a high of an average 16.7 percent between 1980 and 1989.

Data on egresados in the period between 1967 and 1989 reveal two important trends. Egresados were leaving Mexican universities in large numbers, although the rate at which they left decreased over the course of the period, from a high of 105.3 percent under Echeverría to a low of 22.4 percent under de la Madrid.[7] At the same time, there was a remarkable stability in the relative importance of the numerically most significant fields—business, engineering, and health. The series on egresados indicates, then, that unlike in the earlier period between 1940 and 1970, the Mexican economy underwent no fundamental shifts in makeup or direction that would stimulate changes in which fields of professional study were preferred at Mexican universities. Field concentrations maintained the pattern set after the late 1950s, suggesting that the university's reaction to Mexico's major post-1940 social and political crisis, the student movement and repression of 1968, involved quantitative changes in enrollment and graduation rather than relative shifts among professional careers.

Complementary information about how changes in the pattern of professional education affected economic development during the period 1970–85 is provided by data on professional degrees registered by university graduates in the Dirección General de Profesiones (DGP) in Mexico City. Professionals register their degrees for various reasons, but most frequently because employment in certain firms and agencies, particularly in the public sector, is contingent on registration.

Registrations of professional degrees grew particularly fast in three professional fields between 1970 and 1985: health, engineering, and business (Fig. 3–6). The number of health degrees registered increased almost seven times, in business ten times, and in engineering five times. Business, engineering, and health

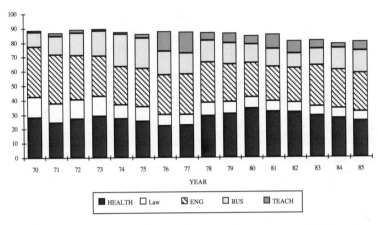

Figure 3–6. Professional Degrees Registered, Five Major Fields, 1970–85. SOURCE: Lorey, *Rise of the Professions*, Table 4; sample data are given in Statistical Appendix, Table 3.

fields together made up an average of almost three-quarters of all degrees registered in the fifteen-year period. Engineering and health alone made up 55.4 percent of all degrees registered. Law underwent a notable decline, from a high of 14.2 percent in 1970 to a low at the end of the period of 6.3 percent. Economics and architecture saw very gradual declines in their relative shares in the 1970s and early 1980s. Science fields remained at a low, averaging less than 2 percent of all registered degrees, while humanities grew gradually, to over 3 percent from under 1 percent through the 1970s. Claiming little more than 1 or 2 percent of all degrees registered prior to 1976, teaching leapt to 15 percent of the total in 1977 and then settled back down to an average of 6.7 percent from 1978 through 1985. As with the data for egresados, the sexenial rate of growth in the number of registered degrees declined over time. From a high growth rate of 80.7 percent between 1971 and 1976, the number of degrees registered increased 39.8 percent between 1977 and 1982 and 48.5 percent between 1983 and 1988.

Data on registered degrees make clear the importance of public-sector employment in stimulating professional study in specific areas. The rapid quantitative expansion of degrees registered in the 1970s reflects the rapid increase of public-sector hiring in that period. Engineering and health, the two fields most in demand by government agencies involved in health care, public construction works, publicly owned or financed economic infrastructure, and parastatal industrial ventures, dominate the professional fields represented.

Professional Degrees, Egresados, and Registered Degrees per Million Inhabitants

One way to put all three of these statistical series in historical perspective is to place each in the context of Mexico's demographic growth in the twentieth century. Here, the number of degrees granted, egresados, and registered degrees in a given year are compared with the Mexican population in the same year (Fig. 3–7).

While there were fewer than 50 degrees granted by Mexican universities per million people until 1934 and about 50 into the early 1940s, thereafter, through 1957, there was a steady increase. After a two-year drop, the number of degrees increased dramatically between 1959 and 1971, from 77 degrees per million inhabitants in 1959 to 256 per million in 1971. In comparison,

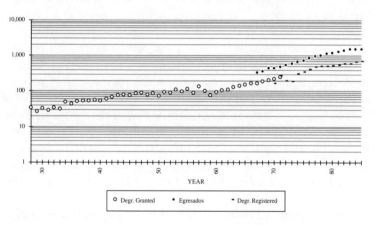

Figure 3–7. Degrees Granted, Egresados, and Degrees Registered per Million People, 1928–86. SOURCE: Lorey, *Rise of the Professions*, Table 7.

the number of egresados per million rose steadily from 334 in 1967 to 740 in 1975, and then experienced a sudden takeoff, from 843 in 1976 to 1,513 in 1983. During the mid- and late 1980s, the number of persons leaving universities with the egresado diploma grew more gradually, to reach 1,618 per million in 1988. Data on professional degrees registered per million between 1970 and 1985 show a steady rise from 188 in 1973, to 303 in 1974, to 482 in 1977. After 1977, there was a gradual slowing through 1980, but between 1981 and 1985 degrees registered per million Mexicans grew again, from 544 in 1981 to 709 in 1985.

The rate of growth of professionals in the context of the Mexican population has changed over time. The number of degrees granted by Mexican universities per million people grew 75.0 percent in the 1930s, 64.2 percent in the 1940s, dipped to 37.8 percent in the 1950s, and climbed to 118.5 percent in the 1960s. During the 1970s, the number of egresados grew 155.6 percent, while the number of degrees registered per million inhabitants grew 203.7 percent. For the five-year period between 1980 and 1985, the number of egresados per million grew 28.1 percent and degrees registered grew 37.9 percent. The remarkable quantitative leap in the number of degrees granted after the late 1950s, noted above in the absolute data, represented a major jump in the number of professionals in Mexican society.

Overall growth rates for the three series clearly outpaced the growth of the Mexican population. While the population grew at 2.8 percent per year between 1928 and 1989, the annual rate of growth of degrees granted between 1928 and 1971 was 4.9 percent, that for egresados was 8.0 percent between 1967 and 1988, and that for degrees registered between 1970 and 1985 was 10.3 percent.[8] Clearly, real gains were made by the Mexican university system after 1929 in producing ever-greater numbers of professionals over time. These gains constitute a major return to government investment in the rapid expansion of places in the university system. Growth in the number of professionals far outstripped population growth over the whole period, although just equaling that growth in the twenty years between 1941 and 1960.

The Development of the Humanities, Social Sciences, Natural Sciences, and Graduate Studies

Another aspect of the data is revealed by examining the fate of smaller professional fields in the period from 1929 to 1989. The complexity and diversity of a developed economy make possible the employment of large numbers of specialists in the humanities and social sciences. Clearly, the most developed societies educate many of these specialists: of university graduates in the United States in 1982, for example, 5.6 percent were in the humanities, 9.5 percent in the social sciences, and 3.3 percent in the fine arts. Comparable figures for Mexico are 0.8 percent in the humanities, 8.3 percent in the social sciences, and 0.8 percent in the fine arts.[9]

In Mexico, university graduates and egresados in the humanities and social sciences have never constituted more than 11 percent of total degrees, egresados, or registered degrees. The average for the period 1964–71, as measured in data on degrees granted, would appear to be about 1.8 percent of all graduates.[10] Data on egresados show an average of 2.6 percent of egresados in humanities and social science fields in the 1967–89 period. The humanities and social sciences make up 5.5 percent of registrations in the 1970–85 period. While the 1970s were characterized by sluggish growth in the humanities and social sciences, the early 1980s were a time of rapid growth in the education of professionals in these fields.

The natural sciences play an important role in economic development, and unlike the humanities are not generally considered luxury fields. Most important perhaps, the natural sciences are essential to the research-and-development functions of modern industrial firms. An average of 5.9 percent of all degrees granted in the 1929 to 1971 period were granted in the natural sciences. In the 1967–89 period, 2.2 percent of egresados of professional fields were egresados of the natural sciences. Even fewer scientists have registered degrees, the average being 1.3 percent of all degrees registered 1970–85. The sciences have experienced very sluggish historical growth in Mexico.[11]

Historical trends in graduate study also contribute to an understanding of the development of the Mexican university system. Only as a society and its economic infrastructure become very complex in organization does the demand for graduates of programs of advanced study develop to a high level.[12] Research and development involves not only specialists in the natural sciences but also in graduate fields in economics, engineering, and management.

Mexico has never educated a large absolute or relative number of graduate professionals. In the 1936–71 period, graduate degrees granted by Mexican universities averaged 1.6 percent of all degrees. Registered graduate degrees made up only 0.6 percent of all degrees registered in the years between 1970 and 1985. Egresados of graduate courses of study in the years 1982–86 made up 4.7 percent of all egresados.[13] The differences between figures for these three indicators reveal important factors in the employment of professionals with graduate training. It is apparently unnecessary to register for a graduate degree in order to find or retain employment, or gain promotion—thus the low rate of registration as compared to egresados and degrees. The relatively high percentage of egresados of fields of graduate study compared to either degrees granted or degrees registered reflects the fact that in the 1980s, only one out of nine entering graduate students achieved the final graduate degree.[14]

The Response of the University System to Changing Government Priorities

Having established the basic trends in the training of professionals at Mexican universities since 1929, we can now place these trends in the context of the evolving policy priorities of the Mexican government. Do the trends in the data reflect the strategies for economic development of presidential administrations after 1929? Or has the university system produced professionals in fields that the government has not found coincident with its plans?[15]

One of the principal ways that the policy priorities of Mexican presidents are expressed, and the most easily quantifiable, is the formulation and publication of the federal budget. Part of a complex policy environment ranging from the yearly state-of-the-union address to strategic travels throughout the country, the president's budget defines his priorities and at the same time creates and encourages objective conditions for the fulfillment of his aims. Public monies spent to advance economic goals, for example, both indicate to the nation the policy emphasis of a president and stimulate the economy—directly, by creating growth and employment, and indirectly, by creating an environment that is favorable to economic expansion.

Historical changes in presidential plans and policy emphasis have been examined by James W. Wilkie. Wilkie organizes central-government expenditure into categories of social, economic, and administrative impact. By comparing proposed budgets with actually executed expenditures, he is able to gauge the relationship between revolutionary rhetoric and the real spending priorities of presidential coalitions. Thus the central government budget can be used both as a guide to a president's rhetorical strategy and as an accurate indicator of policy shifts over time. Six periods between 1910 and 1994 are defined by Wilkie: (1) political revolution (1910–29) in two phases (military, 1910–19, and pacific, 1920–29); (2) social revolution during the presidency of Lázaro Cárdenas (1935–40); (3) economic revolution—the presidencies of Manuel Avila Camacho (1941–46), Miguel Alemán (1947–52), and Adolfo Ruiz Cortines (1953–58); (4) "balanced" revolution in the administrations of Adolfo López Mateos (1959–64) and Díaz Ordaz (1965–70), during which economic and social expenditures were roughly balanced; (5) statist revolution under Luis Echeverría (1971–76) and José López Portillo (1977–82); and (6) restructured revolution under Miguel de la Madrid Hurtado (1983–88) and Carlos Salinas de Gortari (1989–94).[16] Five of these six phases of the Revolution overlap with my data on professionals (Fig. 3–8).

In order to compare the phases of the Mexican Revolution with the data on university graduates, I have organized fields of study into sample "economic" and "social" professions.[17] The historical changes in growth rates of these two basic divisions

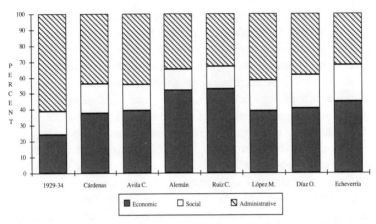

Figure 3-8. Percent of Actual Government Expenditure in Administrative, Social, and Economic Areas, 1929–1976, by Presidential Sexenio. SOURCE: James W. Wilkie, *La revolución mexicana* (Mexico City: Fondo de Cultura Económica, 1978), pp. 66, 322, 354–55, 358.

and in their relation to each other tell us a great deal about the relationship between government plans and the impact of national policy.

The economic grouping comprises business and engineering fields, two professional fields strongly stimulated by increased economic activity. Both business and engineering fields are linked to the growth of the export sector, to industrial development, and to the expansion of internal commerce; they are also highly sensitive to the structure and evolution of Mexico's domestic market. Business administrators and accountants come to be increasingly in demand as firms grow larger and more complex. Engineers with agricultural, chemical, and mechanical expertise are needed as farms and factories step up their production of goods for domestic and international markets. The business field is particularly responsive to the growth of the modern service sector, especially to the rise of public and private firms devoted to financial services.

The social grouping is made up of two sample fields: secondary-school teaching and the health specialties. The provision of basic education and health care has been the primary social goal of leaders since 1929. For this reason, education and health have been the two major areas of direct social expenditure by the central government over the course of the Revolution. The focus here is on secondary-school teachers and persons trained at the university level in teaching specialities, rather than on primary-school teachers, for two reasons. First, the expansion of primary educational opportunities has been studied thoroughly in the Mexican case—rapid quantitative expansion at the most basic level of education seems a clear accomplishment of the Revolution. Second, post-primary educational opportunities have been much more restricted in Mexico than have primary opportunities. Professionals with training in secondary-school teaching thus prove a more refined test of social accomplishments. Changes in the production of teachers for the secondary and higher levels shed light on an important level of preparation of human resources and also on an important aspect in the changing opportunities and quality of life of Mexicans. The health category includes medical doctors, dentists, optometrists, and licentiate-level nurses, all of whom play important parts in improving the breadth and depth of health coverage, and thus the basic social welfare, of Mexicans.

The present classification scheme is simple for several reasons. These four basic fields are the clearest indicators of the historical relationship between economic and social aims and achievements. Economists might have been considered "economic" professionals, and yet economists find employment in a wide variety of public- and private-sector positions hard to categorize as clearly economic or social. Likewise, psychology and social work could have been included under the social-profession heading. But professionals in these fields follow much the same pattern as those in the health field. Anything more complex than these basic indicators gives a false impression of the accuracy of the measurements being undertaken. These sample fields are proxies for economic and social change.[18]

It is necessary to take into account at this point the estimated six-year time lag between students' career-field decisions and time of graduation. Lagging the data on degrees granted and egresados allows a comparison of government expenditure in a given

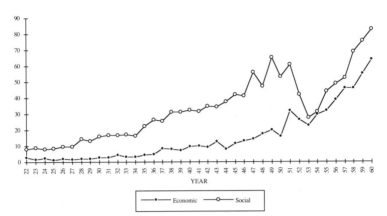

Figure 3–9. Index of University Graduates and Egresados in Economic and Social Fields, 1922–60. Note: This Figure takes into account the six-year time lag between career-field decision and graduation. Dates refer to the year that the student made his or her career-field choice, that is, the year of graduation minus six years. SOURCE: Adapted from Lorey, *Rise of the Professions*, Table 11; sample data are given in Statistical Appendix, Table 4.

period with the decisions of students to follow a certain career in that same period. The figures employed in the following analysis refer to the year students decided to follow certain career paths rather than the year they graduated or left the university as egresados.

The sample economic professional fields underwent significant absolute changes over the course of the period (Figs. 3–9 and 3–10).[19] Sustained growth in economic fields began in 1935 and was steady until 1949. The number of university graduates in economic fields then leapt upward between 1950 and 1951. After a downturn between 1951 and 1953, graduates in economic fields increased dramatically between 1954 and the late 1960s.[20] The 1970s saw the number of graduates in economic professions reach a plateau. Economic professions moved rapidly upward again from 1976 to 1979 and then fell to half their 1979 level during the first years of the crisis of the 1980s.

A very different historical pattern emerges in the sample

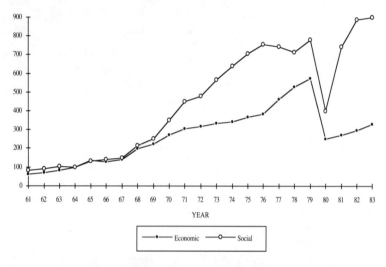

Figure 3–10. Index of University Graduates and Egresados in Economic and Social Fields, 1961–83. Note: This Figure takes into account the six-year time lag between career-field decision and graduation. Dates refer to the year that the student made his or her career-field choice, that is, the year of graduation minus six years. SOURCE: Adapted from Lorey, *Rise of the Professions*, Table 11; sample data are given in Statistical Appendix, Table 4.

social fields. The index of absolute growth in sample social professions shows sluggish growth in those fields from the early 1920s through 1934. In 1935 a sudden increase occurred that continued until 1938. Between 1938 and 1946, the fields settled at a plateau with gradual gains and then grew very rapidly again between 1947 and 1951. After falling sharply in 1952–53, rapid growth resumed in 1955 and extended to 1960. After a steady period of growth between 1961 and 1969, the sample social fields jumped up between 1970 and 1976 to a peak of 757 (1964=100) in 1976. After 1979, the number of participants in the social fields increased once again, reaching 899 in 1983.

Changing relative shares of the groups of economic and social sample fields reveals significant changes in field-concentration patterns over time (Fig. 3–11). The relative importance of the

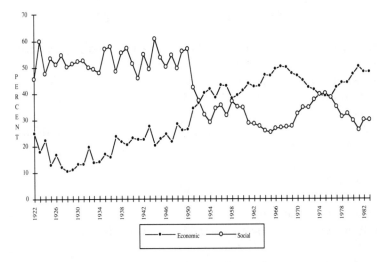

Figure 3–11. University Graduates and Egresados in Economic and Social Fields, 1922–83. Note: This Figure takes into account the six-year time lag between career-field decision and graduation. Dates refer to the year that the student made his or her career-field choice, that is, the year of graduation minus six years. SOURCE: Adapted from Lorey, *Rise of the Professions,* Table 11; sample data are given in Statistical Appendix, Table 4.

two groupings is our most useful gauge of the relative impact of government rhetoric and expenditure and merits detailed consideration.[21]

The evolution of the percent share held by the sample economic fields reveals that the fields rose from a minor position in the early 1920s to become the clearly dominant group of professions by the late 1970s. Although declining from the early 1920s through 1928, economic professions gained slowly but steadily from 11.1 percent in 1929 to reach 15.7 percent of all professional fields in 1936. Between 1937 and 1950 a high plateau was reached—an average of 23.8 percent of all degrees granted were in the sample economic professions. After 1951, economic fields experienced increased growth to peak at more than half of all professional fields in 1967 and 1968. After reaching those peaks, economic professions declined gradually through 1976. The data show then that the most rapid period of growth in the share of the economic professions came in the early 1950s, as Mexico's industrial revolution received its strongest encouragement from presidents Alemán and Ruiz Cortines. The economic fields dominated the professional makeup of Mexican society from this period onward.

The sample social professions experienced a long-term decline in their importance relative to the economic professions. Social professions claimed about half of all professionals between 1922 and 1934. In 1935 and 1936, the social professions jumped to almost 60 percent of all degrees granted. The percent share held by social fields fluctuated between 1937 and 1950, but was generally lower than in the 1920s and early 1930s. Between 1951 and 1954 the social fields experienced a precipitous decline from more than 50 percent in the early 1950s to less than 30 percent by 1954. The percent share of university graduates held by the social fields rose slowly back to 37 percent in the late 1950s, but between 1961 and 1969 slowly declined, consistently accounting for less than one-third of all professional careers chosen by entering university students. Between 1970 and 1975, social professions increased their share to almost 40 percent. After 1976, the percent share held by the sample social professions fell again to settle at about 30 percent of all professions into the 1980s.

Despite this long-term decline, the social fields were greatly stimulated from the mid-1930s through the early 1950s. The social phase of policy emphasis during the administration of President Cárdenas should have had an effect on social professions during the period. The lowest historical point for the social fields was reached during the decade of the 1960s, when the sample economic fields reached their historical peak. The early 1970s saw a resurgence of social professions under President Echeverría that lasted just past the midpoint of the decade.

A statistical test of correlation is useful at this point to establish the strength of the relationship between government expenditure and students' fields of study. We can find the correlation coefficient (the Pearson's product-moment correlation coefficient, symbolized by r) for data organized by sexenio on the growth of the federal budget (actual expenditure) directed toward economic and social ends and data on the growth of university graduates (per million Mexicans) in sample economic and social fields. The correlation coefficient is a measure of the strength of linear relationship between two variables; r can vary from a perfect negative correlation of -1.0 to a perfect positive correlation of $+1.0$, an r of zero indicating no significant correlation. For the eight sexenios between 1929 and 1976 we get a strong relationship of $r=.631$ for economic expenditure and economic professional fields and $r=.653$ for social expenditure and social fields. Because data on professional fields are time-lagged, the direction of causality seems clear.[22]

Analysis of the data thus indicates that the development of the professional fields in Mexico has responded over time to changing policy emphases of Mexican leaders. The production of the universities has followed the lead of government rhetoric, planning, and expenditure. Parallels among the data sets suggest that government expenditure has had a direct impact on the fields of study of Mexican professionals. The social fields were stimulated most strongly during the administrations of presidents whose rhetoric and spending championed social aims—Cárdenas and Echeverría. The most important parallel between the drive for economic revolution after the late 1930s and the functioning of Mexican universities is seen in the rapidly increasing number of professionals with degrees in business and engineering after the strong budgetary shift toward economic revolution in the 1940s.

An interesting test case for examining the relationship between policy aims and university response is the much discussed shift from social to economic aims in 1940, at the time of the transition from the "socially revolutionary" Cárdenas to the "economically revolutionary" presidents Avila Camacho, Alemán, and Ruiz Cortines. The historiography of twentieth-century Mexico has been dominated by a demarcation of two distinct periods on either side of 1940: Cárdenas's attempt to transform Mexico through social reform, and the following "reaction," during which champions of economic revolution concentrated on industrialization to transform Mexico.[23] Many observers believe that the Revolution came to an end in 1940, while others consider 1940 to be its beginning.[24] While this orthodoxy has recently been challenged by scholars of Mexico's economic development, the division is still widely accepted.

The data analyzed here show that there was no clear breaking point in 1940. Instead, Cárdenas emerges as the first of the great industrializing presidents of post-1910 Mexico. It was under Cárdenas that the first large-scale preparation of human resources for economic development began. Seen from this view, many of Cárdenas's social reforms were integral parts of the push for industrial development. The program of rapid land distribution in the 1930s, for example, stimulated the training of agricultural and civil engineers at the university level—engineers who would prove crucial in the expansion and improvement of irrigation and agricultural infrastructure during the first phase of modernization of Mexican agriculture under Avila Camacho and Alemán. Cárdenas's expenditures for economic infrastructure emphasized irrigation and rural infrastructure as would those of Alemán. Both agricultural policy and the education of engineers in the 1930s were central to the "green revolution" that undergirded industrialization in the 1940s and 1950s.

Capitalizing on the political stability created after the political institutionalization of the Revolution in 1929, Cárdenas presided over the beginning of a shift from an economy based on the export of agricultural goods and minerals to one fueled by manufacturing for the domestic market. Shifting government expenditure away from administration and toward economic and social programs, Cárdenas prepared the economy for its sustained growth after 1940. The time series developed here thus push one step further the assertion that "long before the alleged policy shift of the 1940s, the government had been progressing more or less steadily toward the construction of an economic system in which industrial production would play an increasingly important role."[25] Evidence on university graduates shows that the human-resource base for industrialization was a key component of the groundwork laid before 1940. The data also indicate that much of the restructuring of the Mexican economy that made improvements after 1940 possible was already under way by the time Cárdenas came to office in 1934.[26]

Case Study: Engineering Expertise, 1928–85

Engineers constitute a key link between many stated public-policy aims and related accomplishments and thus are well-suited to the analysis of the relationship between economic and social aims and university response. Engineers are central to the development and maintenance of basic economic and social infrastructures, from improvements in agricultural techniques, multi-lane freeways, and the telecommunications network to potable water systems and sanitation. Trends in the education of engineers in Mexico provide a unique tool for studying the complex balance between economic and social emphases within the Institutionalized Revolution in the period after 1929.[27]

The most dramatic change in the education of engineers since the 1930s has been the explosive growth in the field. Between 1929 and 1970, degrees granted in engineering increased to over 31 times the original level. Egresados of engineering specialties quadrupled in the fifteen years between 1970 and 1985, while degrees registered in engineering specialties grew five times in the same period. After 1929, while the engineering field grew rapidly and steadily, graduates and egresados in engineering made up an important part of all professional graduates. The relative importance of the field increased over time, growing from an average of 10.8 percent of degrees granted between 1931 and 1939 to two and a half times that among egresados in the early 1980s. An important sign of the gradually increasing importance of engineering fields in Mexico is the acceptance of engineering degrees in the hierarchy of political power. Mexico has not yet had an engineer become president as have Colombia and Peru in the last few decades. But whereas before 1930 it was rare to find professional engineers in positions of political power, now it is a more common professional background.[28]

How have the relative proportions of specialties within the engineering field changed over time? In particular, have the "classic" specialties of agricultural, chemical, civil, electrical, mechanical, and extractive engineering changed in relation to "new" specialties such as industrial and computer engineering?

Data on degrees granted for the 1928–71 period reveal several significant shifts among the numerically most important engineering specialties. Agricultural engineering and veterinary medicine declined between 1930 and 1938 and then rose sharply between 1939 and 1941. A high point was reached between 1942 and 1950, when agricultural engineering averaged 26.0 percent of all degrees granted in the engineering field. After the high of the 1940s, agricultural engineering and veterinary medicine settled at lower plateaus in the 1950s (19.8 percent during 1951–59) and 1960s (13.7 percent). Civil engineering rose early to a high of 40.2 percent of all degrees granted in engineering in 1934. After that peak, the specialty fell through 1949 by almost half, to 20.4 percent. In the 1950s and 1960s, civil engineering climbed back up to a high average of 29.3 percent in the two decades. The share of degrees in mechanical, mechanical-electrical, and electrical engineering climbed in the late 1930s and reached a high of 37.8 percent in 1939. Between 1941 and 1948, that share fell to an average 16.1 percent. Decline in these three related specialties continued in the early 1950s but was followed in the late 1950s and early 1960s by strong growth to a plateau between 1965 and 1971 of 23.7 percent of all degrees granted in engineering. Finally, the share of degrees in chemical engineering grew gradually in the early 1930s and climbed again through the 1940s. A high point was reached in the 1950s with an average of 17.6 percent between 1951 and 1959. During the 1960s, the share of degrees granted in chemical engineering fell to an average of 12.2 percent.

For the period between 1967 and 1989, the data for egresados of engineering specialties present a picture of major shifts between old and new specialties within the engineering field. Although all specialties showed rapid absolute growth in the 1970s and early 1980s, there were basic changes in the relative importance of engineering specialties. In the fifteen-year period, mechanical, mechanical-electrical, and chemical engineering all saw their shares of all egresados in the engineering field decline by half, while the civil engineering specialty declined more gradually over the period. At the same time, the combined agricultural-engineering/veterinary-medicine specialty grew steadily after 1977. And a new specialty emerged as an important force within the engineering field—industrial engineering. Hidden before 1970 in the "others" category, industrial engineering rose from 6.6 percent of all egresados in engineering between 1967 and 1970 to an average of more than double that—13.0 percent—between 1982 and 1984. Older, smaller fields such as topographic-hydraulic engineering remained stagnant, or like textile engineering, fell sharply, while the new field of computer engineering grew rapidly after 1975. The new electronic-engineering component of the electrical-engineering category slowed the decline of the traditional electrical-engineering field.

Data on egresados, then, show dramatic drops in the relative importance of classical engineering specialties, including civil, mechanical/mechanical-electrical, chemical (which, although it retained its share through 1979, fell off quickly afterward), and extractive engineering in the 1967–84 period. A significant surge was experienced by the new industrial-engineering field, the importance of which doubled from the beginning of the period to the end. Data on degrees registered in engineering specialties reinforce the trends apparent in the egresados series. All fields except chemical engineering showed strong absolute growth in the period between 1966 and 1985. The most dramatic growth, however, occurred in registrations of degrees granted in the industrial-engineering specialty. The share of registrations in this field grew from a negligible percentage in the 1966–70 and 1971–75 periods to 10.8 percent between 1976 and 1980, and to 7.5 percent between 1981 and 1985. Industrial engineering grew at the expense of other registered fields with the exception of civil engineering, which retained its share over the twenty-year period, and agricultural engineering and veterinary medicine, which showed rapid growth in registrations in the years from 1970 to 1985. The three other key industrial specialties within the engineering field—chemical, mechanical, and mechanical-electrical—declined throughout the twenty-year period.

Three important changes in the relative importance of

engineering specialties occurred in the period between 1928 and 1986. First, there was a long-term decline in the importance of the classical engineering specialties, with the exception of the remarkable rise of agricultural engineering and its allied field of veterinary medicine. Second, rapid growth was experienced in new engineering specialties closely related to Mexico's rapid industrialization. Particularly striking was the rise of the new field of industrial engineering, which became one of the "classic" engineering specialties in Mexico after the mid-1960s. Third, while the data reveal moderate long-term growth in diversity, diversity was not one of the most important products of the overall growth in the engineering field. For the most part, the engineering field was dominated by a small number of specialties for the whole period between the late 1920s and the late 1980s.

To assess the historical response of university training of engineers to government policy initiatives, I compared a sampling of the data on the engineering specialties (adjusted for the six-year time lag between entrance and graduation) with trends in federal expenditure. Agricultural engineering and the two industrial specialties of mechanical/mechanical-electrical and industrial engineering were used as sample specialties of social and economic policy, respectively. Although agricultural engineering was included in the economic category in the aggregate analysis of professional fields above, it is useful here as an indicator of social impact because it is the engineering field most likely to be stimulated by government rhetoric and expenditure during social-revolutionary periods given the strong correlation between conceptions of social "revolutionariness" and agrarian reform in Mexico from 1910 to the 1980s. Agricultural engineers are also one of the most nationalistic of professional groups, and for this reason agricultural engineering is one of the professions most closely linked to the socially revolutionary aims of Mexican administrations since 1929.[29] While a majority of agricultural engineers may not take up the career in order to work toward revolutionary aims of social transformation, the small group that does has been very influential among agricultural engineers. For these reasons the agricultural-engineering field provides a view of the complex relationship among rhetoric, expenditure, and the policy impact.

Taking into account the six-year time lag, degrees granted by Mexican universities in agricultural engineering and veterinary medicine indicate the government's strong stimulation of those specialties in the mid-1930s, reaching a plateau between 1936 and 1944. This high point was followed by a drop to a low between 1945 and 1947, but this trough was followed by a resurgence between 1948 and 1954. After a sharp drop in 1955, numbers of agricultural engineering degrees granted increased slowly between 1956 and 1965. Data on egresados in agricultural engineering and veterinary medicine show that the slow climb of the 1960s gave way to a sudden rise in the mid-1970s. Registrations of degrees granted in these two fields show that after a gradual rise throughout the early 1960s, the fields increased their share rapidly between 1975 and 1979.

Degrees granted in mechanical, mechanical-electrical, and electrical engineering rose from the mid-1920s through 1933. From the mid-1930s to 1942, the share of degrees granted in these related specialties reached a low plateau, a period that was followed by great fluctuation in the share of the specialties between 1943 and 1954 with little long-term movement. At the end of the period covered by data on degrees granted, these three specialties moved up to a higher plateau in the late 1950s and early 1960s. Data on egresados show a gradual decline in mechanical and mechanical-electrical specialties, while revealing the rapid rise of industrial engineering, which sustained gradual increases through the early 1960s and then increased its share rapidly in the decade between 1966 and 1976. Finally, registrations of degrees in economic-engineering specialties show mechanical and mechanical-electrical engineering declining between 1960 and 1979, while industrial engineering grew between 1970 and 1974 and then settled at a slightly lower level of relative importance between 1975 and 1979.

The basic trends in engineering specialties in the context of sexenial presidential administrations can be summarized as follows. Agricultural engineering and veterinary medicine were greatly stimulated during the Cárdenas administration during the mid- and late 1930s. This stimulation receded under President Avila Camacho (1941–46), but then increased dramatically during the administration of President Alemán (1947–52). The key industrial specialties of mechanical, mechanical-electrical, and electrical engineering show peaks of development during the administrations of Calles in the late 1920s and during those of López Mateos (1959–64) and Díaz Ordaz (1965–70). Industrial engineering, which grew steadily during the administration of Echeverría (1971–76), was curbed in the late 1970s under López Portillo (1977–82) by the growth in relative strength of agricultural engineering and veterinary medicine. Early on, the education of engineers responded primarily to the construction of economic infrastructure, and this is reflected in the early and sustained importance of the civil and topographical/hydraulic-engineering specialties. From the late 1930s through the 1950s, there was a subtle shift toward industrial specialties such as mechanical, mechanical-electrical, electrical, and chemical engineering. Toward the end of the period under study here, there was another strong shift away from these last-named specialties and toward industrial engineering.

Does the development of the different engineering specialties fit into the policy priorities of the Mexican government established above? Analysis of sample economic and social engineering specialties reveals a distinct period dominated by more typically "social" concerns in the 1930s, evidenced by the growth of agricultural engineering. This period was followed after 1940 by a period characterized by a marked increase in industry-related specialties. In the 1960s, the data indicate a balancing of industrial and agricultural specialties in terms of percentage-share distribution of the specialties. In more recent years, we find the remarkable rebirth of agricultural engineering in the Echeverría years (and its continued strength during the administration of López Portillo with his SAM program for self-sufficiency in food), and the appearance of the dynamic industrial-engineering field.[30]

Data on engineering expertise suggest a complex picture of the relationship between policy priorities and the university system. Cárdenas and Alemán, generally considered at opposite ideological poles of Mexican economic development, both gave strong impetus to the development of agricultural expertise in Mexico. Agricultural engineering declined in importance during the administration of Ruiz Cortines (1953–58), and then slowly gained during the 1960s with the stimulation of President López Mateos's "balanced revolution." Under President Echeverría, who frequently adopted Cárdenas's rhetoric in his pronouncements regarding agricultural development, training in agricultural engineering and veterinary medicine rose to new heights.

Along with the basic correlations between government spending priorities and the education of engineers, it should be noted that the industry-related engineering specialties already were performing well in the 1930s. The data on engineers show the early appearance and strong long-term performance of engineering specialties in areas of "economic" emphasis. The data on engineers confirm that the economic phase of the Revolution was well under way in the 1930s under Cárdenas with the stimulation of industrial and economic-infrastructure engineering specialties such as mechanical-electrical engineering and civil engineering. The modernization of Mexican agriculture was an integral part of the economic phase of the Mexican Revolution; the agricultural foundation of industrialization was laid in the 1930s.

Evidence of the engineering field broadens the conclusion reached above that the human resources needed for economic takeoff after 1940 were created during the earlier, "social" revolutionary phase. The economic revolution begun during the 1940s responded to trends set in motion in society and economy in the 1930s. These trends in turn were based on a rebuilding and partial restructuring of the economy from the mid-1920s to the early 1930s under presidents Obregón (1920–24) and Calles (1924–28, and de facto 1929–34). During the 1940s, presidents Avila Camacho and Alemán recognized and legitimated economic and social priorities and decisions about the path of economic development started during the 1930s under Cárdenas (and quite likely before).

The development of the engineering field after 1939 suggests two conclusions about the historical development of all professional fields: (1) the career-path decisions of engineers have followed government policy initiatives, and (2) the expenditure of government funds in specific areas (to create employment or foster an environment that creates employment) appears to be more important than verbal rhetoric in influencing the choice of engineering fields by university students. This second conclusion is supported by the stimulation of agricultural engineering by both Cárdenas and Alemán, whose explicit economic-development ideology was, of course, quite different. Combining these two conclusions, we can say that both real employment opportunities provided by public and private investment and long-term government strategies for economic development have stimulated directly the development of professional expertise in Mexico.

Summary and Conclusions

The thesis that a current "crisis" in Mexican higher education is primarily the result of the development of the university system as a "state within a state," effectively outside government control, is not supported by quantitative data on university graduates and egresados. Close inspection of the relationship between the university system's education of professionals over time and the policy priorities of the Mexican government reveals a good fit between the two variables. Since at least 1929, universities have followed government initiative, training professionals in line with the rhetoric and spending of a succession of presidential administrations.

Because the university has been responsive to government initiatives since 1929, it is possible that what critics see as a "university crisis" lies with the pattern and process of the economic development that has occurred, rather than with the university's autonomy from government plans. The findings of this chapter suggest that the employment of professionals—employment stimulated in part by the direct and indirect effects of government policy—is key to explaining the historical development of professional expertise in Mexico. In the following chapter, I shift the analysis to the employment side of the equation to examine available data on historical employment opportunities for professionals after 1929. If the demand of Mexican leaders for professional expertise has been met to a significant degree, what about the demand expressed by the economy for professionals? What sorts of professionals has the Mexican economy needed since 1929? And what has been the university system's response to this demand?

CHAPTER 4

From Professionals to Technicians:
The Mexican Economy's
Changing Demand for
University Graduates

Many observers have accused the university system of being unable to educate the professionals that the Mexican economy needs—both in specific fields and at different levels of expertise. The common perception has been that Mexican universities produce too many graduates of "traditional" fields (too many lawyers) and not enough engineers and scientists.[1] A major characteristic of the perceived crisis in the Mexican university system is the idea that the university has not educated professionals in line with the changing demands of the Mexican economy. From the 1930s through the 1950s, the university was hailed as one of the key institutions stimulating economic development in Mexico. Since the 1960s, however, the capacity of the university system, and particularly its public component, to fulfill its role in economic development has been increasingly questioned. By the 1970s, people from both the public and private sectors were calling for closer cooperation between the universities and the economy.[2] President Luis Echeverría responded explicitly during his sexenio to the economic aspect of university crisis, undertaking educational reforms that he believed would provide university graduates with the skills they needed for the country's economic development.[3] This chapter considers two questions: How has the economy's demand for professionally skilled persons changed over time? And how has the university system responded to this changing demand?

Demand for Professionals by Economic Sector

The simplest way to measure the relationship between changing demand for professionals in the Mexican economy and university production of professional expertise is to compare data on the sectoral distribution of the economically active population (EAP) with data on university graduates.[4] If universities respond sluggishly and inefficiently to changes in employment opportunities for graduates, as many analysts of university crisis assume, then there should be an obvious lack of adjustment between changes in professional employment in EAP and shifts in career-field concentrations. On the other hand, if the universities' education of professionals has historically followed the lead of the economy, then EAP and university output should match relatively closely over time.

Using sample professions as indicators of key occupations, university graduates can be organized into primary, secondary, and tertiary economic sectors. The primary economic sector (agriculture) is represented here by agricultural engineering; the secondary sector (mining, industry, construction, and electricity) is represented by engineering fields other than agricultural engineering; and the tertiary sector (transportation, commerce, services, and government) is represented by business, health, teaching, economics, and law. Analysis is restricted to the four decades between 1950 and 1990 because census data prior to 1950 do not include detailed information on the professional and technical makeup of EAP.[5]

Comparison of the data on EAP by economic sector and university education reveals a close relationship between the evolution of professional EAP and the career-field distribution of professionals (Figs. 4–1 and 4–2). Data on both professional employment and university output show that there has been a long-term

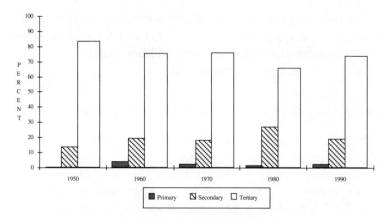

Figure 4–1. Professional EAP in Three Economic Sectors, 1950–90. SOURCE: Statistical Appendix, Table 5.

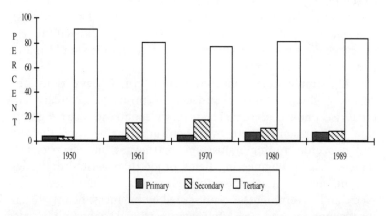

Figure 4–2. Percent of Degrees Granted and Egresados in Three Economic Sectors, 1950–89. SOURCE: Lorey, *Rise of the Professions,* Table 25.

decline in the importance of professionals employed in the tertiary, or services, sector. The share of professionals employed in this sector declined from 83.8 percent in 1950, to 66.1 in 1980, to 74.1 percent in 1990. University graduates in sample fields of the tertiary sector fell from 91.5 percent of degrees granted in

1950 to 81.4 percent among egresados and 72.7 percent among registered degrees in 1980 and 83.9 percent among egresados in 1990.[6] This decline in the relative importance of the services sector is due principally to a rise in the percentage of professionals educated and employed in the industrial sector, a trend reflected in data on both EAP and university graduates. Education of professionals for the primary sector and professional employment in that sector show a rise until 1960 and a gradual decline in 1970 and 1980.

This elementary measuring technique indicates that Mexican universities have historically operated "in tune" with the Mexican economy. The universities have produced professionals in the three basic economic sectors in approximately the same proportions as they have been employed in the economy. There is no evidence of sharp dislocations or even of a noticeable time lag between the two sets of data. Thus the university would seem at first glance to be responsive to the demands of the economy. But it is necessary to explore in detail the extent and nature of this apparent confluence of trends, making reference to specific fields of professional expertise.

Demand for Specific Professional Fields

Observers have often assumed that Mexican universities are "providing an excessive number of professionals in certain careers and very few professionals in others."[7] But the Mexican economy's demand for specific fields of professional expertise has never been adequately examined. Testing of the response of the university system to the changing specific demands of the Mexican economy is hampered by the scarcity of reliable yearly data on employment of professionals in specific occupations. There is no national system in Mexico for following university graduates and egresados into the job market. Nor is there any systematic periodic analysis of employment or lack of employment by career field on either a national or regional basis.[8] Several separate data sets can be employed, however, to create a fairly accurate picture of the relationship between the universities and the Mexican economy over time. Census data provide a historical

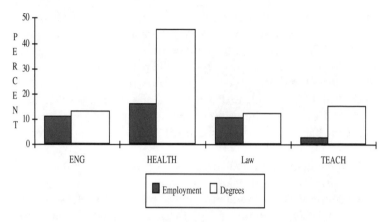

Figure 4–3. Comparison of Employment of Professionals with Degrees Granted, 1950. Note: Upper-case letters indicate career area comprising several degree fields; lower-case letters indicate single-degree career area. For example, HEALTH includes degrees in medicine, dentistry, and optometry. See Statistical Appendix for career-area details. SOURCE: Statistical Appendix, Table 5.

view, while regional data provide more detailed cross-sectional coverage.

Census data for two years, 1950 and 1980, provide insight into the basic relationship between employment and university output. The most straightforward way to measure demand for a professional skill is to examine the employment of professionals with that skill. Detailed data on occupational structure in 1950 and 1980 allow comparison between employment of professionals in a few basic professional fields and university graduates and egresados (graduates in 1950, egresados in 1980) in those fields. The fit in engineering and law was close in 1950; the fit in engineering, health, and teaching was close in 1980. (Figs. 4–3 and 4–4). The data actually indicate a closing of the gap by 1980: apparently, the university system has become increasingly in tune with employment opportunities in the Mexican economy over time. The closeness of the fit also implies that the signals available to students about job opportunities are relatively accurate, since there are no meaningful controls on student career-field choices and little career counseling in Mexico.

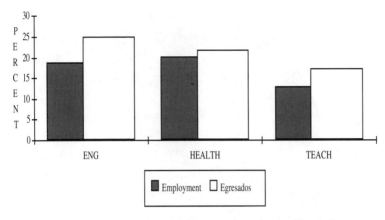

Figure 4–4. Comparison of Employment of Professionals with Egresados, 1980. SOURCE: Statistical Appendix, Table 5.

For a closer analysis of the fit between economic demand for professionals and university output, we can turn to the very small body of studies carried out on the state level by regional universities. It is possible that distortions in different states may cancel each other out at the national level, giving a false impression of a close fit. The best state-level study, because it covers changes over time, even if for only a very brief period, was carried out at the Autonomous University of Nuevo León (UANL) in the late 1970s and early 1980s. The UANL study allows several measurements of demand for professionals other than employment. Various aspects of measurements in the UANL studies create a good general picture of demand in Nuevo León; in addition, the distribution of professionals employed suggests the basic demand for specific areas of professional expertise in the state (Fig. 4–5).[9]

The data reveal that engineering, health, and business professionals were the most commonly employed professionals in Nuevo León in all economic sectors—the three fields together accounted for 70 percent of all employment positions.[10] Engineering alone accounted for 28.7 percent of positions in the state economy; health and business followed with 21.5 and 19.9 percent. Lawyers made up 10.7 percent of employed professionals.

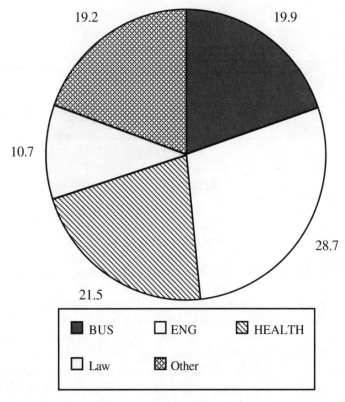

Figure 4–5. Employed Graduates of UANL, Four Fields, 1980. SOURCE: Lorey, *Rise of the Professions*, Table 28.

Among those professionals employed by industrial firms in 1981, engineers and business professionals made up fully 95.1 percent of the total—engineers 56.7 percent and business professionals, 38.4 percent.[11]

Employers' conceptions of needs are revealing. The Nuevo León project collected data from employer questionnaires for 1980 and 1981, and projected needs for 1982 and 1983. Industrial employers' needs fit well with the professionals actually employed. The needs most frequently expressed by employers were for engineers and business professionals: on average, 53.8 percent of all the professionals that employers said they needed were engineers and 38.7 percent were business professionals (as compared to 56.7 percent engineers and 38.4 percent business professionals employed).

A third way to assess demand for professionals in specific fields is to examine wages for professionals. Wages constitute the price of professional services, and prices for goods or services reveal relative scarcity and demand. Employers' perceived needs for professionals in certain areas of expertise are thus reflected in starting salaries for professional employees. Wage data for 1977 from the UANL project indicate that engineers and business professionals were the highest-paid professionals in Nuevo León's industrial sector. In the top 13.7 percent of the wage structure, 63.3 percent of initial salaries went to engineers and 33.1 percent to business professionals. In the top 15.1 percent for all groups of wages, 58.8 percent went to engineers and 29.6 percent was given to professionals with degrees in business fields.

Further insight on demand for professionals in Nuevo León is attained by examining which graduates of regional universities have the best chance of being employed. Professionals with degrees in economics were surest to find employment: all surveyed economists graduating between August 1980 and August 1981 had found work a year later. Business professionals fared almost as well, with 93.9 percent finding work. Almost 80 percent of all engineering graduates were working a year after graduating. Lawyers and health professionals, although also among the most commonly working professionals, had less success as groups, with 79.7 and 65.0 percent working.

Having established the pattern of regional demand in Nuevo León, we need to assess the fit between demands for specific professional-level skills and the functioning of regional universities. Available data suggest that most professionals practice in the state where they receive their training. While migration of professionals to areas with greater demand for their skills plays some part in the distribution of professionals in Nuevo León, its effect is probably minor.[12] There is a fairly good general fit between the demand for professionals and the output of these professionals by universities in Nuevo León (Fig. 4–6). In 1979, business egresados accounted for 18.4 percent of total egresados,

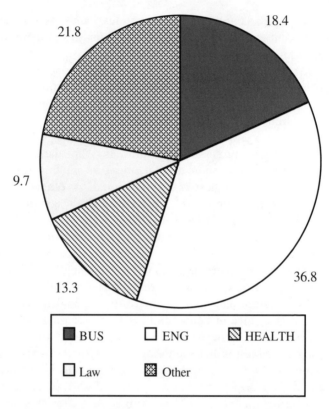

Figure 4–6. Egresados of UANL and ITESM, Four Fields, 1979. SOURCE: Calculated from ANUIES-AE, 1980.

and egresados of law accounted for 9.7 percent. The respective figures for professional employment in these career fields were 19.9 and 10.7 percent, respectively. The fit in health and engineering was not as close as it was nationally, with health professionals accounting for 13.3 percent of egresados and 21.5 percent of employment, and engineers accounting for 36.8 percent of egresados and 28.7 percent of professionals employed.

Although the overall fit between demand for and supply of professionals in specific career areas is close in Nuevo León, this state is unusual in many ways because it is both highly industrialized and located in the Mexican North.[13] Nuevo León can be expected to have a different demand for professionals than other Mexican states, and it is possible that its universities respond well to this demand for reasons that are peculiar to Nuevo León.[14] It is necessary to compare the fit of supply and demand for professionals in the state of Nuevo León with another region of Mexico to gauge whether in general the fit between supply and demand is close.

The case of three states of the Yucatán peninsula—Campeche, Quintana Roo, and Yucatán—form a perfect contrast to the situation in Nuevo León: they are southern, relatively poor, and not as industrialized as Nuevo León. These states are the only other Mexican states for which some amount of reliable regional data tracing university graduates and egresados into the job market is available. As with the data for Nuevo León, the fit between demand and supply is close enough to suggest that regional universities have responded historically to economic demand for professionals in the region. In 1979, engineers made up 30 percent of employed professionals and 25 percent of egresados; business professionals accounted for 15 percent of employed professionals and 20 percent of egresados; and lawyers made up 10 percent of both employed professionals and egresados.[15]

Data for both Nuevo León and Yucatán indicate that the fit between Mexican universities and regional and national economic structure is close. Universities appear to respond to demands on the part of the economy by producing professionals in specific areas of expertise. Given the lack of national-level data for analysis of long-term changes in this fit, it is impossible to conclude with complete certainty that the fit has historically been close or that it is equally close in all parts of Mexico. At the same time, there is no evidence that the fit has changed significantly over time, and the cases of Nuevo León and the Yucatecan states suggest that regional variations would not greatly affect this conclusion.[16]

Even though we have found a strong correlation between demand and supply of professional skills, professionals may not work in the exact areas of their training. One analyst found, for example, that among chemical engineers in 1980, 27 percent were directly involved in production and operations, while 26 percent were found in administration, 25 percent in sales and purchasing, 11 percent in research, and 8 percent in planning and design.[17] A 1963 survey of ten industrial firms found a somewhat less pronounced division: 20 percent of engineers employed in the firms were employed in sales and management positions.[18]

In general, however, it is clear that specific skills are important to employers. An extensive survey of Mexican employers found that:

> For the more senior sub-professionals and for all the professionals, occupationally oriented studies are essential. Three-fourths of our employers took the view that general education, even at the university, was inadequate even for general administration: accountancy, law, business administration, or, in the cases of the engineering companies, engineering, was felt to be a proper preparation for an administrator or manager.[19]

Available data on the professional fields of public-sector employees shed light on the impact of hiring practices on the demand for, and education of, professionals in specific fields (Fig. 4–7). Information on this key aspect of professional employment in Mexico constitutes an important context for both the national picture provided by census data and the regional portraits of Nuevo León and the three Yucatecan states. The average figures for employment by career field in the public sector (taking into account both the central government and the decentralized sector) are as follows: law, 9.8 percent; medicine (medical doctors), 13.6 percent; engineering, 29.2 percent; business, 18.3 percent; and economics, 4.7 percent. There is a strikingly close correlation between this distribution and that of data for both registered degrees and egresados in the same year. The corresponding figures for degrees registered are law, 10.0 percent; health, 25.4 percent; engineering, 26.7 percent; business, 21.0 percent; and economics, 2.1 percent. For egresados, the distribution in 1975 was as follows: law, 12.0 percent; health, 19.0 percent; engineering, 30.3 percent; business, 17.0 percent; and economics, 3.1 percent.[20] Unfortunately, there are no comparable data on public

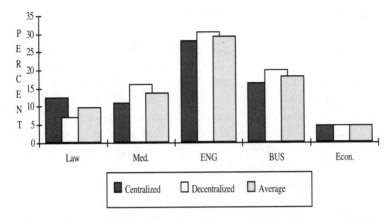

Figure 4–7. Career Fields of Public-Sector Employees in Central Government and Decentralized Sectors, Five Fields, 1975. SOURCE: Lorey, *Rise of the Professions*, Table 29.

employment for earlier or later periods, and so no trends can be discerned in public-sector hiring over time. Yet the clear correlation between employment in the public sector and the professional fields that students select implies that government hiring practices are a key factor in the stimulation of specific professional fields.[21]

The effects of government hiring practices have had an important impact on professional employment trends, and these trends seem, in turn, to have influenced the career-field choices of professionals. Many professionals receive their first job in the public sector and many work in the public sector their whole professional lives. During the administration of Miguel de la Madrid, more than half of the top-level civil servants had studied at the UNAM.[22] In the state of Yucatán, 61.6 percent of professionals surveyed in the early 1980s (egresados of the Autonomous University of Yucatán, 1970–79) found their first job in the public sector, and 67.7 percent were employed by public-sector firms at the time of the survey.[23] Even in Nuevo León, a state thought to be dominated by private-sector interests, almost 15 percent of professionals surveyed in the UANL project worked directly for the government in the late 1970s—a much larger percent if decentralized public-sector industries and services are taken into account.[24]

Two important conclusions can be drawn from these various data sets. First, economic demand has historically had a great deal of influence on student decisions regarding career fields. Second, the university system as a whole has generally responded to economic demand without a great deal of distortion—that is, without producing a great number of unwanted professionals in specific fields. As will be discussed below, Mexican universities may have produced "too many" graduates altogether after a certain time, more than there were professional-level jobs, but the distribution among professional fields has corresponded closely to demand as measured by professional employment.

Student choices and the overall university response in line with economic demand may seem surprising in light of the scarcity of career counseling at Mexican universities. Yet this historical responsiveness shows clearly that students have access to relatively unambiguous signals of which sectors of the economy can provide them employment after graduation. These signals include government rhetoric, government expenditure, and government hiring practice, as well as wages, the saturation of the job market in certain professional fields, and want ads emanating from private-sector firms.[25] The analysis here dovetails neatly with that in Chapter Three. Policy priorities expressed in government rhetoric and expenditure (and government hiring in line with rhetoric and spending) and economic demand have been closely intertwined since 1929. Together, they have had a significant impact on how the university system produces professionals.

Differential Demand for Professionals and Technicians

In addition to its demand for general and specific areas of professional expertise, the economy expresses a demand for different *levels* of expertise. The major distinction to be considered here is that between professionals and technicians. The professional and technician levels, taken together, have made up an increasing part of Mexico's economically active population (EAP) since 1950, the first year for which there is census data by functional classification of occupation. Professionals and technicians grew from 2.5 percent of EAP in 1950 to 7.4 percent in 1980 and 10.6 percent in 1990.[26] But what has been the relationship between professionals and technicians over time? This relationship is of primary importance because the ratio between the two groups, and how that ratio has evolved over time, reveals a great deal about the nature of the economic development in Mexico since 1929.

The difference between professionals and technicians is not to be confused with differences in sector of employment. Shifts within sectors of the Mexican labor force, from agricultural occupations to employment in industry and services, have been well documented.[27] Clearly, there has been a major historical evolution in EAP away from primary activities into secondary and, above all, tertiary employment. But sector of employment is not the same as occupation, and inter-sectoral shifts in EAP are highly misleading if used to gauge historical shifts in the level of occupations of the work force.[28] A close examination of census categories shows that a very large proportion of workers in communications and transport, commerce, and industry have always been self-employed mule-drivers, shopkeepers, and artisans—not professionals or technicians.[29] The most difficult category to analyze as to occupational level is that which has grown most rapidly over time: services. Clearly, many service occupations are not "modern sector" jobs but rather account for domestic workers, as well as vendors of tissue and chewing gum on urban street corners. Thus shifts from occupations in agriculture to jobs in services, communications, and industry do not necessarily indicate growth of highly productive occupational niches. In contrast to inter-sectoral distribution of the labor force, very little is known about the relationship between different occupational levels within EAP.

The historical trends imply that Mexican economic development has created a relatively greater demand for technicians than

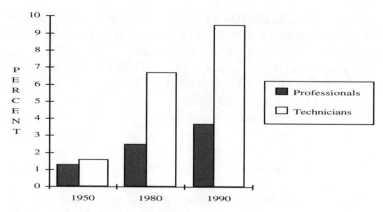

Figure 4–8. Percent of Professionals and Technicians in EAP, 1950–90. SOURCE: Statistical Appendix, Table 5.

for professionals over time (Fig. 4–8). Whereas the absolute number of professional job openings grew 417.8 percent between 1950 and 1980, those for technicians grew 1,055.3 percent during the same period.[30] The Mexican economy thus developed in a way that has led to limited job creation at a very important level of the occupational ladder. The rate of absorption of professionals is if anything overestimated in the census data: because the data are based on the answers of census respondents, they reflect to some degree the supply of professionals (some of whom respond that they are professionals even if they work as technicians) over demand.[31]

The nature of the data series employed in Chapter Three to sketch the evolution of professional fields in Mexico since 1929 supports the thesis that employment opportunities have not increased apace with university production. Data on the ratio of professional-level degrees granted at universities and technician-level degrees granted at universities and secondary schools between 1928 and 1971 show a steady decline after 1940 in the proportion of professional-level degrees to all degrees. The professional share settled at a plateau of an average 32.5 percent between 1941 and 1950, dropped further to an average of 24.4 percent between 1951 and 1957, and finally fell to an average of

17.8 percent between 1958 and 1967. The percentage recovered a bit in the late 1960s to 20.7 between 1968 and 1971. The most dramatic decline came between the mid- and the late 1950s.

The ratio of egresados to registered degrees reveals a large gap between the two indicators, varying from three-to-one to two-to-one with no marked trend between 1970 and 1985.[32] The gap suggests that a large portion of students leaves the university to begin working at the intermediate egresado level. The gap indicates also that many egresados find work as technicians, for it can be assumed that they work primarily in positions where registration of the degree is not required by employers. If persons who register their degrees have already arranged for professional employment or expect it in the near future, then the difference between the number of registered degrees and the number of egresados represents a difference between available jobs and the number of aspirants. The quantitative gap between the two indicators probably indicates a contraction of employment opportunities for professionals sometime after the 1950s. Many observers have noted that since the early 1960s a decreasing percentage of egresados has gone on to achieve the licentiate degree. Various estimates place the percentage of those egresados who did not achieve the final degree in the 1960s at 30 percent, while the ratio can be established as at least 50 percent for the mid-1980s. It seems that a majority of egresados increasingly found work after the late 1950s or early 1960s where they did not need the licentiate degree, most likely as technicians in industry and services. The demand for the more highly trained holders of university degrees would appear to be over-supplied, leading to the increasing production of egresados.

Much secondary evidence, both empirical and impressionistic, supports the conclusion that the Mexican economy grew in a way that did not stimulate demand for the most highly trained university graduates. Many observers noted the differential demand for technicians after the 1950s.[33] The few studies that record these changes suggest that the industries that grew most rapidly after 1955 required a much greater number of technicians than professionals.[34] Such industries as automobiles and automobile parts, electrical machinery and appliances, and nonferrous metals, as well as iron and steel, were among the fastest growing industries, and these industries were important employers of lower- and middle-level technicians.[35] At about 1955, the demand for high-level skills began to diminish in comparison with middle-level skills in many import-substituting industries.[36] In general, the demand for university graduates appears to have been increasingly elastic as compared to that for graduates of other educational levels.[37]

One of the most convincing pieces of circumstantial evidence of a growing differential in demand for professionals and technicians is provided by studies of industrial employment and wage differentials between employed professionals and technicians. A Banco de México study showed that as early as 1961 only 7 percent of employees in middle-level positions were specifically trained for that level: while 54 percent had been brought up from the ranks of workers, fully 39 percent of technicians were university educated.[38] Between 1940 and 1976, white-collar occupational earnings declined relative to blue-collar occupational earnings—a decline that was particularly rapid after the early 1960s.[39] Both this decline and its acceleration by the early 1960s reflect the two interrelated phenomena discussed here: the declining relative demand for professionals and the increasing supply of university graduates.

We can compare the rates of growth for employment positions for professionals and technicians in the census data with the rates of production of professionals at Mexican universities (Fig. 4–9). As noted above, employment positions available in the economy for professionals grew 417.8 percent between 1950 and 1980; positions for technicians, on the other hand, grew 1,055.3 percent. Between 1950 and 1960, the number of degrees granted in all professional fields grew 75.1 percent; between 1960 and 1970, 232.1 percent. Between 1970 and 1980 the number of egresados grew 266.5 percent and registrations of degrees 149.1 percent. No single series on university graduates covers the entire time span between 1950 and 1980, but the three series together make the essential trends clear.

The growth rate of degrees granted was matched fairly closely by the growth rate of professionals until 1960. Between 1950 and

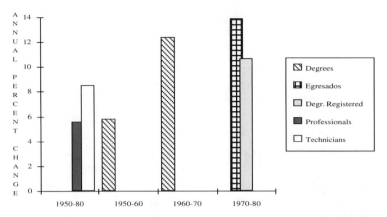

Figure 4–9. Growth of Degrees Granted, Egresados, Degrees Registered, Professionals, and Technicians. SOURCE: Statistical Appendix, Table 5.

1980 the annual growth rate of professional EAP was 5.6 percent compared to 5.8 percent for degrees granted between 1950 and 1960. Between 1960 and 1970, however, the number of degrees granted grew at an annual rate of 12.4 percent. The annual rate of growth of degrees granted for the entire period from 1950 to 1970 was 9.0 percent. By the 1960s, the universities were clearly producing graduates at a rate much faster than the rate of job creation for professionals in the Mexican economy.[40] The number of degrees registered grew at an annual rate of 10.7 percent between 1971 and 1980, very close to the growth experienced by degrees granted in the 1960s.[41] The growth rate of egresados, on the other hand, was significantly higher than that of either degrees granted or degrees registered and thus seems to reflect the higher growth of positions for technicians. While the number of positions for technicians in EAP grew at an annual rate of 8.5 percent between 1950 and 1980, egresados grew at an annual rate of 13.9 percent between 1967 and 1980.

A comparison of census data with series on university graduates indicates that employment for technicians grew much more rapidly than for professionals after 1950. The growth rates of technicians and professionals in EAP were mirrored in the growth rates of egresados and degrees granted and registered. It seems clear that the major difference between university egresados and university graduates in the job market is that egresados are more likely than graduates to be employed at the technician level.

Analysis of these various data sets on professionals and technicians points to four general conclusions. First, the ability of the Mexican economy to absorb university graduates at the professional level has not grown as fast as has the number of university students. Second, the demand for technicians has grown at a much faster rate than that for professionals. Third, the universities have produced both professionals and technicians at rates significantly greater than the rate of job creation. Fourth, the mismatch between demand and output and the differentially greater demand for technicians than for professionals appears to have been particularly marked since the late 1950s.

Implications for Economic Development Since 1929

What do the historical trends in university graduates and employment opportunities for professionals outlined above tell us about the nature of economic development in Mexico since 1929 (and particularly about the process of industrialization after the late 1930s)? Why has employment for professionals been as limited as it has been since the late 1950s?

Until the late 1950s, the expanding industrial and commercial sectors and the growing state apparatus absorbed most university-trained professionals relatively easily. The perception of observers in the late 1950s that there was a shortage of engineers, business managers, highly skilled workers, and scientists was generally correct.[42] Demand for engineers and business managers was especially high, because the Institutionalized Revolution focused economic development efforts on industrialization and the modernization of commercial networks. The fact that many working people at the technician and lower occupational levels were promoted to professional positions implies a vacuum at the professional level during this period.[43]

Government employment of professionals accounted for a large part of this professional employment boom. Professional employment in the public sector received its first real boost with the rise of the active state in the late 1920s and in the 1930s under Cárdenas. The expansion of state employment benefited a broad cross section of Mexican society, but particularly the professionally trained offspring of the growing middle sectors. All the great projects of the early years of Mexico's economic revolution—land distribution, banking, transportation, irrigation, and the establishment of myriad government agencies and enterprises—required a great many professionally skilled persons for management and direction. The public sector needed professionals with experience in "modern production engineering, in the careful computation of costs and returns, in market analysis, [and] in the scientific appraisal of alternative opportunities."[44] For example, the demand for professionals for public-sector banking services—due to the government's establishment of a string of credit institutions to finance economic development between 1935 and 1957[45]—was an important stimulus to professional education.

After the late 1950s, the economy became unable to produce jobs for professionals at the rate that professionals were graduating from the universities.[46] Professionals generally did not find themselves unemployed, but rather increasing numbers of professionally trained university graduates found work as technicians. High rates of GDP growth (6.9 percent per year in the 1940s, 5.6 percent in the 1950s, 7.0 percent in the 1960s, and 5.5 percent in the 1970s) provided the economy with many jobs, but job creation at the professional level did not keep pace with job creation at lower occupational levels. By the 1970s, the reduced capability of the economy to produce jobs for professionals led to overt government concern under President Echeverría. Echeverría attempted to stimulate the direct creation of employment at the professional level in the private sector and at the same time greatly expanded public-sector job opportunities for university graduates.[47]

I suggest that the post-1950 trend of increasingly depressed demand for professionals relative to technicians is related to three main characteristics of the historical development of the Mexican economy. These three factors, and others of less importance, worked in concert to influence major changes in the university system's functioning after the late 1950s. All were the unintended, unexpected, and perhaps unavoidable results of government policy and the pattern of economic development.

First, employment opportunities for professionals were restricted by historically high levels of protection of Mexican industry. Protection of industrial concerns had its roots in the Porfiriato; protection after the Revolution began in earnest in the late 1930s and increased rapidly and steadily until the mid-1980s. Mexican industries received a wide range of protections, particularly an overvalued peso from the early 1940s through 1954, quantitative control of imports thereafter, and generous tax breaks and implicit subsidies throughout. The employment-creating effects of the dynamic economic growth after 1940, growth that was engendered by such protective policies, were much diminished by the late 1960s, a fact reflected in Echeverría's stopgap attempts in the 1970s to increase employment at the professional level.

Protection from domestic and international competition allowed Mexican industry to produce goods with outmoded equipment, minimal investment for research and development, and limited innovation: it limited the need for new technology and associated professional knowledge,[48] because Mexican entrepreneurs had little incentive to innovate to raise productivity.[49] Limited spending for research and development restricted job creation in a key area of professional employment. The use of outmoded technology, and the reliance for economic growth during the 1940s and 1950s on increased utilization of installed capacity idle up to the late 1930s, greatly reduced both the number of professionals needed by the economy and the level of professional training at the universities. Little of the economic growth that occurred in Mexico during the process of import-substituting industrialization was due to technological change.[50] Most of the technology used in industrial plants in the 1980s continued to be obsolete or lag behind state-of-the-art innovations.[51]

A second factor that restricted the employment opportunities for professionals was the historical pattern of importation of capital goods, and thus of technology developed outside of Mexico, as a basis for industrial expansion. Importation of professional expertise embodied in foreign-made machines constricted employment opportunities for Mexican professionals because technology in industry is not an independent, abstract body of knowledge but rather a function of machines and their development.[52] Capital-goods industries have a much greater need for professional-level employees than do other manufacturing firms, requiring preinvestment studies, complex technology, quality control, credit, and marketing.[53]

Reliance on imports of machines and the sluggish development of the Mexican capital-goods industry were not chance occurrences but rather were a result of the economic development strategies followed after 1940 and particularly after the devaluation of 1954. During the period of "Stabilizing Development" (1954–76), one of the primary preoccupations of economic policymakers was satisfying the desire to import machines while trying to keep capital purchases within the limits imposed by the goal of domestic price stability.[54] Government subsidies—from accelerated depreciation and investment tax credits to exemptions from tariff laws—encouraged the private sector to import capital goods.[55] After 1955 the Mexican peso was continuously overvalued, facilitating the importation of machinery. Between 1960 and 1978, the percentage of Mexican imports of machinery and other equipment grew from 1 to 10 percent of all imports.[56] Even in periods of rapid growth in the manufacture of capital goods (like the late 1970s, when production of capital goods increased by 67.8 percent), the importation of capital goods (124.7 percent) far exceeded that growth.[57]

The reliance of Mexican industry on imported capital goods meant that the primary stimulus to professional education took place in the countries that produced advanced capital goods for domestic use and for export,[58] a tendency strengthened by the pattern of foreign investment in capital-intensive industries. Foreign investment, particularly by large, multinational corporations, came to dominate "in areas demanding sophisticated technology and large amounts of capital, such as rubber, chemicals, fabricated metals, electrical and nonelectrical machinery, and transportation."[59]

A good example of the relationship between foreign investment and demand for professional expertise is the Mexican auto industry. This industry, generally an important employer of professionals in the developed world, has created only very little demand for highly trained professionals in Mexico, since the vast majority of innovation continues to take place in the United States, Japan, and Europe. The auto-parts industry, the sector of the Mexican auto industry most stimulated by the development of car manufacturing for export, although it has had some positive effects on increasing demand for professional expertise, expresses relatively weak demand for professional-level employees compared to what an independent terminal auto industry could.[60]

Because a capital-goods industry developed only very slowly in Mexico, it should not be surprising that Mexican universities have not educated the large numbers of graduate-level experts in sciences and technology associated with advanced, competitive economies. Professionals in these areas, particularly those trained to the graduate level, have not been demanded by the Mexican productive apparatus because Mexico continues to concentrate its productive capacities in the consumer-nondurable, consumer-durable, and intermediate-goods sectors.[61] And because of the prominent role of foreign investment in development of the Mexican capital-goods sector, the economy could come to have an important capital-goods component without exerting a strong demand for highly trained professionals. One observer sums up the relationship this way: "Overinvestment in capital goods was [consistently] combined with underinvestment in management skills and labor training."[62]

Such effects of protection and dependence on imported capital goods are apparent in the case of the textile industry of Mexico, particularly the cotton-textile industry concentrated in the states of Puebla and Veracruz. Because of protection and concentration on the domestic market, the Mexican textile industry was able to operate profitably with prerevolutionary equipment imported from Europe and little innovation in production or management through the 1960s.[63] Protection, along with other factors, meant that a strong incentive to reinvest in research and development or in the physical plant did not exist.[64] Because of these factors, textile manufacturing in Mexico did not lead to the development of a textile-machine industry, which would in turn have provided demand for machine-tool and specialty-steel industries.[65] The concomitant sluggish growth of the textile-engineering field, to be expected in such a situation, was noted in the previous chapter.

These first two factors have made it possible for the Mexican economy to get by with a smaller relative number of professionals than that found in the developed world, probably without a great effect on productivity in the industrial sector.[66] Because of government protection and the importation of capital goods, Mexican employers have been able to save on costs by reducing investments in research and development and by upgrading workers through formal and informal on-the-job training. Thus Mexican industrialists have not been forced to reduce the higher labor costs associated with employing professionals by improving technology or raising the productivity of professionals. Neither have they been faced with incentives to develop original technology or adapt advanced technology to Mexican markets. Instead, protection and importation of technology have made it possible for producers to save on labor costs by hiring fewer professionals. Attempts to upgrade Mexico's technology-innovating infrastructure were notably weak: CONACYT (Consejo Nacional de Ciencia y Tecnología) was established in the early 1970s but never was provided the level of funding necessary to achieve its goals. All of these factors were bound in a vicious circle in which the reduced need to innovate limited opportunities for highly trained professionals and the lack of these professionals raised the supply price of innovations in Mexico. When the sluggishness with which Mexican industry evolved technologically came to be understood as one of the economy's critical points of weakness in the 1980s and 1990s, it would prove difficult to break the circle.[67]

A third factor complicated the employment situation of professionals after the late 1950s: the pattern of government employment of university graduates. Much of the increase in Mexico's professional/technical EAP after the late 1930s occurred in state or parastatal concerns, the number of which mushroomed after the 1950s. In both centralized and decentralized sectors after the late 1950s, the government absorbed those professionals produced by the universities but not really needed by either the public or the private sectors. Over time, the government grew into the largest employer of university graduates and egresados. The state's importance as a first employer of professionals who later find employment in the private sector continued to be very great into the 1990s.

Many of the agencies and state-controlled industries that hired professionals had limited real needs for the skills of highly trained professionals but were under political pressure to expand employment.[68] This dynamic produced the illusion of rapidly growing professional cadres, while the real need for high-level professional skills probably stagnated. This mismatch is reflected in the differential demand for professionals and technicians since the late 1950s discussed above.

The rapid expansion of the public sector after the 1930s was driven in part by the need to create jobs for professionals from middle-sector backgrounds. The growth of public-sector hiring of professionals reached a peak in the late 1970s and early 1980s; public-sector employment exploded by 82 percent between 1975 and 1983. By 1983, public-sector employees accounted for 20.4 percent of all Mexican employees. Three-quarters of this growth in public-sector hiring occurred in the centralized sector (more than half in the central government itself), and one-quarter in the decentralized agencies and industries. Three-quarters of public-sector employees were employed in services.[69]

Since the 1950s, the real demand for highly trained professionals in the public sector has not been particularly high. Government employment in key areas of infrastructure—such as the nationalized railroad, petroleum, and electricity industries in the 1930s, 1940s, and 1950s—required a certain number of experts at the top. But later developments in these sectors did not increase the demand for professionals proportionally. The government needed a few specialists for the top ministry positions and for important posts in the decentralized agencies, but the majority of government employees in professional positions did not need a high-quality professional background.

An excellent example of the underlying pattern in government employment of professionals is found in Mexico's oil industry after the expropriation of 1938 and the creation of the government petroleum monopoly PEMEX. The petroleum industry requires a great deal of capital investment but creates proportionally few professional jobs. After 1938, PEMEX expanded employment greatly even during times of stagnating production and, since the mid-1940s, has probably employed roughly twice as many persons as needed at all levels of expertise.[70] During the late 1970s, PEMEX again expanded its employment beyond its real needs as it was increasingly incorporated into government plans for economic growth and social transformation.[71] Employment at PEMEX almost doubled between 1975 and 1983.[72]

The oil industry, the motor of Mexico's economic growth from the late 1970s to 1982 and a key prop to the economy during the crisis of the 1980s, developed in an inefficient and noncompetitive way, relying for its profitability on high prices for oil and on imported technology. PEMEX spent very little on basic research or the development of secondary petroleum products.[73] This pattern of development is reflected in the lackluster growth of the petroleum engineering field noted in Chapter Three. President Salinas's purging of the corrupt leadership of the petroleum workers' union in 1989 was a move toward making operations more efficient. A key aspect of plans to improve efficiency was to reduce the drain of overlapping and superfluous jobs at the professional level. The great sponge constituted by 60 years of government hiring became saturated and by the 1990s was being squeezed to shake out excess professionals.

These three interrelated factors, which link the employment of professionals to Mexico's economic development, reflect the most problematic aspects of the evolution of the Mexican economy. Limited real demand for professionals reflects the uncompetitive, inefficient nature of Mexican industry and its reliance on the Mexican government for protection and on foreign capital-goods producers for technological innovation.[74] It is the historical pattern of economic development that has limited demand for professionals, not any absolute lack of professionals or relative lack of professionals in specific fields that has limited economic development.[75]

The sluggish growth of the sciences sketched in Chapter Three supports these conclusions, indicating that expenditure for research and development by Mexican firms grew only slowly after 1929. Even after 1940, private-sector firms did not need a large number of scientists for research. Some of this inertia may be due to the influence of foreign enterprises, which generally find it efficient to carry out their research and development operations in the developed countries. Principally, however, the sluggish growth in the education of scientists followed from the strategy of import substitution adopted by the Mexican leaders after 1940. The relatively uncontrolled flow of foreign capital goods—machines and equipment for manufacturing—led to an almost complete neglect of basic research and a weak scientific and technological infrastructure.[76] In the 1970s, while the number of research institutions and specialists increased with government support, "A comparable demand for these services from industry never materialized, despite tax and loan incentives. The prospects of abundant petrodollars and easily obtainable technology, capital goods, and intermediate products from abroad made the national effort rather extraneous."[77] Additionally, scientists have not played an important role in public-sector policy research or implementation. In general, the public sector has relied on the private sector, both foreign and domestic, for technological innovations.[78]

Neither the history of graduate study nor that of undergraduate study in the humanities, social sciences, and natural sciences reveals a Mexican economy characterized by a high degree of diversity or complexity. There has been little demand for highly trained professionals with graduate preparation. The economy has not historically had the ability to produce employment for specialists in the humanities or social sciences—"non-productive," or not directly productive, professionals. The supply of professionals with skills in these areas has not increased over time, but rather appears to have remained fairly stable since 1929.

The absorption of large numbers of professionals into the economy from the late 1930s through the 1950s did not indicate the beginning of indefinitely expanding employment opportunities for professionals. This earlier phase of employment expansion was itself illusory in good part. The example of employment during World War II and immediately afterward is instructive: while the economy expanded, and with it employment opportunities for professionals, the structure of the economy underwent no radical change—the increases in production and employment were due principally to increased utilization of idle capacity. Because there was no change in the nature of the machinery used and no increase in expenditure for research and development, the employment of professionals underwent no dramatic qualitative change. The absolute numbers of professionals in the wartime workplace may have increased, yet their *relative* numbers did not increase significantly.[79]

Analysts of the Mexican economy have tended to confuse growing employment in "modern" sectors of the economy since 1940 with a "modern" occupational profile. The secondary and tertiary sectors of Mexico's economy may have expanded, yet that expansion was characterized by the continuation of rather traditional needs for professional skills. This continuity implies that the Mexican economy, although highly developed in some aspects, did not achieve an industrial development characterized by innovation and competitiveness. The economy developed without stimulating an independent capital-goods and research-and-development infrastructure. And without the development of a self-sustaining capital-goods industry and domestic research-and-development networks, opportunities for professionals were severely limited.[80]

While it is clear that the proportion of all skilled labor increased in the Mexican economy between 1950 and 1980, this general trend obscures the differential growth of less-skilled labor (technicians) within the skilled group.[81] While GDP grew rapidly during the 1960s (at 7.0 percent per year) and during the 1970s (at 6.6 percent each year), employment for professionals did not increase at a similar rate. Economic, social, and political stresses have arisen from this unintended result of Mexico's economic development that were not foreseen by optimistic observers of the "Mexican Miracle." And in looking back, analysts have inaccurately attributed these stresses to the internal faults of the university system rather than to the pattern of economic development.

Effects of Economic Change on the University System

Many more students enter the universities with professional careers in mind than there are professional career spots available in the job market: most of them will have to take jobs as technicians. In contrast to the sluggish trend in professional employment as compared to rapid increase in employment for technicians, university enrollment in professional fields has been increasing continuously since the 1930s and particularly since the late 1950s. This growth became a problem only after the late 1950s, when absorption of university-trained professionals in the economy began to slow.[82] The virtual explosion in the number of university students who finish coursework but do not attain the degree reflects a rational response to the mismatch between the number of professional jobs and the number of aspirants.

The changing structure of the economy and the changing nature of its demand for professionals and technicians were not reflected in university fee structures or admissions policy. The fee structure in the public university system sent incorrect signals about the Mexican economy and the demand of that economy for university-educated professionals after the late 1950s. Before that time, the low cost of public university education reflected more or less accurately the need for a great quantity of professionals in "traditional" and "nontraditional" fields. Student pressures, based in the revolutionary rhetoric of universal and free education, kept fees low and the doors to applicants open at the public universities from the 1930s through the 1980s. Low private costs for attaining professional status and skills attracted a growing number of applicants; at the same time, most aspirants were admitted to the universities.

Government subsidy of higher-education costs has historically been the determining factor in university pricing policy, even though the universities are formally outside direct government control.[83] Government subsidies have been used to make up for the low level of university fees and have led directly to the massive influx of new aspirants to professional employment. Employers have also gained a great deal from this arrangement, because the government subsidy of low fees has been passed on as a major subsidy to employers of university graduates.

Like university pricing policy, university admissions policy has not responded to the economy's preference for technicians over professionals. Evidence of trends in enrollment at professional and technician levels shows a ratio far removed from the reality of demand for professionals and technicians. In the 1958–63 period, for example, there was a 20 percent increase in secondary enrollment at the IPN, but an 80 percent increase in enrollment at the university level.[84] The predominance of college-preparatory programs in secondary school has encouraged secondary-school graduates to enter the university and follow a professional course of study.[85]

Neither have public-sector wage and hiring policies adjusted over time to changes in the demand for professionals in the Mexican economy. The government bureaucracies were locked for several decades into pay scales that placed a premium on formal educational training. Agency directors and others who hired in the public sector demanded university degrees for positions in the bureaucracy regardless of modest needs for high-level expertise. Public-sector hiring and promotion practices favored those applicants with professional training. The government contributed to the confusion sown by its subsidies to the public universities by paying relatively high wages to professionals in the public sector and by linking employment in government bureaucracies to educational attainment rather than to the ability to perform discrete tasks. The effect of government intervention was widespread because public-sector wages have a great impact on private-sector wages, and because public-sector hiring policies affect hiring in the private sector. All these factors added to demand for higher educational opportunities.[86]

A gradual, and until the 1980s, subtle, change in the status of university degrees followed from the mismatch between graduates and jobs. Because so many opportunities for professionally trained persons were actually at the technician level, a professional degree, or at least some formal professional training, was frequently needed to find work, particularly in the public sector, but the specific professional skills and knowledge formally associated with the degree or training often were not. For the student there was little incentive to achieve the skills associated with the formal degree if he or she would most likely find employment as a technician. A paper chase ensued. While positions for professionals were increasingly closed at the top, an egresado diploma or even a licentiate degree was increasingly needed to find work as a technician.

Differences between declining demand for university graduates with degrees and increasing enrollment at the professional level led to conflicts over academic standards. General downward pressure, exerted primarily through student strikes, tended to minimize admission requirements and levels of academic achievement expected of students. Students exerted this pressure on academic standards primarily as an attempt to square academic requirements with the requirements of the job market. This pressure was largely implicit and existed in addition to students' general desires for less-demanding academic criteria. Comparison of data on job opportunities for professionals and on university production of professionals (above) suggests that the achievement level at Mexican universities settled at roughly the average level needed in the labor market over time.

This complex web of interrelated processes can be summed up as follows. Because of the relatively slow rate at which the Mexican economy produced places for upper-level professionals after the 1950s, and because of the continuing low private cost of public university education, the university increasingly produced egresados who would be employed as technicians. Since the majority of students did not need the knowledge behind the licentiate degree to work as technicians, they exerted a downward pressure on achievement standards at the university. This downward pressure reflected above all the differentially greater economic demand for technicians than professionals in both the public and private sectors.

Summary and Conclusions

The historical relationship between the university and economic development in Mexico must be reassessed. Many observers of Mexico's economic growth have complained of a dearth of trained professionals in what they see as the "right" fields; they have seen the lack of professionals in certain fields as an obstacle to economic development. And, for the most part, they have seen this problem as stemming from shortcomings in the Mexican university system and thus as a part of a university crisis in Mexico.[87]

A careful review of trends in university production suggests that the development of the Mexican economy produced the patterns of professional education revealed in statistical data. Thus, we should not blame the Mexican university for not producing "enough" professionals or for not producing professionals in the "right" fields of expertise. Professionals were educated as their skills were needed in Mexico. This pattern follows that of the now-developed countries, which did not begin their industrial drives with "enough" skilled professionals or with university graduates trained in just the "right" professional fields, but rather educated them as they went along.

The demand of the Mexican economy for professional expertise, in different fields and at different levels, has been met by the university system to a greater degree than believed. The university, its structure and function, evolved very much in tune with the process of economic development as it unfolded after 1929. Until the late 1950s, the expanding industrial and commercial sectors, and the growing state apparatus, absorbed the bulk of the universities' production of professionals. Demand for a steady supply of scarce professionals was reflected in high wages for professionals in both public and private sectors and low costs for higher education through low, government-subsidized fees at the public universities. In a cyclical fashion, high wages and low private costs for education stimulated growing enrollments at the universities.

After the late 1950s, a differentially greater demand for technicians as opposed to professionals led to several key changes in the structure and function of the university, as the end of the period of emphasis on economic revolution in 1958 coincided with a leveling-off of the growth of employment opportunities for professionals. The government might create public-sector jobs for many professionals, but without strong growth in the private sector of the economy, employment could not be provided for all. Even Frank Brandenburg, generally optimistic about the achievements of the Revolution with regard to the employment of professionals, noted in the early 1960s that "there is some doubt whether private enterprise is . . . providing attractive jobs in sufficient number to satisfy the job appetites of college and technical-school graduates." [88]

The Mexican university system has responded to the greater relative demand for technicians by producing large numbers of egresados to fill technician positions, taking over in part the role of secondary or technical education. While there may be nothing inherently wrong with such a substitution of universities for secondary schools in the function of training technicians, it is unlikely to be the most efficient allocation of resources. University education imposes by far the highest social cost of all levels of education in Mexico. [89] But I suggest that this fundamentally inefficient university system accomplished important social and political objectives. How and why the university system responded the way it did to the economy's demand will be taken up in the following two chapters.

CHAPTER 5

The "Crisis" of Quality in Mexican Higher Education and the Rise of the Private Universities

Much of the debate surrounding the university crisis in Mexico has focused on the issue of the quality of the education received by students—the quality of the university's professional output. The assumption that a historical decline in the quality of university education had reached crisis proportions by the 1980s is almost universal among scholars and policymakers.[1] Accepting declining quality a priori, some political analysts have seen the rhetorical debate about quality as obscuring a struggle between the government and students for domination of the university.[2] But almost no scholarly work has been devoted to the question of quality in historical perspective or to the relationship between the quality of university education and long-term trends in Mexico's economic development.

Quality: Measurements and Implications

The central difficulty in any discussion of the quality of university education in Mexico is the measurement of such an elusive concept. How can we gauge quality at Mexican universities? What are the implications of changes in quality over time? Has a crisis in quality developed since 1929? Why are there differences in quality among institutions of higher learning in Mexico?

Three fairly reliable ways to gauge quality at the university level can be developed from available statistical data: (1) per-student expenditure on higher education; (2) teacher-student ratios; and (3) ratios of full-time faculty to teaching staff hired on an hourly basis.[3] Unfortunately, there is no way to measure accurately or consistently many other aspects of university education that contribute to quality—faculty qualifications, average class size, the level of reading materials, the sophistication of assignments or exams, the state of the physical plant (including libraries and laboratories), attendance, or trends in grading. Standard aptitude or achievement tests do not exist for Mexico.

The picture we get using the above three indicators will of course be incomplete. No claim is made here that these data reveal a complete picture of quality; rather they are valuable proxy variables that should be considered in any discussion of quality. It is unlikely that expenditures per student could go up, that there could be fewer students per teacher, and that the ratio of full-time to all faculty could increase without some positive change in the quality of education for students. Most importantly, these are the only existing data that shed any light on historical quality issues in Mexican higher education. Some critics may argue that quality is an entirely "subjective" characteristic of educational systems and cannot be gauged by any "objective" means. I do not claim that the data here allow for an entirely objective view of changes in quality at Mexican universities, but that they provide a less-subjective, and longer-term, perspective. Subjective measures by themselves—the opinions of educators or students, or interviews with other persons presumably affected by educational quality issues—must be used with great caution.

Expenditure per student at public universities in Mexico rose in real terms in the period from 1930 to 1980 (Fig. 5–1).[4] Expenditure levels (in 1970 pesos) were fairly stable at an average of 1,760 pesos between 1930 and 1955. This expenditure had increased to an average of 1,927 pesos per student enrolled between 1965 and 1975, and remained high in the early 1980s with

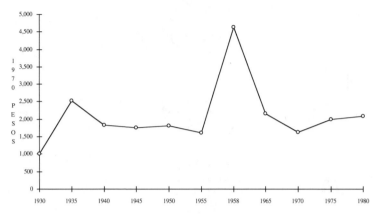

Figure 5–1. Mexican Universities' Real Expenditure per Student, 1930–80. SOURCE: Statistical Appendix, Table 6.

the influence of the oil-boom expenditures of the central government. There was no sudden drop after the late 1950s or late 1960s, when many observers have suggested a "crisis" in quality began; in fact, government expenditures kept pace with the rapid rise in student enrollment during those periods. This basic conclusion is supported by alternate, shorter-term data from UNESCO for the years 1961 through 1985, suggesting, as do my data series (drawn from many different sources) that one peak of expenditure came at the end of the 1950s and another in the early 1980s.[5]

Does the average number of students per faculty member at Mexican universities between 1928 and 1985 reveal a crisis in quality (Fig. 5–2)?[6] The ratio of students to teachers began high at almost 22 students per teacher in 1928 and then fell to a low average of 5.1 in the early 1950s. After the early 1950s, the ratio began to increase slowly, from an average 6.9 in the late 1950s, to 7.6 in the early 1960s, to 11.9 in the late 1970s, to a plateau averaging 10.6 students per teacher between 1980 and 1990.[7]

There was no sudden, dramatic leap in the ratio of students to teachers at any point between 1929 and 1990. Rather the ratio of students per professor improved gradually from a high of 21.8 in 1928 to a low of 4.4 in 1951. The ratio of students to teachers

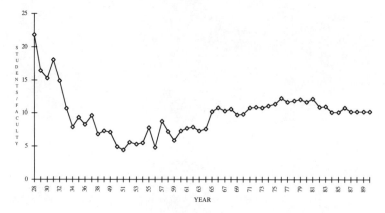

Figure 5–2. Students per Faculty at Mexican Universities, 1928–90.
SOURCE: Statistical Appendix, Table 6.

then began to grow, doubling between the early 1950s and 1981. As with the data on expenditure per student, no crisis in quality is suggested by these data. They reveal instead a slow reduction of student-faculty contact at Mexican universities.

The ratio of full-time faculty to all faculty is perhaps the most telling measure of quality.[8] There is little doubt that in any educational system, the effectiveness of education is determined by the dedication of quality teachers and their contact with students. This is particularly true at the university level, where expert teachers, fully employed and actively involved in their fields of expertise, are extremely important. At Mexican universities, faculty are hired on a full-time, part-time, or hourly basis. Historically, a great majority have been hired on an hourly basis, which means they are paid for the hours they spend lecturing and receive no compensation, direct or indirect, for preparation or research. Full-time faculty are paid considerably more than their part-time and hourly colleagues. They have much greater contact with students, because, unlike hourly faculty, they do not as frequently have to hold down other jobs to make ends meet. Full-time faculty are also able to devote more time to their research.[9]

Data on full-time faculty at Mexican universities show that

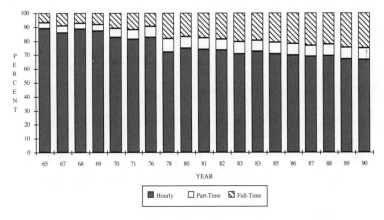

Figure 5–3. Mexican Universities' Full-Time (FT), Part-Time (PT), and Hourly Faculty, 1965–90. SOURCE: Statistical Appendix, Table 6.

the relative weight of full-time faculty in all faculty increased dramatically between 1967 and 1990 (Fig. 5–3). From a low in 1968 of 7.2 percent of all faculty, full-time faculty members reached a high of 25.1 percent of all faculty in 1990, while hourly faculty fell from 88.7 percent in 1968 to 66.6 percent in 1990. While the number of students per teacher increased slightly, then, the number of full-time teachers grew at a rapid rate.

The same quality indicators for the UNAM, long Mexico's largest university and the flagship institution of the public higher-education system, reveal important trends. Expenditure per student increased in real terms from the mid-1920s through the late 1930s to a low plateau in the 1940s and early 1950s (Fig. 5–4). In the late 1950s, expenditure began to rise again and increased rapidly after the mid-1960s. After a decline in the early 1970s, per-student expenditure jumped to new highs by the early 1980s and declined only slightly following the crisis of 1982.[10] The ratio of students per faculty at the UNAM from 1931–58 was fairly stable at between 6.5 and 8.5 students per faculty member from the mid-1930s through the late 1950s (Fig. 5–5).[11] After 1958, there was a marked jump to an average of 10.1 students per faculty member between 1959 and 1969. The early

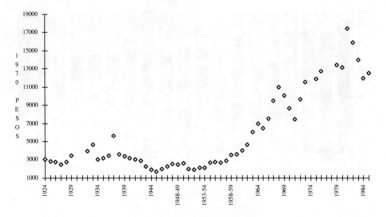

Figure 5–4. UNAM Real Expenditure per Student, 1924–85. SOURCE: Lorey, *Rise of the Professions in Mexico*, Table 36.

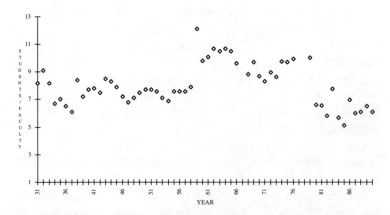

Figure 5–5. UNAM Students per Faculty, 1931–90. SOURCE: Lorey, *Rise of the Professions in Mexico*, Table 37.

1970s saw an average of 8.9 students per teacher. During the late 1970s, the number of students per teacher climbed slightly to an average of 9.9 and then fell to 6.3 in the early 1980s. The growth of the percent share of full-time faculty at the UNAM was dramatic, increasing almost four times between a low point of 3.0 percent in 1969 and 12.0 percent in 1990 (Fig. 5–6). During the

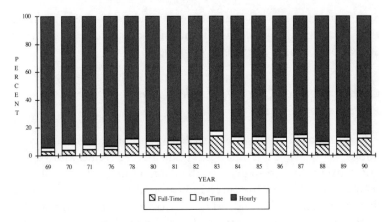

Figure 5–6. Full-Time (FT), Part-Time (PT), and Hourly Faculty at UNAM, 1969–90. SOURCE: Lorey, *Rise of the Professions in Mexico*, Table 38.

same period, the share of faculty hired on an hourly basis fell from 93.8 percent to 85.0 percent. Between 1967 and 1988, the share of the UNAM budget that has gone to pay teachers' salaries has increased from 30.6 percent of the total budget to 64.6 percent.[12]

The data developed and analyzed here indicate unambiguously that a "crisis" in quality has not occurred. There is no sudden change in the evolution of quality indicators between 1929 and the 1980s. Moreover, some of the data sets indicate historical improvement in quality at Mexican universities. Per-student expenditures have grown slowly since the 1920s, with more rapid growth after the late 1950s. The number of students per teacher at Mexican universities has apparently grown somewhat between the 1950s and the 1980s, with a considerable leap in the early 1960s. But at the same time, the ratio of full-time to part-time teaching staff has doubled since the 1960s, suggesting that there may have been a gradual improvement in the contact between full-time staff and students over time. If anything, then, there has been a leveling-off of increases in quality begun in the 1940s and a gradual decline in quality since the late 1950s.

Significant upturns in the late 1970s and early 1980s indicate that some of the proceeds of the oil boom went to improve educational quality at the university level.

Comparisons of Quality at Public and Private Universities

It is important to distinguish between changes in quality at public and private universities, because these trends allow us to differentiate their responses to the demand for professionals and technicians. Two of the three indicators discussed above can be developed for public and private institutions: the ratio of students to faculty and the ratio of full-time teachers to all teachers at the professional level. I have chosen sample groups of public and private universities for 1970, 1980, and 1990. The sample for 1970 includes 20 universities, 15 public and 5 private; for 1980 and 1990, the sample is 22 universities, 16 public and 6 private.[13]

Data on students per faculty and students per full-time faculty at sample public and private universities for 1970, 1980, and 1990 show significant differences between the two types of institutions (Fig. 5–7). In 1970, the public universities in the sample had 10 students per faculty member but 205 per full-time faculty member. Private universities, on the other hand, showed 8 students per faculty member and 85 per full-time faculty member. In 1980, the number of students per faculty member had risen for both public and private universities in the sample group: to 16 for public institutions and 11 for private. At the same time, however, the number of students per full-time faculty member had fallen dramatically in both cases, to 90 at public institutions and 31 at private, suggesting that the number of full-time faculty per student has increased over time. In 1990, public universities showed significant improvement, with 13 students to all professors and 52 students to full-time professors compared to 10 and 67, respectively, at the sample private universities. In the 1970s, private universities surpassed public institutions in providing contact between students and faculty. Between 1970 and 1980, however, the number of students per full-time faculty declined

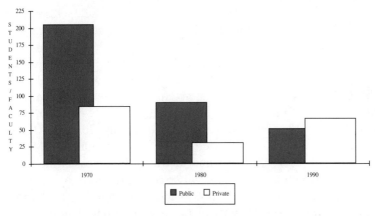

Figure 5–7. Students per Full-Time Faculty at Public and Private Universities, 1970, 1980, and 1990. SOURCE: Statistical Appendix, Table 7.

by 63.5 percent at private schools compared to 56.1 percent at public schools. By 1990, public universities had closed the gap considerably.

Data on the ratio of full-time faculty to all faculty reveal similar trends in differences between public and private institutions. In 1970, when the overall average of the sample was 10.9 percent full-time faculty members, at public universities in the sample group 8.5 percent of faculty were hired full-time, while at private universities fully 18.0 percent were employed full-time.[14] In 1980 the sample average was 24.9 percent; at public universities, the average was 21.7 percent full-time, at private universities 33.5 percent full-time. Between 1970 and 1980, public universities' percentage of full-time faculty grew 155.3 percent, while private universities trailed with a growth rate of 86.1 percent. By 1990, public universities could boast 28.9 percent full-time faculty compared to 25.6 percent at private institutions. It must be noted in reference to changes by 1990 that trends after the economic crisis of 1982 are complicated by the apparent practice at public universities of granting full-time status to faculty while lowering salaries. The opposite may have happened at private schools: real salaries did not slip as much as at public institutions, while fewer full-time faculty were hired.

A revealing insight into the significance of these data is gained by separating out exceptional universities in both categories. Exceptional public and private universities are those that do not share the basic characteristics of the largest institutions in each category. Many of Mexico's small private universities do not have enough students to hire a large proportion of full-time staff. A few large public universities, founded relatively recently, have emphasized the employment of full-time faculty. The UAM (Universidad Autónoma Metropolitana—Autonomous Metropolitan University), established in the early 1970s, is the most notable exception of this sort and an innovator in many other aspects of university curriculum, teaching, and research. Removing such exceptions from the data yields a sample of universities that are typical in the sense that they dominate the experiences of the majority of Mexican university students.

Separating out the exceptions in both sample groups, we find that in 1970 the two oldest and largest private universities— the ITESM (Instituto Tecnológico y de Estudios Superiores de Monterrey—Technological Institute of Monterrey, Nuevo León) and the UAG (Universidad Autónoma de Guadalajara–Autonomous University of Guadalajara[15]) could boast an average of 38.7 percent full-time faculty. The older public universities, in contrast, supported only 6.6 percent full-time faculty.[16] The UNAM, the largest public institution in the country, supported just 3.8 percent full-time faculty members. In 1980, the full-time faculty at typical public universities had grown to 17.0 percent, while at the two largest private universities the ratio had grown more slowly, to 48.9 percent full-time faculty. The public universities improved at a quicker rate than the private universities: a 157.6 percent change during 1970–80 compared to 26.3 percent for private institutions.

The quality gap between public and private institutions, large in the 1970s, apparently narrowed in the 1980s. The ratio of full-time to all faculty at private institutions exceeded that at public institutions by two times in 1970 and by one-and-a-half times in 1980. Much of the overall improvement at public universities by the 1990s was due to the growth of the UAM and improvement in the full-time ratios at a few public institutions, particularly the IPN (Instituto Politécnico Nacional—National Polytechnic Institute), UANL (Nuevo León), and UAP (Puebla).[17] Even in the 1980s, the difference between the oldest and largest institutions in the public and private categories remained significant; the private universities still maintained an edge.

There are other quality differences between public and private universities that are difficult, if not impossible, to quantify given the available data. The most important of these differences relate to the characteristics of faculty. At public universities, professors are frequently employed as generalists who must teach both inside and outside their specific field of interest and academic experience. There is little employment of specialists with graduate-level training who practice combined teaching and research in their areas of expertise. Many professors, particularly at the large public universities, are themselves recent graduates or even egresados.[18] Some university students are hired to teach while they work to finish their licentiate degree.[19] At the UNAM, there may be more licenciados teaching classes than professors with graduate degrees. Private universities have apparently led the field in hiring professors with advanced (M.A. or Ph.D.) professional training.

Available data on faculty salaries at public and private institutions show important differences in both the level of pay and the ratio of salaries among faculty members on different pay scales. Evidence for 1970 indicates a large gap between high salaries at private universities and low salaries at public universities. Additionally, the ratio of full-time to part-time to hourly salaries is about 6 to 3 to 1 at private universities and about 4 to 2 to 1 at public institutions.[20] Because there is a higher ratio of full-time to part-time and hourly teaching staff at the private universities, a greater number of teachers make more money at private universities; this factor has important implications for faculty morale and camaraderie.

The difference in salaries has had an important effect on exceptional public universities like those in the UAM system, which have lost many highly qualified faculty to better-paying positions at private universities. The rector of the UAM's campus at Azcapotzalco has commented that this "internal brain drain" is much more harmful to Mexican public universities than the loss of scholars to the United States or Europe.[21] While some of this loss has been offset by the Sistema Nacional de Investigadores (SNI), a program established in 1984 that provides additional salary to advanced scholars at selected public institutions, the flight of researchers from public to private schools continued throughout the 1980s. There are other differences between public and private universities that have an important impact on quality. Evidence indicates, for example, that the physical plant is newer and more technologically advanced at private institutions, particularly at the large ones.[22] Private universities clearly have an advantage as regards the full-time status of students; while most public university students work part- or full-time, most private-university students do not. And, unlike public institutions, private universities have been able to set ceilings on enrollments and screen entrants on the basis of standard entrance examinations.

The historical quality gap between public and private universities indicated by these various gauges is to some extent expected. The principal reason that private schools have more full-time teachers and pay them more (the keys to quality education as gauged above) is that private universities receive higher fees from matriculating students. With greater income per student than public universities they can afford to hire expert, full-time faculty and draw good teachers away from public institutions. Private universities have funds for improving their physical plant that many public universities, particularly those in the provinces, do not have. In addition, public universities must devote large sums to the expensive task of producing the vast majority of Mexican professionals in expensive social areas such as medicine and sanitary engineering. The public universities must also spend large amounts on research in medicine and the natural sciences, areas where research efforts by private universities have generally been weak.

Explaining Changes in Quality

The three indicators developed above suggest that the quality of education at Mexican universities probably remained substantially at the same level during the entire period under discussion. Changes in quality have not taken place at a rapid rate—there were no sudden rises or declines after the late 1950s, for example. No sudden drop in quality occurred during the period of most rapid growth in enrollment, from the mid-1960s to the early 1980s, and none at the largest and most frequently criticized public institution, UNAM. If quality has not declined precipitously, however, neither has it shown steady long-term growth. What has caused the sluggish change in quality over time?

Observers have attempted to explain what has been seen as a crisis or rapid decline in quality in various ways. One expert on Mexico's twentieth-century history, for example, has seen the "quality crisis" as a direct result of the university's autonomy: "The autonomy of the university, intended to protect it from government interventions, and student participation in the running of university affairs eventually proved harmful to the quality of education. The faculty and administration could not raise standards or limit admission without protest and heated opposition from the students."[23] Other observers have seen expanding enrollment and consequent overcrowding of campuses as the main culprits. According to this view, exploding enrollment has had a negative effect on the quality of the education received by professionals at the large public universities because enrollment has outstripped expenditure, an assumption questioned above.[24] Sometimes quality problems at the universities are blamed on deficient secondary education. In this interpretation, poorly prepared university entrants make poor university graduates. It is increasingly common to hear university students themselves blamed for the purported crisis in quality: they are seen as too "politicized," or as "not wanting to study."

The common element in all these various explanations (as in others I have not listed) is that they all look to the university and its structure to explain changes in quality. In searching for an explanation for an ill-defined crisis, analysts have blamed the university, the university bureaucracy, university students, and in general, "the system," but have not examined the basis of that system—economic development since 1929.

The analysis of Chapter Four directs us toward other kinds of explanations for long-term changes in quality at Mexican universities, explanations having to do with historical demand for professionals in the economy. Student pressures for change at Mexican universities have responded historically to the fact that high-level skills are not those in greatest demand in the Mexican economy. Logically, then, we can suggest that if Mexican students found higher achievement at the university necessary to find work, pressure would be exerted (more likely pressure applied by employers and the state than by students) to produce graduates with different skills. The historical resiliency of the system suggests that quality has adapted to the level of demand.

If the quality of educational achievement is linked directly to the job market and career expectations, we must look to those factors to explain differences in quality. Quality is not primarily determined by the size of the student body of an institution or its autonomy—examples of large, independent universities that graduate quality professionals abound.[25] Rather, characteristics of the market for professionals and technicians determine the quality of their university preparation.

We must redefine the problem as one of sluggish growth or stagnation in quality rather than a rapid decline in quality throughout the system, and we must relate this sluggish growth to the demands of the economy for professionals and technicians. The indication that the sluggish growth of the Mexican economy is attributable principally to very slow growth of quality at public universities leads us to consider next the comparative experiences in the job market of graduates of Mexico's public and private universities.

Private Versus Public University Graduates in the Job Market

The final arbiters of the quality of higher education in Mexico are the employers of professionals and technicians. After all, the most basic qualitative difference among university graduates and egresados—that between professionals and technicians—has historically reflected the demands of public and private employers. The foregoing analysis suggests that a basic difference between graduates of public universities (particularly those located in the provinces) and graduates of private universities is that they are viewed differently in the job market.

Employers have come to control the quality of job entrants in some overt ways. They sometimes administer entrance exams or demand that applicants have a certain number of years of practical experience. Rather than trust in the degree granted by the university or accept at face value the ambiguous egresado status, employers certify the level of applicants' preparations. Some analysts have noted an increase in newspaper want ads that require applicants to have considerable experience to back up their degree status.[26] Significantly, work experience remains more important for egresados or graduates of public universities than for those of private institutions.

Many private- and public-sector corporations provide training for new employees to make up for deficiencies in their university background. IBM of Mexico, in advertising training-program grants in 1987, required that applicants have a university grade point average of 8.0 (scale of 10) and be available for full-time study. Both are demands that Mexican public universities cannot make of their students—they correspond most closely to professional training at private universities. IBM offered the program equally to both egresados and degree-holders as long as they had proven high levels of aptitude and achievement with high grade-point averages.

Available evidence indicates that many employers, particularly in the private sector, have come to prefer graduates of private universities for the best employment positions—those involving the most responsibility and the highest level of skills. Privately educated professionals clearly take the elite positions in the private sector. Graduates of private universities have also become increasingly prominent in the public sector. Job-entry exams for both public- and private-sector corporations seem to favor Mexican students educated privately.[27] Employers may have actually begun to discriminate against the product of public universities on the basis of institutional association alone, and graduates of different institutions are assumed to have certain personal as well as professional traits.

While employers have increasingly demanded graduates of

private universities, private-university students have shown a great interest in private-sector jobs. Data from one study of social class and career patterns at Latin American universities show that the desire of Mexican students to work in the private sector increases as their class increases. Twenty-eight percent of survey respondents with upper-class backgrounds had plans to work in the public sector. Among lower-class students, 37 percent were planning a career in government.[28]

Employers' preference for graduates of private universities has been expressed perhaps most clearly in the close relations between private-sector employers and private universities. The private sector has historically been active in the creation of Mexico's most important private institutions of higher education, both older institutions like the UAG and the ITESM and newer institutions such as the ITAM and the Universidad de las Américas.[29]

Why are employers attracted more to graduates of private rather than public universities? Private universities are different in two main ways from their public counterparts: their programs are much more closely tailored to the actual supply of professional jobs than are those of the public universities, and their admissions and achievement policies are more closely geared to quality product. For both these reasons, the links between private universities and both public- and private-sector employers (particularly the latter) have been increasingly close since the late 1950s.[30]

Data on private universities indicate that in 1980 only 5 percent of private-university students were studying medicine, and only 2 percent agriculture, while 33 percent were studying engineering and 78 percent social sciences (a category dominated by business administration and accounting at private universities).[31] These are clearly the professional fields most in demand in private-sector industry and business.[32] This basic difference was clear as early as the late 1950s, with private institutions showing an explosion of enrollment in business fields by the early 1960s.[33] The public universities, on the other hand, show much greater emphasis in the fields of medicine, law, and agriculture—fields with stronger employment in public-sector agencies.

Significant quality differences between public and private institutions were discussed above. The high percentage of full-time professors in the faculty and the low ratio of students to full-time faculty compared to that at public institutions is the key factor in this difference.[34] Additionally, private universities had an efficiency rate (graduates as percentage of their entering class) of 63 percent, roughly twice that of public universities.[35] Students at private universities move through their course of study more rapidly due to different requirements and the fact that they do not have to work as many hours a week as public-university students, if they must work at all to support their studies. These factors make it possible for private universities to be closely attuned to the market for professional expertise.

There are two more subtle, but extremely important, advantages that graduates of private universities typically gain from their professional training. Not only are they better educated in fields that are in demand, but they receive a socialization that makes their integration into professional work easier for them and more valuable for employers. This socializing process is important for employment in both the private and public sectors.[36] The graduate of a private university can operate with languages (particularly English) and computer skills in a modern business environment. The typical business-administration graduate of a provincial public university, on the other hand, does not read or speak English well and has had little advanced training with computer systems or software. Some more subtle advantages held by private-university graduates, such as interview skills and general comportment, may also be related to differences in curriculum content at public and private universities.[37] In general, private-university graduates carry in their university experience the promise of being able to adapt to a modern firm's organization and maintain or increase productivity levels with both specific expertise and the ability to adapt to the corporate environment.[38]

The political orientation of private-university graduates is also likely to be more acceptable to private-sector employers, while the political views of public university graduates are in many cases antithetical to private-sector employers.[39] There has clearly been a historical lack of understanding or rapport between private-sector employers and the public-university system due to the prevalence of Marxist analysis as a guiding academic ideology at public universities. This ideological focus has always rubbed Mexican business the wrong way. Private universities, in contrast, promote a nonpolitical environment for professional study.[40] Private-university graduates are trained to avoid Marxist approaches in favor of other perspectives and methodologies, particularly when it comes time to enter the professional job market.

The public sector also leans toward graduates of private universities at its top levels, and for many of the same reasons as those held by private-sector employers. A trend toward granting high political posts to graduates of private universities since the late 1970s has been noted by many analysts.[41] Support of private higher education is a response on the part of the government to the differences between public- and private-university graduates outlined above. As is frequently noted, the Mexican state's approach to economic development has had much more in common with mainstream Western economic thought than with the radical teachings of the public universities.[42] The government, like the private sector, has found that it needs the very highly skilled product of the private-university system to run the affairs of state and finds its ideology more in line with that of the private universities. By the early 1990s, public universities seemed to be gradually adapting to the demand of the public sector for professionals sympathetic to the government's project for economic development by changing curricula and degree requirements in many disciplines.[43] The economics department at the UNAM, for example, one of the most radical of departments in Mexico, was undergoing a major process of internal restructuring by the early 1990s; a central problem of the 1980s was the inability of the faculty's graduates to find work in the public sector.

Differences in quality at public and private universities would appear to be determined primarily by two factors: (1) the demand of private-sector and certain public-sector employers for high-quality professionals, and (2) the development of the differential demand for professionals and technicians discussed in Chapter Four. Public and private universities came to be driven by qualitatively different labor markets as the demand for high-quality professionals in the private sector, and at the upper level of the public sector, grew faster than quality at public universities. Public universities were not able to respond to that demand because of the need to fulfill their social commitment (discussed in Chapter Six). Private universities expanded their output to fill the gap left between demand and public-university supply. The low rate of increase in quality at public universities sharply curtailed their traditional dominance in the production of the most highly qualified professionals.

Public and private institutions fed the demand for different levels of expertise. Private universities and the best public universities came to fill the need for top-level professionals while most of the public universities, particularly the public universities of the provinces, produced large numbers of egresados who did not complete the degree and worked primarily as technicians. The largest public university, the UNAM, is a hybrid of sorts, producing both high-quality professionals for employment in the public and private sectors and a large number of dropouts and egresados who will work as technicians. The labor markets fed by public and private universities were not mutually exclusive, of course, and there was undoubtedly some crossover. Graduates of private universities sometimes worked at lower levels in the public sector and graduates of public universities sometimes worked in the highest echelons of public and private affairs. But the general effect of demands for different levels of professional expertise was to favor the development of private universities to supplement the production of professionals by public universities. Why this task has fallen to the private universities, or why it has been actively taken up by them, must be understood in the context of the historical deconcentration of the Mexican university system.

Implications of Historical Deconcentration

The perceived over-centralization of higher educational opportunities has taken a prominent position in public-policy debate since the 1970s.[44] What was the historical course of concentra-

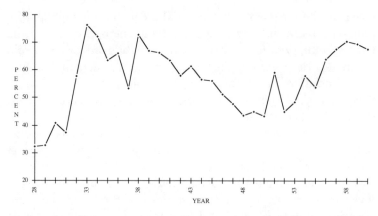

Figure 5–8. Enrollment at UNAM and IPN as Share of Total University Enrollment, 1928–60. SOURCE: Lorey, *Rise of the Professions in Mexico*, Table 42.

tion and deconcentration of the Mexican university system? What differences were there between the evolution of private and public universities? (In the following discussion I use the term "deconcentration" rather than decentralization to emphasize the declining importance of the historically largest and oldest institutions rather than trends in the geographical location or financial status of universities.)

In 1929, the UNAM was prominent in the education of Mexican professionals, claiming a third of all enrollment at the professional level (Fig. 5–8).[45] The UNAM came to dominate Mexican university training only after 1932, when it rose to 57.7 percent of all enrollment. The IPN was founded in 1937 as the nation's flagship polytechnic school. The two institutions—the UNAM and IPN—consolidated their hold on university education and by 1938 reached an all-time high of 72.7 percent of all enrollment at the professional level in Mexico.

During the period from 1929 to 1960, UNAM and IPN dominated all aspects of professional training—they were the largest institutions of higher education and at the same time were closely associated with government policy. Most other universities in Mexico were established in a way that made them juridically dependent on either the UNAM or the IPN. This dependence, particularly of public universities in the provinces, had its roots in the link between study in the states and study in the capitol. The curricula of provincial universities were incorporated into those of the two large public institutions of the capital to allow students from the provinces to transfer easily to the universities in Mexico City. This original advantage led to the domination of the entire higher-education scene by the two public-university giants and to the flow of students from the states to the capital.

After 1938 the UNAM and IPN's share of enrollment began to fall, descending gradually to a low of 44.9 percent in 1952. The mid-1950s saw an upturn, and enrollment at the two giants reached another high of 70.5 in 1958. The late 1950s appear to have been a time of rapidly growing pressure on the position of these two major institutions of higher learning. This pressure resulted from accelerated enrollment at provincial public universities and private institutions, which was associated with the growth of the Mexican economy after the late 1930s. After the late 1950s, the dominance of these two institutions was greatly eroded. Available data series for the late 1950s and early 1960s are contradictory as to the proportions of this decline, but agree on the general downward trend in the percentage of Mexican students attending the UNAM and the IPN. By the mid-1960s, the UNAM and the IPN could no longer claim even half of Mexico's enrollment.

Reliable enrollment data for private universities, first available for the late-1950s, show that the private share of university enrollment grew from 10.3 percent of the total university enrollment in 1959 to 14.9 percent by 1964 (Fig. 5–9). This trend seems to be exactly the inverse of the trend at the two largest public universities and probably explains a good part of their declining enrollment share.

Trends in the number of egresados of fourteen sample universities, public and private, from 1967 to 1989 reveal significant deconcentration of the Mexican university system during the 1970s and 1980s.[46] Although these fourteen institutions were Mexico's largest and most important centers of higher education, their share of total egresados at the professional level declined

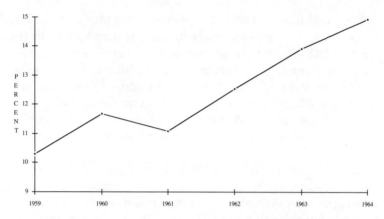

Figure 5–9. Enrollment at Private Universities as Share of Total University Enrollment, 1959–64. SOURCE: Lorey, *Rise of the Professions in Mexico*, Table 43.

steadily over time. From a high of an average of 77.4 percent during 1967–69, the share of these schools fell to an average of 75.2 percent in the early 1970s, to 75.8 percent in the late 1970s, to 66.9 percent in the early 1980s, and finally to a low of 59.8 percent of all egresados in 1985 and 1989. The long-term decline in the share held by the fourteen most important public and private universities implied a rapid deconcentration and diversification of the whole system.

The most important characteristic of this progressive deconcentration in the Mexican university system since 1929 is that it had both public and private dimensions, each of which is important for understanding the economic and social roles the university played after 1929 and particularly after the 1950s. The eleven public universities in the sample have seen their share of all public-university egresados fall from 95.1 percent in 1967 to a low of 65.0 percent in 1989. And the oldest and largest private universities have fallen to less than one-quarter of all private university egresados by the late 1980s from a high of 61.7 percent in 1967.

The Mexican government was never comfortable with the overwhelming weight of the UNAM in the higher education arena. When the government wanted the UNAM to further the aims of "socialized" education in the 1930s under Cárdenas, the UNAM was seen as being: "conservative to the point of being reactionary. It is not only out of touch with national life . . . but it is actually engaging in the negative work of raising up a generation either entirely indifferent to the revolution or for which the revolutionary principles are an anathema."[47] The government generally supported attempts to diminish the power of the UNAM after the early 1930s. The IPN was created to a large extent to balance, and thereby reduce, the political strength of the UNAM, as well as to balance the UNAM's emphasis on non-technical careers. The establishment of these two institutions touched off a rivalry between the two institutions that continues to the present day.[48] Between 1933 and 1937, the government attempted to set up a Government University (Universidad del Estado), completely dependent on the government, to fill government needs for professionals. More recently, the UAM was created in the early 1970s under Echeverría to counterbalance the political importance of the public university giants in the Federal District, as well as to solve problems of overcrowding. The share of the public-university giants, UNAM and IPN, fell from 44.7 percent in 1967 to a low of 19.6 percent in 1989 (Fig. 5–10).

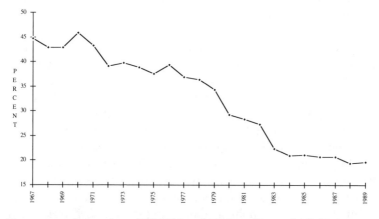

Figure 5–10. Egresados of UNAM and IPN as Share of All University Egresados, 1967–86. SOURCE: Statistical Appendix, Table 8.

As early as the late 1930s, private universities were founded in Mexico. In the 1940s the rate of foundation of private universities picked up pace, and after the late 1950s, they gradually came to achieve real importance, cutting into the traditional dominance of the public universities. In 1929, Mexico had only five universities, all public. By 1958, it had 125 universities, 53 of them private; by 1982, 315 universities, 148 of them private; in 1987, 362 universities, 191 of them private.

Private universities were founded for two essential reasons: (1) to provide instruction that was not infused with socialist ideology, and (2) to fulfill needs for highly qualified professionals, primarily in the private sector. For these reasons, the Mexican middle and upper classes played an important part in the foundation and support of private universities from the beginning. The UAG was founded as the first university outside of central government control in 1938 after a prolonged struggle pitting the conservative leaders of the state of Jalisco against the Cárdenas regime and its education policies. Both the UAG and the Universidad Iberoaméricana were established as alternatives to UNAM's general level of politicization and what was seen as its specific political orientation. According to at least one recent analysis, it was the gradual adoption of Marxist-oriented curricula and research agendas at public universities that undermined the prestige of public-university graduates over time.[49]

Economic demand for professionals was as important a stimulus as ideological orientation in the establishment of private universities. The ITESM, for example, owes much to the development of the regional economy of Nuevo León and was founded to fill specific regional needs for professional skills. Responding to the need for professionals and technicians by "Mexico's Detroit," the ITESM adopted the California Institute of Technology and MIT as models and introduced new fields such as banking and industrial accounting.[50] The more recently founded ITAM (Instituto Tecnológico Autónomo de México—Autonomous Technical Institute of Mexico) was established in Mexico City to produce non-Marxist business managers and economists to supplant the radical economists emanating from UNAM.[51] Another example of the same trend is the UPAEP (Universidad Popular Autónoma del Estado de Puebla—Popular Autonomous University of Puebla State). The UPAEP was established with middle-class support to provide an option to the UAP (Autonomous University of Puebla), which was characterized by student radicalism and frequent strikes in the 1960s. With high matriculation fees, the UPAEP attracted students from middle-class Pueblan families and quickly became an important force in the private sector of the regional economy and society.[52]

Since the late 1950s, the Mexican government has lent various kinds of direct and indirect support to private universities. The ITAM and the ITESM in particular developed with the backing of the government. Support was forthcoming because of the widespread conviction among policymakers that the public universities were not producing enough graduates of the sort necessary in the highest echelons of the public sector. Private schools, on the other hand, explicitly established goals in line with both government policy and the needs of specific economic sectors.[53] Government support for private institutions was thus consistent with government needs for professional expertise.[54] At the same time, encouragement of private-university growth was one of the main expressions of government support for middle-class social aspirations. Private universities greatly increased their share of all egresados after 1967, so that in 1976, private-university egresados accounted for 14.4 percent of all egresados.[55] By 1985 they reached a high of 19.8 percent of the total (Fig. 5–11).

The shift at the end of the 1950s away from public institutions, particularly the oldest and largest, and toward private universities and regional public universities coincided with the shift in the economy's demand for professionals and technicians toward a relatively greater demand for technicians. The response of the public and private universities as a system to this change in demand was to play different but complementary roles. It was not possible for most public universities to both keep the doors to university education open to all aspirants and at the same time produce the most highly qualified graduates. The private universities stepped in to carry out this latter task. It was an

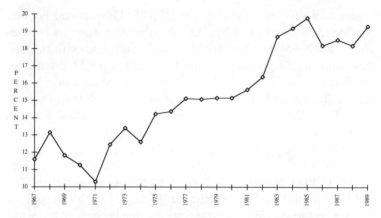

Figure 5–11. Egresados of Private Universities as Share of All University Egresados, 1967–89. SOURCE: Statistical Appendix, Table 8.

expensive undertaking, and private universities were able to raise fees to match demand. While the two largest private institutions—the UAG and the ITESM—prospered, private institutions in the central region and particularly the Federal District boomed, stimulated by the desires of employers in Mexico's most dynamic industrial and service region for private-university graduates.[56] The expansion of regional public universities partially relieved the tremendous pressure on the public-university giants in the Federal District by keeping a good part of increased demand for higher educational opportunities confined to the provinces rather than letting it flow to the capital. This flow has also been stemmed by the passing of stricter laws regarding transfer from the provincial universities to UNAM and IPN. By the mid–1980s, provincial students could only transfer easily to the UNAM or IPN if their desired field of study could not be pursued in their home state.[57]

Summary and Conclusions

Trends in the quality of Mexican university education and the historical deconcentration of the university system are related.

Large historical differences in quality between public and private universities, insofar as such differences in quality can be gauged, indicate that public and private universities responded to the needs of different markets for professionals and technicians. This response drove the deconcentration of the system after the 1950s.

Both changes in quality and the deconcentration of the university system reflect an increasingly tight market for professionals. Private universities took advantage of the fact that higher expenditures per student, higher ratios of full-time faculty to students, and less politically infused study environments produced graduates who were more attractive to employers than most egresados of public universities. The development of private universities also reflected an attempt by students and their families to increase employability in a tight market for professional expertise. As professional positions declined relative to the number of students beginning professional careers, private universities increased the quality of their education, greatly reducing the historical dominance of public universities.

Public and private universities thus function together as a system in Mexico. Provincial public universities produce more dropouts and egresados than graduates, and most of their egresados find employment as technicians. Private universities in Mexico's most economically dynamic regions produce the highest-quality degree holders, most of whom go on to work as professionals, the majority of them in the private sector. The oldest and largest public universities like the UNAM and IPN perform both tasks, producing high-quality graduates as well as large numbers of egresados. There is surely some crossover in these roles: public universities like the UAM and the UANL show high-quality indicators and are linked closely to the labor market for highly qualified professionals. Clearly, the public sector's ability to compete is not inherently lacking.

The development of a Mexican university system, including both public and private institutions working together as described here, has been difficult for observers to explain. To some, it has seemed inefficient, to others, unjust. But this pattern of public and private differentiation has proven useful in Mexico because of the importance of the social role of public universities in rhetoric and policy. The public university system as conceived in 1929 had as one of its principal purposes the advancement of social mobility. The historical meaning of this social role and its effects on university education after 1929 are examined in Chapter Six.

CHAPTER 6

The University System, Social Mobility, and Social Status

The fundamental social goal of the university system after 1929 was deceptively simple: to promote upward social mobility by providing access to the professional job market. It was thought by policymakers, and hoped by the public, that university training would increase the attractiveness of job applicants to employers by increasing their skills and molding their values. Professional jobs would result in higher incomes and make it possible for university graduates to join the ranks of the middle and upper classes.[1] These ideas, associated with analysts of the human-capital school, had a major influence on individual and family decisions to pursue higher education long before the development of an academic literature on human-resource development in Mexico.[2]

The social demands on the university were reinforced by government rhetoric and were accepted as goals by administrators of the university system.[3] Over time, the aim of providing social mobility became linked explicitly with both the autonomy and the open-door admission policies of the large public universities. Jorge Carpizo, rector of the UNAM in the mid-1980s, stated that "the responsible exercise of autonomy converts us into a factor of mobility and social change."[4]

Many observers have accepted as historical fact that the Mexican university system was a purveyor of significant social mobility. And many analysts have seen the social role of the university system as being equal in importance to its educational role. Leslie B. Simpson wrote in 1952 that the university's historical success in turning out large numbers of graduates "did not necessarily represent a thirst for knowledge on the part of the recipients. The university offered an opportunity for the ambitious or the talented to join the ranks of the privileged. . . . A very considerable number of the students were poor."[5]

Writing a decade later in 1963, William P. Glade shared the opinion that the university had brought significant social mobility to Mexico: "The investment in education had an important effect in fostering upward social mobility and growth of a middle class and in increasing sharply the supply of Mexican nationals available for filling positions in the economy requiring higher technical competence."[6]

More recently, critics of Mexico's university system have come to accept as historical fact just the opposite. In this view, the university has always served the middle classes by giving them the advantages of low fees and easy entrance requirements. Alfonso Rangel Guerra, for example, wrote in 1978 that "so long as the enrollment in institutions of higher education is composed of students coming from the upper and middle classes of society, it cannot be said that access to higher education is an important factor in social mobility."[7] This perception that the social goal set for the university after 1929 was not met is an important part of conceptions of "university crisis," particularly among analysts on the left, who have generally emphasized the university's social role over its role in producing professional expertise for economic development.[8]

This chapter weighs these opposing views by asking four questions: How much mobility into professional strata has there been in Mexico since 1929? Has the university system promoted social mobility?[9] How have Mexican universities, public and private, responded to the increasing demand for social mobility? What have been the larger social implications of the university system's response? Unfortunately, we cannot answer questions about social mobility through professional education by analyzing comprehensive data on the backgrounds of students or on their career histories: such data have never been collected in a comprehensive or systematic fashion. Further complicating matters, there exist only a few reliable secondary works on social mobility in Mexico in the twentieth century, and almost none of these studies are based on primary research. The purpose here is to attempt to link for the first time patterns of social mobility and the evolution of the functioning of the university system, taking into account the evidence and conclusions of previous chapters.

Class Structure and Social Mobility

One effective way to assess historical social mobility in Mexico is to analyze available data on class structure in the twentieth century. Census data on income and occupation can be examined for clues to the nature and rate of upward mobility over time. These data also allow us to focus specifically on mobility into the middle and upper levels of society, where professionals are concentrated. It is at these levels that university education can be assumed to be important in attaining higher income and in modifying occupational status.

Changing patterns of income distribution should not be used alone to gauge social mobility, although this is commonly done. Data on income distribution are generally analyzed using the Gini coefficient to gauge the degree of equity of income distribution and the Theil decomposition index to assess the importance of various factors affecting distribution. The central problem with the use of these techniques and with the use of data on income distribution on their own is that it is possible to have social mobility into the professional echelons of society under conditions of both improving and deteriorating distributions of income.[10] Two aspects of class structure and social mobility are examined here: income distribution and occupation. They are considered separately and in combination. Data on both aspects, derived ultimately from the Mexican decennial census, were adapted from both the census and various secondary sources.[11]

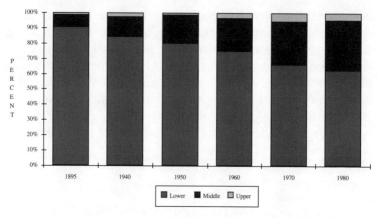

Figure 6–1. Mexico's Changing Class Structure, 1895–1980. SOURCE: Lorey, *Rise of the Professions in Mexico,* Table 49.

Mexico's class structure changed dramatically between 1895 and 1980 (Fig. 6–1). Both the upper and the middle classes grew greatly during the eighty-five-year period; there appears to have been sustained social mobility from working classes into higher strata over the course of almost a century. While the working class declined from 90.7 percent of the total in 1895 to 61.8 in 1980, the middle class grew steadily from 7.8 percent to 33.0 percent of the total in the same period.[12] The upper class grew from 1.5 percent at the end of the nineteenth century to 5.3 percent in 1980. These key changes, particularly at the middle levels, reflect long-term trends of migration from subsistence agriculture to the economy's modern sectors and a general shift in the composition of employment to higher paying industrial and service occupations.[13]

The rate of growth of the upper- and middle-class categories between 1940 and 1980 is noteworthy. The data suggest that the upper class declined between 1940 and 1950 (slumping 41.4 percent over the decade), grew very rapidly between 1950 and 1960 (123.5 percent), grew 50 percent between 1960 and 1970, and declined by 8.8 percent between 1970 and 1980. The middle class grew rapidly in two periods: between 1940 and 1950 (42.9 percent) and between 1960 and 1970 (32.9 percent). The middle class grew more slowly from 1950 to 1960 (16.7 percent) and from 1970 to 1980 (12.9 percent).

To look within these basic trends, it is necessary to disaggregate the data in three ways. First, the implications of changes in the absolute data as well as in the percentage data must be considered. Second, it is necessary to isolate certain intermediate class levels within the broad "upper," "middle," and "working" class categories. We want to focus on the "stable" sector of the middle class and the "semi-leisure" sector of the upper class, because it is in these sectors that professionals are found.[14] Third, we must consider trends in income and trends in occupation as well as the trends in combined data on income and occupation.[15] These three disaggregations are performed simultaneously.

Absolute data on the number of positions at different social levels, generally neglected by scholars, are at least as revealing as the relative share of each stratum.[16] Positions in the Mexican upper classes (measured by combined income and occupation data) grew at a rate of 127.8 percent from 1950 to 1960, 124.5 percent from 1960 to 1970, and 43.3 percent between 1970 and 1980. Compared to this upper-class growth, the middle classes grew more slowly, 30.7 percent between 1950 and 1960, 82.2 percent between 1960 and 1970, and 84.0 percent between 1970 and 1980. If we compare the semi-leisure stratum of the upper class with the stable sector of the middle class, we see that growth of the semi-leisure class has decreased over the course of the three decades, while positions at the stable middle-class level have grown fairly rapidly and the rate of change has increased over time (Fig. 6–2).

The combined income-occupation average figure obscures important differences. In the period from 1950 to 1970, increases in the absolute number of persons in the two professional class strata gauged by income were greater than increases in the numbers of persons at the same level gauged by occupation in three out of four cases. From 1970 to 1980, the trend reversed, with occupation the more important factor by a small margin. The data imply that social mobility into Mexico's professional classes in the 1950s and 1960s can be attributed primarily to changes in income rather than to changes in occupation.

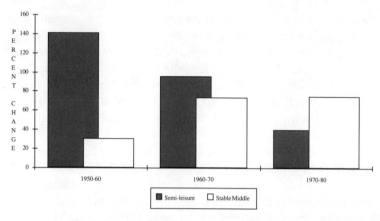

Figure 6–2. Growth of Persons in Two Social Strata, Combined Occupation and Income, by Decade, 1950–80. SOURCE: Lorey, *Rise of the Professions in Mexico*, Table 51.

While absolute data give an indication of the overall increase of positions at each stratum of society, they do not necessarily indicate that social mobility is taking place. The data could reflect the natural growth of population at each level with no net relative gain and no mobility. Both absolute growth in the numbers of available positions and relative growth of upper classes are preconditions for social mobility. Only if there is long-term decline in the working class and long-term growth of the middle class in both absolute and percent-share terms can we assume that persons of working social background are moving up into the professional strata.

Historical social mobility as reflected in the changing relative relations between class strata has been dramatic (Fig. 6–3). The share held by the middle class increased at a rate of 16.7 percent from 1950 to 1960, 33.3 percent from 1960 to 1970, and 12.5 percent from 1970 to 1980 (data for combined income and occupation). The stable sector of the middle class has maintained a growth rate of about 35 percent in all three decades, although the rate has declined slightly over time; the stable middle class increased at a rate of 36.7 percent from 1950 to 1960, 34.3 percent from 1960 to 1970, and 33.3 percent from 1970 to 1980. In

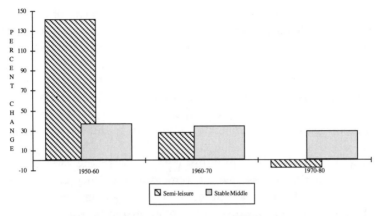

Figure 6–3. Change in Percent Shares of Two Social Strata, Combined Occupation and Income, by Decade, 1950–80. SOURCE: Lorey, *Rise of the Professions in Mexico*, Table 52.

comparison with the middle class, the upper class has seen its share decline precipitously. While growing rapidly at 123.5 percent between 1950 and 1960, the growth of the upper class slowed to only 50 percent between 1960 and 1970, and declined by 7.0 percent between 1970 and 1980. The semi-leisure stratum has mirrored the decline of the overall upper class, falling from a high growth rate of 141.7 percent between 1950 and 1960, to 27.6 percent between 1960 and 1970, to –10.3 percent between 1970 and 1980.

Close examination of differences between income and occupational mobility within these averages reveals a fact of great significance. Social mobility into Mexico's professional classes can be attributed primarily to change in income rather than to change in occupation. Whereas the share of persons at the middle stable level by income grew 50 percent from 1950 to 1960, 64.4 percent from 1960 to 1970, and 40.5 percent from 1970 to 1980, the occupation share grew by little more than half those rates (28.8 percent from 1950 to 1960, 17.6 percent from 1960 to 1970, and 29.0 percent from 1970 to 1980). At the semi-leisure level, the income share grew 187.5 percent between 1950 and 1960, 28.3 percent between 1960 and 1970, and decreased by

27.1 percent between 1970 and 1980. As to the share of persons in the semi-leisure stratum by occupation, it grew 50.0 percent from 1950 to 1960, 58.3 percent from 1960 to 1970, and 36.8 percent from 1970 to 1980.

Now that the basic trends have been established, we can compare these rates with rates derived from our other data sets. How do these rates of mobility into the professional classes compare with the growth in numbers of university graduates, egresados, and degrees registered since 1929 (developed in Chapter Three)? How do rates of social mobility compare with the rates of job creation at the professional level (measured in Chapter Four)? A comparison of data on social mobility with data on these historical trends provides a gauge of the relationship between the university and social change over time.

As shown above, the professional sectors of Mexican society opened at a relatively rapid rate in the 1950–80 period. The absolute number of stable-middle-class slots grew at 469.3 percent over the period, while those in the semi-leisure stratum grew 562.3 percent—average annual rates of 6.0 and 6.5 percent, respectively.

The universities, however, were producing graduates and egresados at at least twice those rates over the same period of time. The number of university graduates was increasing at an annual rate of 9.9 percent between 1950 and 1971, egresados at an annual rate of 10.6 percent between 1967 and 1989, and registrations of professional degrees were growing at a rate of 10.7 percent annually between 1971 and 1980.[17] Clearly, slots were not opening up fast enough to satisfy the ambitions of many university graduates and egresados.

This fundamental historical mismatch between social change and the university's education of professionals can be periodized by comparing the growth rates of positions in the stable-middle-class stratum with the growth of the number of university graduates, egresados, and degrees registered from 1950 to 1980 by decade (Fig. 6–4).[18] As was clear in previous data sets, there is a break point at the end of the 1950s. During the period from 1950 to 1960, degrees granted by the universities and the two professional class sectors grew at roughly the same pace:

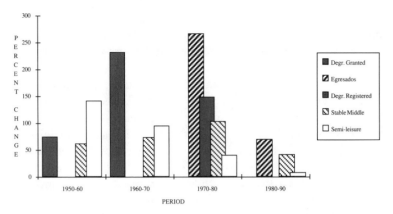

Figure 6–4. Comparison of Growth of Persons in Two Class Strata with Growth of University Graduates, Egresados, and Degrees Registered, 1950–90. SOURCE: Statistical Appendix, Table 9.

while degrees granted grew 75.1 percent over the decade, the absolute number of places in the stable middle class grew at 61.5 percent and the semi-leisure class at 141.2 percent. During the next two decades, however, the pace of university production far outpaced that of social mobility: from 1960 to 1970, degrees granted grew 232.1 percent while positions in the stable middle class and semi-leisure upper class grew at only 73.6 percent and 95.7 percent, respectively; from 1970 to 1980 egresados and registered degrees grew 266.5 percent and 149.1 percent, respectively, while positions in the stable middle class grew at 103.1 percent and those in the semi-leisure upper classes increased by 40.4 percent. Although growth of places in Mexico's professional classes was more rapid during the 1970s, then, the rate at which those places were created was still superseded by the number of university graduates.

A comparison of data on economic demand with rates of social mobility supports the idea of a historical mismatch. The annual growth rate of positions in the economy was 5.6 percent for professionals and 8.5 percent for technicians during the 1950 to 1980 period. The annual rate of growth of slots in the professional middle- and upper-class strata was 6.0 percent for the stable middle class and 6.5 percent for the semi-leisure class. These growth rates coincide closely, and are much lower than the annual growth rate of university graduates, indicating relatively fewer real opportunities for professionals to work and move up in society.

Three basic conclusions can be derived from a comparison of Mexico's evolving class structure with data on university graduates, all key for understanding the university's historical response to social demand. First, there has been some social mobility into the professional strata of Mexican society over time. Between 1950 and 1980, the share of the professional strata of society grew by a little less than two times; the stable middle class grew 136.7 percent, while the semi-leisure stratum grew 183.3 percent. In absolute terms, the number of persons in the stable middle class stratum increased almost five times, persons in the semi-leisure stratum almost six times.

Second, shifts in income were generally more important than shifts in occupation in producing social mobility at the professional level of Mexican society. Regarding the university's response to demand for social mobility, it is significant that social mobility by way of occupation was historically less important than by way of increases in income.[19] University education, of course, affects both occupation and income. But its main impact is generally on occupation (doctor or accountant) and occupational level (professional or technician). In most cases, university education accounts for the most important occupational change in the working lives of professionals.[20] But the data examined here indicate that most Mexicans who experienced upward mobility into the upper-middle or upper classes between 1929 and 1980 did so by being paid more for what they did rather than by any qualitative change in what they did or in their training.

Third, the growth rate of university graduates, egresados, and degrees registered has exceeded the rate of creation of social places for university graduates and egresados by a factor of roughly two. Chapter Four showed that the relative number of employment positions for professionals decreased over time. Data on social mobility analyzed in this chapter indicate that at the same time the growth of places for professionals in the upper echelons of Mexican society slowed.

The overall implication of this analysis is that the university has been increasingly less successful over time in satisfying the demand for social mobility into the middle and upper classes by way of professional careers. While universities did have a positive effect on social mobility until at least 1960 through their role in forming graduates for professional occupations, after that time university production of egresados and graduates outpaced the capacity of economic development to create a rapidly growing professional middle and upper class.

Clearly, the university's decreasing ability to promote upward social mobility was not the fault of the university system. Rather, the university's role in promoting social mobility was restricted by decreasing opportunities for the professionals it graduated. After the late 1950s, Mexican universities were confronted with an impossible challenge: to respond to a demand for social mobility that could not be met given the pattern of Mexico's economic development. The response of the university system was a logical adaptation to a historical bottleneck born of constricted opportunity. The implications of this response will be discussed following examination of two further aspects of the role of the university in social mobility.

The Social Origins of University Students

Mexican public universities are frequently seen as catering primarily to the middle classes; private universities explicitly fulfill the needs of middle- and upper-class families. The university system as a whole is often criticized for not serving Mexico's working classes. Without being granted the opportunity to prepare for one of the professions needed by the developing economy, children from working-class Mexican families cannot achieve their (and their families') aspirations, and one of the basic social goals of the Revolution goes unfulfilled.[21] But it is necessary to test the assumption that Mexico's public universities have historically favored the middle classes; unless it is tested, the assumption is implicitly perpetuated. It is possible that the Mexican university system has served different groups of students in different ways.

Any attempt at measuring the class backgrounds of university students must begin by noting that the amount of reliable, consistent data on socioeconomic variables in Mexican university education is extremely small; no national-level data of any value exist, and no data that allow for long-term historical analysis can be constructed easily. All comments or analyses of the class background of Mexican university students, all the sweeping generalizations one reads, are based either on small and unreliable statistical data sets or on subjective impressions and hearsay.

What evidence is available for examining the social background of Mexican university students? Two indicators can be constructed for the UNAM to allow partial analysis of the problem: (1) the highest level of schooling or profession of students' fathers, and (2) the monthly income of the students' families.[22] These two indicators, based on student responses to university questionnaires in 1949, 1963, 1970, and 1979–80, give a picture of the background of those UNAM students who chose to answer the questionnaires. Student responses, however, can be misleading. Many students answer some questions (number of persons in student's family) while leaving others unanswered (whether or not they work, for example). Many students, of course, do not answer the questionnaire at all and we know nothing about them. And for specific questions, the opinions of students cannot be entirely trusted. Most students tend to underestimate their family's income, and most students are unsure of their father's occupational qualifications and background: they tend to underestimate the years of schooling their fathers received. If Mexican universities have historically provided mobility into the ranks of the middle and upper classes, we would expect to find a significant portion of students from working strata in their programs. If the degree to which the university advances social mobility into the middle and upper classes has increased, we would expect to find an increasing percentage of students coming from working-class backgrounds.

The longest historical view is provided by data on the highest level of schooling achieved or occupation of the responding student's father (Fig. 6–5). The data have been made comparable by considering a university education a professional background (data for 1949 and 1963 are for highest level of schooling achieved by

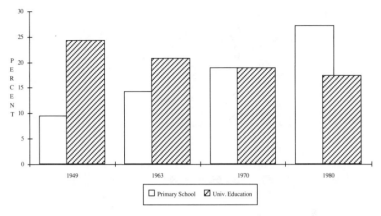

Figure 6–5. Educational Level Attained by Fathers of UNAM Students, 1949, 1963, 1970, and 1980. SOURCE: Statistical Appendix, Table 10.

student's father, whereas data for 1970 and 1980 are for occupational levels). These data show that there has been a historical decline in the relative number of middle-class entrants and a historical increase in the relative number of working-class entrants to the UNAM. There was a significant long-term decline in the percentage of responding students whose fathers were professionals or had university educations, from 23.6 percent in 1949, to 20.8 percent in 1963, to 19.0 percent in 1970, to 17.4 percent in 1980. Matching this trend of decreasing numbers of UNAM students with middle-class backgrounds is the increase in students whose fathers left the school system after completing primary school, a percentage that grew from 9.5 percent in 1949, to 14.3 percent in 1963, to 19 percent in 1970, and 27.3 percent in 1980. A similar trend can be found in data on completion of secondary school, which rose from 7 percent in 1970 to 10.4 percent in 1980.[23]

Data on monthly income of UNAM students' families make it possible to organize responding students into classes for three years: 1963, 1970, and 1980 (Fig. 6–6). Because of the necessity of deflating 1963 and 1980 pesos to 1970 values, the categories do not overlap exactly and thus the figures must be considered approximate. A marked increase in the percentage of middle-class students between 1963 and 1980 would seem at first glance

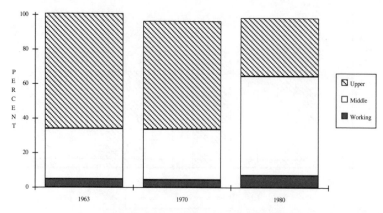

Figure 6–6. Class of UNAM Students' Families Gauged by Monthly Income, 1963, 1970, and 1980. SOURCE: Statistical Appendix, Table 10.

to confirm a growing predominance of the middle classes at Mexican universities. But the data show that the percentage of working and transitional middle-class students has increased from 14.2 percent in 1963 and 13.3 percent in 1970 to 37.3 percent in 1980. On closer inspection, then, it is clear that middle-class growth has been centered in the transitional, or non-professional, middle class. The representation of the upper classes at the UNAM has fallen over time from 66.4 percent in 1963, to 62.5 percent in 1970, to 33.6 percent in 1980.

Trends in data on family income and father's schooling and occupation throw doubt on the conclusion that the UNAM has always favored the students of middle-class origin. It appears that there was a significant increase in the representation of students from non-professional backgrounds at the university in the 1970s. (Whether these students drop out, reach the egresado level, or go on to achieve the final degree is another question, discussed below.) The university has opened over time to allow more students from working-class backgrounds the chance to study. Success in providing opportunities to enter the university has been the main purpose and most important accomplishment of the historical open-door admission policy.

The expansion of university enrollment to admit applicants from working-class backgrounds began after the 1950s. It thus follows a period during which real mobility by way of the university was more pronounced than it was to be later, as shown above. Data from an informal survey carried out in the process of research for this study shed additional light on the periodization of the university's opening. In a non-random sample of 25 professionals with whom the author had contact, there was a distinct break in social origin along generational lines. Respondents were asked detailed questions about their professional training and about the occupations of their parents, among other variables. Older professionals (50 years and more) were much more likely than younger professionals to have come from working-class backgrounds and to have, by way of university education, experienced intergenerational mobility.[24] These informal survey data mirror the data on class structure examined above. Since the rapid quantitative expansion of enrollment can be dated to about the end of the 1950s or the early 1960s, it seems that the university began opening its doors to working-class students after the time of greatest experienced mobility. And it was after the late 1950s that the middle classes began to favor private education for their children, indicating that private education had become a surer ticket to a middle-class lifestyle.

Giving students from working-class backgrounds the chance to study at a Mexican university, however, does not by itself imply that these students will be able to take advantage of that opportunity. Do students from working-class backgrounds remain at the university long enough to become egresados? Do they graduate? As one observers has noted, "Gainfully employed professionals remain those that come from privileged classes, which, according to Mexican political rhetoric, is one [of] the outcomes that mass professional education is supposed to avoid."[25] The overall implication, based mostly on impressionistic observations, is that students from working-class families tend to be the first to drop out and the most unlikely to become recipients of licentiate degrees. The students who are best prepared at entry, who can afford to devote themselves to full-time study, and who eventually achieve the degree, probably came from predominantly middle- and upper-class backgrounds. The most obvious example of this pattern is the popular hope of professional employment in engineering and technical fields, fields that have been hailed as the popular professional preparations par excellence since the 1930s. University training in such fields usually takes longer than that for other fields, however, and frequently demands full-time study, which only students from well-to-do backgrounds can afford.

In the social-class origins of university students in Mexico, there is a split within the university system. The data on the UNAM examined above are not representative of all Mexican universities, for few public universities are as middle-class as the UNAM and the IPN. Most provincial universities have a larger proportion of working strata among students than the institutions in the capital. Such would be the implication of any informal comparison of appearance at Mexico's regional universities with those in the capital and with regional private universities.[26] The upper class and the upper-middle class are best represented at private universities in the provinces and Federal District where high fees are levied. The almost complete absence of government or university grants to support the study of working students at private universities means that student populations at the private universities are relatively homogeneous.

Expanded enrollment and low matriculation fees at the public universities in the capital and in the provinces do not by themselves mean that students from working-class families will be able to succeed. In fact, in championing the twin goals of open doors and low fees, the university system and student leaders may have had even the opposite effect. The enrollment of working-class students has apparently increased and fees have remained at a symbolic level, but the system may in other ways work against the eventual success of these students. The reasons for this irony are discussed in more detail after consideration of the special case of women professionals.

Women Professionals as a Measure of Social Mobility

The success of Mexican women in achieving social mobility over time has been studied very little. Most studies of social mo-

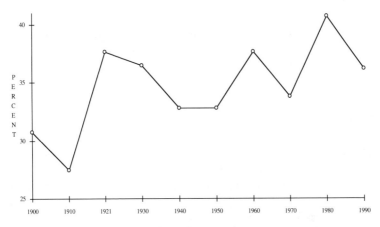

Figure 6–7. Professional and Technician Women in EAP, 1900–90.
SOURCE: Lorey, *Rise of the Professions in Mexico*, Table 58.

bility focus on males or families. Here, data on female professionals are examined as a clue to the mobility of women and to general trends of social mobility in Mexican society. The careers of women professionals lend a valuable window on general issues of social mobility because women working outside the home respond directly to basic realities of economic development.

Mexican census data on women professionals and technicians show little change in their share of professional employment over the course of the twentieth century (Fig. 6–7). Between 1900 and 1990 women occupied roughly the same share of professional and technician positions, as measured at ten-year intervals. The average for the entire period is 34.6 percent, with a standard deviation of only 3.9 percentage points. But, as noted in Chapter Four, the censuses do not generally differentiate between professionals and technicians. In one year for which there is reliable data on male and female shares of both professional and technician positions (1980), women could claim only 18.4 percent of the professional category within EAP, while women constituted 40.7 percent of jobs in the technician category. By the broader definitions of professionals and technicians employed in Chapter Four, women made up 11.2 percent of professionals and 45.8 percent of technicians in 1980. Overall, women made up

27.8 percent of EAP in 1980, so their share in the professions was well below their average share in all occupations, and their share of technician positions was well above average.

Two long-term series on the percent share held by women students at the UNAM show remarkably little change over time. Degrees granted to women averaged 21.1 percent of all degrees granted from 1910 to 1966. While this share did rise slightly from 16.3 percent in the period before 1915 and reached a high of 28.0 percent in the five-year period from 1930 to 1935, the overall standard deviation is only 5.8 percentage points across the entire period. The high point in data on degrees granted to women in the early 1930s is reflected in enrollment data as well during these years, with women achieving a high of 26.9 percent of all enrollment. Similarly, in data on female students enrolled at the UNAM between 1930 and 1966, the overall average is 20.3 percent and the standard deviation only 3.5 percentage points. After the early 1930s, there is a slow decline in the relative share of female enrollment at the professional level to an average 16.9 percent in the five-year period from 1955 to 1959.

At least as important as the relative share of women at Mexican universities is how their fields of study have changed over time. Here, data on the career fields of women professional students at all Mexican universities are compared in 1969, 1980, and 1990 to gauge how the nature of women's work at the professional level has evolved in Mexico over two decades (Fig. 6–8).[27] The share of women in fields traditionally dominated by women grew over the course of the two decades under study. In health fields, a traditional stronghold of female professionals, female enrollment grew from 20.6 percent in 1969 to 43.9 percent in 1990 in medicine, from 44.9 percent to 64.8 percent in dentistry, and from 70.5 percent to 76.0 percent in psychiatry and social work. The female share fell slightly, from 76.6 percent to 68.3 percent, in pharmaceutical chemistry. In another area of professional study traditionally dominated by women—humanities— the share held by women fell, from 61.5 percent in 1969 to 55.0 percent in 1990.

At the same time, women made significant headway in breaking into professions traditionally dominated by men in Mexico.

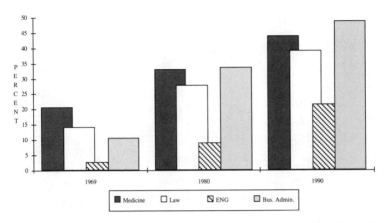

Figure 6–8. Women Enrolled in Selected Fields as Share of Total Enrollment in Those Fields, 1969, 1980, and 1990. SOURCE: Statistical Appendix, Table 11.

In law, the field with the longest tradition of male dominance, the female share of enrollment grew steadily from 14.3 percent in 1969, to 27.8 percent in 1980, and to 39.1 percent in 1990. Even in engineering, in which women were underrepresented at 21.6 percent in 1990, the share of female students rose significantly from an average of 2.8 percent in 1969 and 9.0 percent in 1980. Women also found their way into some of the newer professional fields that expanded rapidly after 1940. In business fields women have made significant gains, rising from 10.7 percent of all students enrolled in business administration in 1969, to 33.7 percent in 1980, to 48.8 percent in 1990, and in accounting from 17.8 percent, to 37.2 percent, to 50.2 percent.

Another way to approach data on female professionals is to examine shifts among occupations within the female university population (Fig. 6–9). Women moved away from the traditional female fields in the twenty years between 1969 and 1990. The percentage of women studying to be secondary-school teachers of all women professional students, for example, fell from 21.3 percent in 1969 to 17.2 percent in 1990; the share in medicine fell from 11.0 percent in 1969 to 4.9 in 1990; and the proportion in pharmaceutical chemistry declined from 3.9 percent in 1969

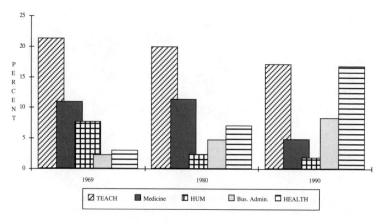

Figure 6–9. Women Enrolled in Selected Fields as Share of Total Women Enrolled, 1969, 1980, and 1990. SOURCE: Lorey, *Rise of the Professions in Mexico*, Table 63.

to 2.1 percent in 1990. In humanities the portion of all women declined from 7.7 percent in 1969 to 1.9 percent in 1990. And a large share of women students have shifted toward nontraditional and new professional fields. The share of all women enrolled in business administration, for example, almost quadrupled, from 2.3 percent in 1969, to 4.8 percent in 1980, to 8.4 percent in 1990. In engineering, only 3.0 percent of all women were studying engineering in 1969; by 1987, 16.8 percent were studying engineering specialities. These data indicate that women made significant gains in most professional fields, even in those traditionally dominated by men. Undoubtedly these increases in enrollment translated into female egresados and female degree recipients, and thus it is clear that women as a group experienced an important degree of social mobility by way of university education. More women have joined the professional ranks over time.

Data on degrees registered by women from 1970 to 1985 reveal the same widespread movement of women into new professions over time (Fig. 6–10). Overall, the number of degrees registered by women grew from 8.6 percent of all degrees registered in 1970 to 19.3 percent in 1985. In business and medicine, women roughly doubled their percent share and attained a relatively

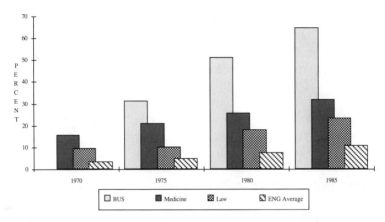

Figure 6–10. Degrees Registered by Women Professionals, Selected Fields, 1970–85. SOURCE: Lorey, *Rise of the Professions in Mexico*, Table 64.

important influence in these fields. In architecture, law, agricultural engineering, and veterinary medicine, women increased their shares but remained relatively unimportant as compared to men. In engineering this pattern is most clear: while women increased their shares from the low average level of 3.5 percent in civil, industrial, and chemical engineering in 1970, they reached an average level of only 10.9 percent by 1985. In dentistry, psychology, social work, sciences, and teaching (at both primary and secondary levels), women continued to register many more degrees than men in 1985. The average for these fields was 51.5 percent in 1975 and 69.5 percent in 1985.

The evidence of women's presence in the professional fields contradicts the findings and guesses of older literature on the topic. Most analysts have not perceived important changes in the field concentrations of women at the professional level, emphasizing instead the continuation of female professionals in "female" careers. For example, having examined the cases of dentistry and pharmaceutical studies, three analysts hypothesize that: "These two fields might be considered in the purview of women because of their 'helping' characteristics and could thus be considered in the same dimension as nursing. . . . One could also contend that pharmacy and dentistry are available to women because men have channeled their attention to the older and more traditional status-conferring fields of medicine, law, architecture, business, and engineering.[28]

These interpretations, however, do not fit the evidence of the data developed here, nor, in fact, do they fit these authors' own broader conceptions of the Mexican case. The authors classify medicine, philosophy, and science as the "high-status" professions in Mexico and economics, law, and engineering as "low-status." Yet it is clear in the data developed above that women have made significant inroads in the "status-conferring" fields of medicine and business and have greatly increased their importance even in law and architecture.

More complex explanations of women's movement into the professional fields since the 1960s are needed. While the data analyzed here are not comprehensive enough to lead to conclusive answers, they suggest at least one important possible interpretation. Drawing from the analysis of Chapter Four, we know that professional employment for women, like that for men, will be determined ultimately by the development of the Mexican economy, by the number of jobs available at the professional level. And we saw in Chapter Four that the relative number of jobs opening at the professional level has been increasingly restricted over time. Working against a shrinking market for professional skills, women have been able to find their way into the professional fields.

The foregoing analysis implies that women may well have entered the professional marketplace in part because more professional families have had to rely on double incomes in order to survive or move up the social ladder. Upward mobility for women as individuals indicates decreasing opportunities at the level of the family economy.[29] It may seem surprising that women have had as much success as they have, because they were taking positions in fields historically dominated by men. The data developed here suggest that the infamous Mexican machismo is not a determinant cultural trait but rather follows from environment; in this case, careers for women in new professional fields have become necessary and desirable because of an increasing squeeze on professional family economies since the late 1950s.

The University System and the Demand
for Social Mobility

We have considered three quantifiable aspects of the relationship between the university system and historical patterns of social mobility in Mexico. It has been established that while a good degree of social mobility by way of university education may well have been present in the 1940s and 1950s during the first two decades of Mexico's "Industrial Revolution," mobility had slowed considerably by 1960. The essential mobility bottleneck was economic. The growing Mexican economy did not create enough jobs to satisfy all or even most university graduates; growing demand for social mobility coincided with declining relative numbers of opportunities for professional employment. As a result, a high degree of real, long-term social mobility through university preparation for professional jobs was not possible. A similar pattern is apparent in other Latin American countries: "The aim [of the students] is to get a 'middle class standard of life' with a good suburban house and a car, a standard hitherto enjoyed by a favoured minority. Now it is patently impossible for an ever-growing number of graduates to enjoy a standard of living which is five to ten times the per-capita income of their countries."[30]

The principal response of the Mexican public universities to the mobility bottleneck has been to accept all applicants, keep fees low, and maintain achievement standards at minimum, relatively undemanding levels.[31] The rapid growth of the university system since the early 1960s is generally attributed to Mexico's rapid population growth and to the expansion of the educational system at lower levels. But an expanding population or rising numbers of secondary-school graduates do not necessarily mean that enrollment at universities must increase. The reality is that public-university policy has been the main cause of rapid growth in enrollment. University policy was influenced greatly by both the goals set for the university system in 1929 and by student activists' insistence on low- or no-cost "universal" education. One of the key nonnegotiable demands of the student movement in 1968 was that the universities be opened to the "popular sector" regardless of formal entrance requirements. In fact, rapid growth was desirable primarily because it meant that the myth of social mobility could be kept alive.

Who benefited from this growth in enrollment at the public universities? The data analyzed above indicate that students from working-class backgrounds benefited in the sense that they were allowed places in the entering classes. The rapid expansion of university enrollment occurred disproportionately at the working end of the social spectrum after the late 1960s. But while working-class students may have benefited by being allowed places at the universities, these places by themselves did not guarantee that working students would receive the licentiate degree and enter the job market with professional qualifications: "The open admission procedure which has been established in most [Mexican] institutions does not imply that, because of the mere fact of making entrance easy, the universities are providing more opportunities for education, nor does it mean that these opportunities would be reduced if rigorous admission standards were established."[32]

Likewise, low fees did not inherently provide opportunities for social mobility to students from working-class backgrounds. It is clear from the earlier analysis of Mexico's class structure that social mobility for Mexico's working-class aspirants to professional employment did not follow automatically after 1960 from low fees at public universities.[33] Government subsidy of low public-university fees meant that private cost was equal (even though negligible) for all students. But those students for whom the opportunity cost of attending university was higher—in other words, students from working socioeconomic strata—frequently could not study full-time and thus often were unable to progress as far or as fast as those from middle- and upper-class backgrounds.[34]

Giving students of working-class backgrounds the opportunity to enter the university was not in general followed by financial support for their studies. The differential impact of low fees has been reinforced by the absence of a working system of quotas and grants to actively recruit and support promising students from working-class backgrounds. It should be no surprise that students from working-class backgrounds make up the majority of dropouts; they probably also constitute a majority of those egresados who do not continue on for the degree.[35] The students who remain in school for the full licentiate career are generally those who can afford to study full-time, and this is particularly true of professional fields that necessitate a long period of study—engineering and medicine, for example.

Open enrollment was paired with a system of open exit from public universities. Students are free to leave their studies anytime (their personal investment in it by way of fees is minimal anyway), and university administrators make little serious effort to retain students (they are a financial burden). Letting students drop out at the end of their first year, or after two or three years, is in fact an implicit system of selection.[36] It was reported that at the UNAM in 1988, for example, fully 72 percent of entering students left the university without achieving the licentiate degree.[37] Because this "system" of selection works to separate those who will be able to continue from huge entering classes, it has not been necessary to restrict entrance to the university by the imposition of stiff entrance requirements or aptitude exams. Taken together, admission, fee, and support policies have reinforced a university system that has come to favor the children of better-off families since the late 1950s. At the same time, the rhetoric and appearances of low-cost education have obscured the real social function and impact of the system.

Equally to the point, giving students from working-class backgrounds the opportunity to enter the university cannot substitute for providing them employment opportunities. The absence of jobs for professionals has been the ultimate cause of the universities' implicit and prejudicial selection process. As competition for scarce opportunities increased, the university system came to favor those students who could afford the higher indirect and direct costs of university education. Historical trends imply that the government will only step in (with its subsidy and encouragement) to spur social mobility for students of working classes when more jobs for professionals exist than there are middle- and upper-class applicants, as was the case in the 1940s and 1950s. After that time, public universities expanded enrollment from working-class segments of the population even though increasingly few of the entrants from these strata would be able to finish their studies.

The great accomplishment of the public universities in this situation of mismatch between the Mexican economy's demand for professionals and the social demand for upward mobility has been their success in providing working entrants with the social status that accrues to university students, whether or not they graduate with the licentiate degree. The provision of social status has been the primary purpose and the principal benefit of keeping the doors of the public universities open. Because almost anyone can enroll at a public university, the status associated with attendance at university is easy to gain. At the same time, this admission policy reinforces the image that social mobility is indeed possible by way of university education. Some analysts have seen the granting of social status to students as the primary function of Mexico's public universities: "Admission policy supports the thesis that professional training is not the primary purpose of university programs. Rather, the university is a means of providing temporary activity and prestige to young adults from poor socioeconomic backgrounds who, if they did not attend the university, would be marginally employed, if at all, and possibly engage in anti-social behavior or actions against the political system."[38]

A year or two at a university helps poor students achieve some measure of status in lieu of real upward mobility. The number of Mexicans of college age who are "presently studying" in a professional field but who have not been to a class in years is enormous. Because of the prestige lent a student by any amount of time spent at a university, or by continuing enrollment, the government's attempts to stimulate terminal secondary programs that would lessen the pressure of an increasing number of applicants on the universities have been unsuccessful.[39] One or two years at a university can also help working students find work at the technician level. The university advancement system is set up so that students can drop out whenever their aspirations match employment opportunities: for many working students this equilibrium is reached rapidly. In this way, the university can be a factor of real social mobility, albeit at a low level: "A scale can be imagined, at one end of which the university is seen as having meaning only as a full cycle ending in graduation, while at the other end it is visualized from the very moment of admission as an ante–room in which the student will stay only just long enough to enable him to find employment." [40]

Study in certain professional career fields, whether active or intermittent, lends social status to students even if the degree in that field is never received. This is an important reason for choosing a "traditional" career over a new career. Employment in many new fields is uncertain (particularly for the egresado or graduate of a public university), and little prestige is attached to professions such as sanitary engineering. Even though gluts may exist in some traditional professions, then, traditional careers and specialties provide a good measure of prestige, independent of whether the profession is ever practiced. It is frequently commented that Mexico produces far more lawyers than it needs, for example; but the continued popularity of law (although the field is much less popular now than it was historically) reflects in part the lack of career opportunities for professionals in general and the social status associated with the field. It is principally for this reason that Mexico's public universities have dominated professional education in so-called traditional fields such as law and civil engineering.

Public and private universities have played complementary roles in their adopted task of providing social status in a historical context of declining professional opportunities. Increasingly, public universities have conferred social status to students of working-class backgrounds, while private universities have focused on the reinforcement of middle- and upper-class status through the provision of high-level professionals to both the public and the private sectors. The preference of more wealthy Mexicans for private education because of the poor quality and low reputation of public universities (poor quality translates into reduced ability to find a high-paying job) increasingly leaves public university education to students seeking social status and jobs as technicians—students who cannot afford private education.

Are Students to Blame for the Problems of the University System?

Students are frequently blamed, implicitly or explicitly, for the problems of the Mexican public university system and, in a more general way, for the purported university "crisis." Many observers are troubled by the involvement of students in university and national politics, seeing this involvement as problematic because it seems a more serious commitment for students than their participation in the university learning process. The perennial student demonstrations and sympathy strikes at Mexican universities appear to make it more difficult for the learning process to go forward. Some observers see the public universities as primarily places of political maneuvering and recruitment: "These students don't study, but try to initiate a political career at the university, thus the public system has deteriorated rapidly. So, the students who really want to study go to private schools. The importance, then, is the division taking place between the politically motivated student and the academically motivated student."[41]

Far from causing the problems of the university system, students are the victims of Mexico's economic development and its impact on the university's structure and function. In the context of the historical evolution of opportunities presented here, the behavior of university students in Mexico, and particularly their political activities, should be seen as symptoms rather than as causes of university crisis. The working-class students aspiring to a higher station in life are the victims of a university system that lets them through the door but fails to support their studies to the licentiate level.

A majority of university students face a tight job market in which they will be unable to find work, have to accept work at the technician level, or be "qualitatively underemployed."[42] Many public-university graduates go through a difficult period of adjustment after graduation as they scale down their expectations and aspirations to the level of employment needed by the public and private sectors. The psychological effects of this adjustment to job-market reality has important backward links.

High dropout rates (about 65 percent at the UNAM and IPN) and the difficulty of finding work with a university degree, for example, affect study and achievement levels and encourage students to actively search for employment exits throughout their university careers.

Students in Mexico both want to believe in the possibility of social mobility and are aware of the real limitations to mobility by way of professional careers. Data on the career expectations of Mexican students show that while 95 percent anticipate higher social status within 10 years (thus seeming to accept the reality of real social mobility), only 38 percent expect a higher economic status than that of their families and only 23 percent anticipate "many opportunities."[43] The fact that they hope for mobility but know it to be limited means that social status will be sought as the next best thing.

In order to cushion the economic, social, and psychological effects of scarce opportunity, students develop ways to make sense of their situation and may press for political change. The government feels a need to contain these pressures so they do not have destabilizing social and political consequences. Such pressures reached uncontainable proportions by the late 1960s, coming to a head as part of the student uprisings of 1968. Consequences of this sort have in general been avoided or been contained by recourse to the provision of social status by the universities. After the events of 1968, access to the university was greatly expanded and attempts, many successful, were made to co-opt students into the system.

The interest of public-university students in reformist and radical models for change, also sometimes seen as a cause of university crisis, must be interpreted in this larger context. Reformist or radical creeds provide the most accessible explanations for the fate of graduates in the employment market. Most importantly, they provide a way for students to externalize blame for their situation.[44] The diffusion of these creeds might be perceived as one of the major achievements of the university system, rather than a symptom of its deterioration. But these creeds can also prove threatening to the country's leaders and cause outright repression of students, as was made plain in 1968. Student criticism of university policy must also be interpreted in the light of these factors. Believing that open doors and low admission and advancement standards are to blame for the problems of the universities, university administrators have tried to reform the university at various junctures. Students have seen such attempts to reform the university from the top down as authoritarian and non-democratic.

Neither reform-minded students nor administrators have been aware of the importance of the critical fact suggested by the analysis here: reforming the university system can, by itself, accomplish little because historically the university has been shaped by the process of Mexico's economic development. Reform of the university system, particularly in terms of fees, admission and advancement requirements, and student support, might bring the university in line with the economy and with the social goals of the university set up in 1929, but such measures cannot by themselves solve the larger problems of Mexico's economy.

In sum, students unable to find professional-level work are the victims of the long-term pattern of Mexico's economic development. Universities do provide social status to an important number of university students, however; in lieu of a ticket to professional employment, students are beneficiaries of a university system that has adapted its function to economic reality. The reformist and radical creeds common at the public universities represent an important psychological benefit because they teach students not to blame themselves for a situation over which they have no control.

Summary and Conclusions

The integration of the university system with the process of economic development brought some real social mobility through the late 1950s. But the expansion of opportunities and university production of graduates could not continue in this symbiotic relationship, given the constraints of Mexican economic development. The pace of social mobility from the working classes into the professional classes of Mexican society slowed as occupation came to contribute less to this movement than did income over the period 1950–80. Because of external constraints, the Mexican university was increasingly less able to act as a conduit to the middle and upper classes of Mexican society after the 1950s.

As the pace of mobility slowed, Mexico's public universities opened their doors and increased the enrollment of students from working-class families. This access by itself, however, did not mean that social mobility by way of the university was available to these students: working-class students dropped out and stopped their study at the egresado stage more frequently than did students from middle- and upper-class backgrounds. Likewise, the apparent mobility of women into the professions obscures increasing strain on professional families because women had to add their incomes to that of their spouses to maintain the socioeconomic standing of the family.

Pressures on the university system grew by the 1960s because it could no longer provide the same degree of social mobility as it had previously. The result was a transformed university system characterized by a differentiation between the functions of public and private universities. Public universities came to provide social status to increasingly large numbers of students of working-class backgrounds, while private universities concentrated their efforts on the reinforcement of middle- and upper-class status.

The impact of social demand on the university has thus come to be as profound as that of economic demand. And social demand has become much more important than economic demand in influencing the expansion of the number of places at universities. Analysts may be technically correct in pointing out that the way the Mexican university system has developed in response to social demand is inefficient, expensive, and wasteful. But to do so is to ignore the key place in official rhetoric and the popular imagination held by the promise of social mobility. We cannot underestimate the social and political importance of the commitment to produce social mobility or, failing that, to reinforce the myth of social mobility by way of university education.

CHAPTER 7
_____

Conclusions

Since 1929 the Mexican university system has been shaped by the interrelated demands of policy priorities, economic development, and social change. Policymakers have insisted that the university respond to government initiative; employers have expected the university to provide them with professionals and technicians; and a broad spectrum of Mexican society has looked to university education for upward mobility. These demands have echoes in three major aspects of the "university crisis" perceived by academic and non-academic observers of the Mexican university system. In the crisis view, universities operate independently of government plans for development, are out of touch with the demands of the Mexican economy, and fail to promote significant social mobility.

Contrary to dominant popular and academic perceptions, Mexican universities have not drifted far outside the guidelines set by government plans for economic development since 1929. The university system has produced graduates in professional fields in a way entirely consistent with the policy priorities of Mexican leaders. Furthermore, given the lack of direct government intervention in university affairs, it seems clear that students' decisions guide the university system's response to policy. Government rhetoric and spending create an environment suitable for a certain pattern of economic development; students' perceptions of professional opportunities, their career decisions, and thus the functioning of the university system evolve in step with this policy environment.

As Mexico's state-led industrial revolution gathered steam in the late 1930s, the university system began to expand its output of professionals who could be employed in the effort—business administrators; accountants; economists; and industrial, mechanical, and electrical engineers. Whereas before 1940 the professional profile of the country was dominated by health, law, and engineering (in that order), by 1960, engineering, health, law, and business had become the most important professional fields numerically (in that order). By 1980, engineering led health, business, and upper-level teaching; law was a distant fourth. Mexico's professional profile became more diverse at the same time that traditionally important fields gave way to newer fields directly oriented toward industrialization.

The demand of the Mexican economy for professional expertise in different fields and at different levels has been met by the university system to a much greater degree than believed. The data developed for this study show that graduates and egresados leave Mexican universities in substantially the same fields in which they are needed. Employers in both the public and private sectors are able to make their needs felt among university students and their families as they select professional career areas.

By far the greatest challenge to the university system posed by the evolving Mexican economy was its need for an increasingly greater relative number of technicians compared to professionals. After the late 1950s, the ability of the Mexican economy to absorb university graduates at the professional level did not grow as fast as did the number of egresados produced by the universities. The Mexican economy's changing demand for professionals and technicians is one of the most significant and useful findings of this study because it makes possible new interpretations of the relationship between economic development and the university system. The economy's demand for university graduates had a profound effect on the Mexican university system and helps explain its current difficulties.

Until the late 1950s, the expanding industrial and commercial sectors and the growing government apparatus absorbed easily the bulk of the universities' production of professionals. Demand for a steady supply of scarce professionals was reflected in high wages for professionals in both public and private sectors and in low costs for higher education through low, government-subsidized fees at the public universities. The implicit subsidy to employers constituted by government support of university fees was part of a system of direct and indirect infrastructure subsidies that included education, electrical energy, petroleum products, communications, and controlled food prices. In a cyclical fashion, high wages for professionals and low private costs for education stimulated growing enrollments at the universities. Government employment of professionals accounted for a large part of the professional employment boom, particularly in fields such as medicine and teaching.

After the late 1950s, however, there was a precipitous decline in the ability of the economy to produce jobs for professionals at the rate that students entered the universities. The public sector might create jobs for many professionals, but a growing majority of students with aspirations to professional work and status could not be employed in either the public or the private sector as professionals. Increasingly limited opportunities for professionals after the end of the 1950s reflected the uncompetitive and inefficient nature of Mexican industry as it developed between the late 1930s and the early 1980s. The period of sustained economic growth was based on an industrialization process that relied heavily on the Mexican government for protection and on foreign capital-goods producers for technological innovation. As an unintended consequence of these policies, the Mexican economy did not forge an industrial plant characterized by innovation and competitiveness in the world market and did not create an independent capital-goods and research-and-development infrastructure. Without innovations in the machinery used in manufacturing or an increase in expenditure for research and development, the education and employment of professionals could undergo no dramatic structural change. These factors had the greatest impact on professionals trained in engineering, business, and the sciences. While some critics continue to argue that there are not enough Mexican university graduates per capita to fuel development, low graduates-per-capita ratios accurately reflect the nature of economic development achieved in Mexico since 1929.

How did changing demand for professionals and technicians affect Mexican universities? The university system's most significant response was to produce a small number of graduates to fill the need for the most highly qualified professionals and a much larger number of egresados to fill the need for technicians. The government's emphasis on increasing enrollment capacities at public universities in the 1940s and 1950s thus paid off in an unintended way: it made possible the university system's twin roles of training professionals and technicians.

Two important impacts of the economy's evolving demand for university graduates can be seen in changes in the quality of professional education and the deconcentration of the university system. By producing very different sorts of graduates, public and private universities acted together in responding to the economy's demand for university graduates and egresados. A "system" of public and private universities evolved after the 1940s as the two types of institutions came to feed different labor markets.

A secular leveling-off of quality at Mexican universities was one noticeable result of the changing demand of the economy. Although a "crisis" in quality did not occur in Mexican higher education, the impressive increases in quality of the 1940s did not continue after the late 1950s. Because they mirror the timing of changes in the economy's demand for professionals and technicians, changes in quality constitute one aspect of the university system's response to shifts in that demand.

Within the general trends of changes in quality, important differences developed between public and private universities. The demand in the private sector, and at the upper level of the public sector, for the best-trained professionals grew faster than quality at the public universities after the late 1950s. The size of enrollments and the rate of graduation at private universities increased rapidly to fill the gap. Public and private institutions came to play complementary roles in training students to different levels of expertise. Graduates of private universities and some graduates of the best public universities filled the need for top-level professionals. The public universities, particularly the public universities of the provinces, produced large numbers of egresados who generally did not complete the degree and who found work primarily as technicians. Regional public universities partially relieved the tremendous pressure on the public university giants in Mexico City by keeping a good part of increased demand for higher educational opportunities confined to the provinces. The deconcentration of the university system, like changes in quality, was driven by the tighter market for professionals as compared to technicians in a context of rapidly expanding enrollment.

The development of a university system characterized by different roles for public and private institutions bore a striking resemblance to the differentiation of public and private sectors in the Mexican economy. The drive after the crisis of 1982 to reduce public-sector spending by selling off publicly owned firms (under presidents de la Madrid and Salinas de Gortari) made relevant several questions regarding the public component of the country's university system: Was the public university system an efficient producer? Did it produce a competitive, quality product? Had protecting the university from market forces (by government subsidy of low fees) helped or harmed Mexican society?

As in the case of other decentralized agencies and parastatal firms, it could be said that after the late 1950s the public-university system became an increasingly inefficient producer of the most highly qualified professionals. Private universities experienced very strong development after the 1950s because there was only weak competition from the public universities in filling the demand for high-quality professionals. Ironically, however, the public universities were successful in becoming efficient producers of technicians, and in doing so they fulfilled a necessary function given the development of the Mexican economy.

It might seem that the government played a negative role in manipulating the price mechanisms of university education through its subsidy of public-university education, at least in the period after the late 1950s. Government support of low fees encouraged demand for places in the university system to grow much faster than opportunities for professionals in the economy. The practice of filling the gap between nominal university fees and the real costs of educating professionals with government subsidy meant that public universities did not have to restrict admissions in line with the demands of the market for quality professional expertise. The irony here is that the cost of producing the most highly qualified professionals gradually shifted to the private sector, leaving the less-expensive task of educating technicians to the public sector.

The intervention of the government in the price mechanism of higher education and the "inefficiency" of the public universities were both determined by the demand for social mobility—the key social role of the university system in the implicit university-government pact of 1929. The three basic types of challenges to the university system—policy, economic, and social—come together around the demand for social mobility, because fundamental to the interaction of these three demands is a disparity between aspirations to professional careers and the opportunities brought by development.

Over time the demand for upward mobility and middle-class status increasingly came into conflict with the reality of Mexico's economic development. Eventually, as the process of economic development created a progressively smaller relative number of jobs at the professional level, the university's ability to satisfy expectations for social mobility became restricted. While universities did have a positive effect on social mobility until at least 1960 through their role in readying students for professional occupations, after that time egresados were produced twice as fast as they could be employed at the professional level.

The university system evolved to meet this strain. As the possibility of social mobility decreased, public universities opened their doors to entrants from working-class backgrounds and became less efficient at producing professionals. After the late 1950s, the public-university system adopted the function of providing social status rather than social mobility to most university students of humble backgrounds, while private universities came to focus on the reinforcement of middle- and upper-class status through the provision of high-level professionals to both public and private sectors. It was this new role for the public university that prevented it from meeting the quality demands of the economy. Government subsidies were spent on supporting huge entering classes and providing the maximum number of university places for the first few years of university education.

The adaptation of providing social status in place of significant upward social mobility was extremely important because it assured the survival of the myth of social mobility and perhaps the survival of the university system itself. Different roles for public and private universities and a fundamental "inefficiency" thus proved useful in Mexico because of the importance of the social role of the public universities. This response on the part of the university system was entirely in line with the universities' responsibilities under the implicit pact of 1929 and completely consistent with the reality of changing opportunities for university graduates.

The historical adaptation of the Mexican university system to changing economic and social realities is central to the political history of the university. It is widely believed that the government has supported open doors in order to offer an escape valve for unemployable youth. One observer commented that the large numbers of entering students who could not find professional employment were not casualties of the education system as much as successes for the political system.[1] Such a scheme, even if implicit, would appear to have backfired, because the dissatisfaction of students with the university's failure to provide a path to professional employment has led to broad student involvement in extra-university political issues.

The political activity of Mexican university students must be interpreted in the light of the historical limitations facing them in their professional careers. Students benefit from the system in some important ways: the universities provide social status to an important number of university students in lieu of a ticket to professional employment, and the reformist and radical creeds instilled at the public universities represent an important psychological benefit because they teach students to externalize blame for limited employment opportunities. But in the long term, university students, unable to find professional-level work, are the victims of Mexico's economic development. The university cannot change this situation even with thorough internal reforms: the determining factors are beyond the control of university administrators or students.

It was once common to interpret student politics and relations between the state and the university in purely political and legal terms. In that view, struggles between the government and university students were seen as conflicts over the university's hard-won autonomy from direct government intervention in its internal affairs. But relations have been much more complex, as is borne out by the principal differences between two key periods in the political relations between the university and the state since 1929: the period of relative peace between students and the state from roughly 1940 to 1958, and the period of overt conflict and violent confrontation after 1958 that came to a head during 1968.

Traditional interpretations do not adequately explain the long period of relative political peace between the university and the state from roughly 1940 to 1958. The focus on juridical aspects of the struggle between university and state led one author to view the lack of state-university tension in the 1940s and early 1950s as due to the effectiveness of the organic university law of 1944. For the 1950s, the same analyst observes that "why UNAM students remained calm in spite of the numerous opportunities provided by the strikes and demonstrations of 1956 remains as much a mystery as why so many outbreaks occurred." The explanation forwarded for this latter period of relative calm is that students lacked unity: "The postwar expansion of higher education . . . fragmented student culture, making the creation of a common cause difficult."[2]

The present study suggests that the principal reason for the political peace between the university and the state during the 1940s and 1950s was an underlying integration of the pattern of economic development and the universities' production of professionals to plan, guide, and execute that development. Because of this integration, there existed a commonality of interest between government policies for economic development and the university's structure and function. The economy expressed a strong and steady demand for professionals and provided a significant degree of social mobility.

Public employment of professionals played an important part in creating the political calm of the 1940s and 1950s. Providing employment for professionals may never have been an explicit goal of policymakers, but there was a tremendous increase in the number of posts in the public sector with the rise of the active state after the mid-1930s. Although this trend began in the 1930s, it became increasingly important as the economic revolution went forward in Mexico during the 1940s. The employment of many thousands of professionals in the state apparatus is one of the major understudied factors in the growth of the Mexican state and associated bureaucracies after 1929. The central and decentralized sectors of the Mexican state apparatus became top heavy for the same reason that the Mexican military is brass-heavy: both institutional networks provide employment for persons who cannot be readily absorbed by the economy. The sociopolitical function of employing critical and vocal professionals in the public sector should be clear: in this as in other ways, the nexus between the university and the public sector is "an instrument of legitimization" and "an engine of consensus."[3] In a detailed listing of implicit pacts between the Mexican government and sectors in Mexican society, one observer sees the principle benefit of a government-university pact to university graduates as an "ever-expanding pool of job opportunities in the centralized and decentralized agencies as well as [an] opportunity to advance into politics and become government consultants."[4]

The success of the "Institutionalized Revolution" in providing employment for professionals should be seen as one of its signal accomplishments. Political pressure from unemployed professionals had previously constituted one of the principal challenges to political stability in Mexico. Professionals who had been left out of the economic growth of the Porfiriato played an important role in the Revolution of 1910. One of the principal purposes of the state apparatus after the political consolidation of the Revolution in 1929 was the maintenance of a high employment level for professionals, and this purpose is seen in the dramatic growth of government bureaucracies and public enterprises over time.

But while the Mexican state apparatus was able to expand to provide significant employment opportunities for a large number of university graduates, its ability to create professional jobs at the rate that students left the university system has become increasingly limited over time. The case of professionals in health care fields is instructive. While there were a total of almost 15,000 egresados in health fields in the late 1980s, the number of residencies in Mexican hospitals hovered around 2,000. The ABC Hospital in Mexico City (a private hospital with an important charity clinic) received over 2,000 applications for its roughly 60 residencies. Some observers estimate that as many as 70,000 doctors were unable to find residencies in Mexico in the 1980s.[5] The situation of young doctors without job prospects is sadly ironic, because the majority of Mexicans continue to suffer from myriad preventable diseases and have limited access to quality health care.

The relationship between economic development and social mobility outlined in this study lies at the root of post–1958 political conflicts involving the university system in Mexico. One of the great debates surrounding the violent events of 1968 in Mexico involves the ultimate causes of the students' activism and the reason that students received such broad support from Mexico's middle classes. Many authors are at a total loss to explain student discontent and protest:

> There had been no major change in the students at UNAM or in academic regulations prior to 1968. The economy experienced no sudden downturn and in fact was growing faster than ever at a rate of 7 percent a year, making Mexico's growth one of the world's fastest. There had been no sudden changes in Mexico's foreign policy nor was there any threat of war on the horizon. No social movement or political party had launched a campaign against the PRI in the months before July 1968.[6]

The analysis of the present study suggests that the growth rate of GNP is not the most useful signal for examining the link between the university and economic development: the economy can grow without creating enough jobs for professionals to absorb all seekers. While GDP grew rapidly during the 1960s (at 7.0 percent per year) and during the 1970s (at 6.6 percent a year), employment for professionals did not increase at similar rates. This disparity is a key factor in explaining the students' activism and their broad support within the middle classes in the late 1960s. Discontent with the implications of historical economic development among professionals, and within the middle class from which most came, was widespread and profound. The inherent tension between the number of opportunities and the number of university entrants and egresados was a nationwide phenomenon. The disturbances of 1968 were not isolated to Mexico City but spread across the nation. The final crisis and massacre of students in October of 1968 in the Plaza of Three Cultures in Mexico City was preceded by large and violent student protests in the states of Sonora, Puebla, and Morelos.

The logic of the present study implies that increasingly scarce jobs for professionals would tend to focus university politics on issues involving the provision of social status. And since at least 1958, political struggles have revolved around issues of entrance and advancement at the universities. Higher qualitative norms and more restrictive admission policies, while perhaps improving the quality of professional expertise produced by the universities, also make higher education less accessible. Student protests in the winter of 1986–87 were triggered by the resolution of UNAM's administration to raise academic standards. Even the 1968 reform movement, which spread far beyond the original protest of secondary and university students over the violation of autonomy to become a watershed in Mexican political history, had substantial roots in student objections to attempts to raise academic standards a few years earlier.[7]

The data developed here also shed light on the disciplinary location of political activity and protest. Political activity among students at the UNAM, for example, has historically been centered in the schools of law, economics, social and political sciences, and philosophy. These schools are physically adjacent to one another but are separated by the main quadrangle from the "politically quiet" faculties of architecture, business, and engineering.[8] These two groups of schools represent professions for which demand has declined generally since 1929 on the one hand and professions for which demand has expanded rapidly since the late 1930s on the other. Trends in employment also divide the politically active students of the UNAM from the less-active engineering students of the IPN. Political activism on the part of students studying to be lawyers, and the relative lack of it among those studying to be business managers or engineers, is perhaps not caused primarily by the personal characteristics of students in these fields or by the nature of the fields of study themselves. Job opportunities have historically been an essential, yet unrealized, ingredient in the political awareness and political protest of Mexican university students.

The idea that the politics of the Mexican university system follow some internal dynamic conditioned principally by struggles over autonomy or democracy needs to be modified greatly. The present analysis of the impact of economic development on job opportunities, mobility, and the functioning of the university system suggests that the historical pattern of economic development explains important aspects of the functioning of the university system in Mexican political life.

The disparity between the number of persons desiring to enroll at universities and the number of university places grew steadily after the late 1970s as the open-door policy created a university system of massive proportions. While the university system responded with flexibility to the challenge of burgeoning social demand, the overall situation remained grave. The UNAM, for example, could only make room for half of all applicants by the late 1980s. In August of 1988, 500,000 students who had been denied entrance to the IPN marched through Mexico City.[9] And the contraction of the Mexican economy in the 1980s left its mark on employment of university graduates: at the Autonomous University of Nuevo León in Monterrey, for example, the percentage of egresados employed one year after leaving the university fell from 76.2 percent in 1980–81 to 49.1 percent in 1986–87.[10]

The drastic reduction of government jobs for professionals after the economic crisis of 1982 meant that pressures within the system would continue to build. With the dramatic restructuring of the Mexican economy during the 1980s and 1990s, and particularly the increased foreign investment and free-trade initiatives pursued by President Carlos Salinas de Gortari, many professionals were certain to be laid off and replaced by new, largely imported, technological introductions.[11] In privatizing parastatal enterprises, the government planned to transfer perhaps a third of the work force to the private sector, which in turn would reduce superfluous labor.[12] Mexico's entrance into the GATT in 1985 and the emphasis on maquila and other assembly operations for export has done little to stimulate professional opportunities. While in the long term professional employment may well be enhanced by a Mexican economy that is more competitive internationally, the outlook for professionals in the short term (perhaps to the end of the century) is not bright.

The dominant image of a Mexican university system beyond government control, at odds with the economy, and unable to provide social mobility, must be revised. The development of the university system cannot be understood outside the context of the evolution of the Mexican economy since at least 1929. The Mexican university system as a whole, including public and private universities, has proven resilient, responsive to government policy and the realities of historical economic development and social change. The pattern of university response to historical challenges reveals the unintended consequences of government priorities and the protected, uncompetitive nature of the Mexican economy.

What has been described as a university crisis is the reflection, at the level of professional education, professional employment, and social mobility, of a broader and deeper crisis in Mexican development. It is the particular pattern of Mexico's economic growth that has produced such characteristic features as overcrowded campuses and the differentiation of public- and private-university functions. Because the fundamental causes of these conditions are external to the universities, only a greatly modified trajectory of economic development or a new consensus on the role of the university system in society, or both, can resolve the university crisis in Mexico.

Reference Matter

Categorization of Professional Fields and Specialties

In the past, most data on the university system in Mexico have been organized into highly aggregate groupings of career fields such as "health," "social sciences," and "engineering and technical" professions. Some of these groupings, such as "philosophy and letters," have been retained from the names of university faculties organized in colonial times. The "philosophy and letters" category includes careers that are now generally considered both social sciences, such as history and geography, and humanities, such as philosophy and literature.

The basic organizing principle for the categories developed in this study is the employment of professionals. Fields of study are placed in categories according to the sector in which university graduates in those fields will most probably work. Thus, veterinary doctors, sometimes found in the data with other medical professionals, are here grouped with agricultural engineers; actuaries, who are trained in mathematics, law, or engineering departments, have been placed in the business category because they generally work for insurance firms.[1]

All major data series are presented by calendar year. This form of presentation is most accurate for data on degrees granted, egresados, and registered degrees, the three basic series analyzed in this study. In contrasting data on expenditure and enrollment, which are generally tabulated on the basis of the academic year after 1970, with other data series, I use the later calendar year. For example, expenditure data for the academic year 1975–76 are compared with data on egresados for 1976. The decision to compare 1975–76 with 1976 instead of 1975 does not lead to any major changes in the interpretation of the series.

The field abbreviations used in tables and charts are included after the field name. Upper-case letters (e.g. "BUS") indicate an aggregate field, lower-case letters (e.g. "Econ.") a field made up of a single degree.

Makeup of Professional-Field Categories Used in Text, Charts, and Statistical Tables

DEGREES GRANTED[2]

Business (BUS)
Commerce
Business Administration
Accounting
Actuary

Engineering (ENG)
Agricultural Engineering
Chemical Engineering
Civil Engineering
Electrical, Mechanical, and Mechanical-Electrical Engineering[3]
Extractive Engineering
Other Engineering (Not Specified in Source)

Health Professions (HEALTH)[4]
Medicine
Dentistry

Sciences (SCIENCE)
Chemistry
"Scientific Professions"

Teaching Professions (TEACH)
Secondary-School Teachers
University Professors

Other
Psychology[5]
Diplomacy
Pharmaceutical Chemists
Various Other Professions[6]

EGRESADOS[7]

Architecture and Design (Arch.)
Architecture
Architectural Engineering
Design

Business (BUS)
Business Administration
Accounting
Communications
International Relations
Industrial Relations
Commercial Relations
Public Relations
Tourism
Sales and Marketing
Customs
Public Administration[8]

Engineering and Applied Sciences (ENG)
Agricultural Engineering
Chemical Engineering
Civil Engineering
Computer Engineering
Earth Sciences
Electrical and Electronic Engineering
Extractive Engineering
Industrial Engineering
Mechanical and Mechanical-Electrical Engineering
Other Engineering (See Lorey, *Rise of the Professions*,
    Chapter 4)

Health Professions (HEALTH)
Medical Doctors
Dentistry
Nursing
Optometry
Pharmaceutical Chemists
Bacteriology, Parasitology

Humanities and Arts (HUM)
Dramatic Art
Dance
Scenery

Philosophy
History
Language
Letters
Music
Religion

Psychology and Social Work (Psych./SW)
Psychology
Social Work

Sciences (SCIENCE)[9]
Biology
Biochemistry
Atmospheric Sciences
Marine Sciences
Geology
Physics
Mathematics
Chemistry

Social Sciences (SS)
Sociology
Anthropology and Archeology
Archival and Bibliographical Studies
Geography
Political Science
Political Science and Public Administration
Latin American Studies
Sports Organization

Teaching Professions
Egresados of Normal Superior (Higher Teacher Training) courses
Education
Pedagogy

REGISTERED DEGREES[10]

Business (BUS)
Commerce
Business Administration
Accounting

Engineering (ENG)
Agricultural Engineering
Chemical Engineering

Civil Engineering
Electrical and Electronic Engineering
Extractive Engineering
Industrial Engineering
Mechanical Engineering
Mechanical-Electrical Engineering

Health Professions (HEALTH)

Medicine
Dentistry
Nursing
Optometry

Humanities and Arts (HUM)

Philosophy
Language and Letters
Music
Visual Arts

Psychology and Social Work (Psych./SW)

Sciences (SCIENCE)

Physics
Mathematics
Biology

Social Sciences (SS)

Sociology
Anthropology
History

Teaching Professions (TEACH)

Other

All other degrees

Field Breakdown by Function Used in Chapter Three

SOCIAL

HEALTH

TEACH

ECONOMIC

BUS

ENG

Field Breakdown by Economic Sector Used in Chapter 4

PRIMARY SECTOR—AGRICULTURE

Agricultural Engineering

Veterinary Medicine

Topographical/Hydrological Engineering

SECONDARY SECTOR—INDUSTRY

Mechanical Engineering

Electrical Engineering

Chemical Engineering

Textile Engineering

Industrial Engineering

Biochemical Engineering

TERTIARY SECTOR—SERVICES

Civil Engineering

Computer Engineering

Other Engineering

Earth Sciences

Arch.

BUS

Econ.

HEALTH

TEACH

Psych./SW

SCIENCE, SS, HUM

TABLE I

University Degrees Granted, Nine Fields, 1930–1970

Year	Arch.	Econ.	HEALTH	TEACH	Law	BUS[a]	ENG	SCIENCE	Other	TOTAL
1930	6	0	249	0	138	0	117	15	0	525
1935	5	3	381	21	264	0	87	23	0	784
1940	22	3	428	74	286	0	148	88	0	1,049
1945	7	10	677	280	248	90	253	110	0	1,675
1950	15	9	865	291	238	130	256	97	0	1,901
1955	9	9	1,355	653	381	290	651	240	0	3,588
1960	113	32	795	169	588	380	1,013	239	0	3,329
1965	321	143	1,786	537	904	488	1,903	192	166	6,440
1970	522	281	2,305	776	1,440	1,386	2,965	360	636	10,671

SOURCES: Data were derived from Dirección General de Estadística, *Anuario estadístico* and *Compendio estadístico*, various years and Secretaría de Educación Pública, *La educación pública en México, 1964/1970* (Mexico City: SEP, 1970); for complete series, see Lorey, *Rise of the Professions*, table 1.

[a]Business category estimated 1940–60. Numbers of business degrees in these years rounded to nearest ten degrees.

TABLE 2

University Egresados, Eleven Fields, 1967–89

Year	Arch.	BUS	Econ.	ENG	HEALTH	HUM	Law	Psych./SW	SCI	SS	TEACH[a]	TOTAL
1967	1,080	3,111	530	3,583	2,798	169	1,986	148	312	285	1,265	15,267
1970	1,010	5,384	736	6,647	3,608	259	2,820	326	454	283	1,068	22,595
1975[b]	1,790	7,580	1,370	13,480	8,470	500	5,330	900	900	650	3,560	44,530
1980	2,556	13,819	1,722	20,798	18,051	622	6,154	2,545	1,586	783	14,167	82,803
1985	4,182	28,101	1,859	27,135	17,205	1,168	9,516	4,339	2,873	2,025	21,697	120,100
1989	5,857	34,990	2,111	32,694	14,789	1,426	11,465	4,372	3,191	2,280	27,265	140,440

SOURCES: Derived from ANUIES (Asociación Nacional de Universidades e Institutos de Educación Superior), *Anuario estadístico, Enseñanza superior en México,* and *Educación superior en México,* various years, and unpublished ANUIES data; for complete series see Lorey, *Rise of the Professions,* table 3.

[a]Secondary teaching only, 1967–80; for 1985 and 1989 the data include all licenciate-level egresados of teaching fields.
[b]Data for 1975 were partially estimated to adjust for incomplete coverage in source.

TABLE 3

University Degrees Registered, Eleven Fields, 1970–85

Year	Arch.	BUS	Econ.	ENG	HEALTH	HUM[a]	Law	Psych./SW	SCI	SS	TEACH	TOTAL
1970	510	840	190	2,920	2,330	0	1,180	0	90	170	100	8,330
1975	1,010	4,450	440	5,650	5,380	220	2,120	250	350	720	610	21,200
1980	1,160	4,460	670	8,580	12,060	290	2,800	750	520	2,090	2,260	35,640
1985	2,020	8,500	1,000	15,040	14,000	1,680	3,480	1,300	390	4,470	3,770	55,650

SOURCES: Data derived from unpublished manuscripts and tabulations at DGP. Data are rounded to nearest ten degrees registered. See Lorey, *Rise of the Professions*, table 4.

[a]It was not required that humanities degrees be registered until 1974.

TABLE 4

Graduates and Egresados in Sample Economic and Social Fields

PART I: Average Index and Percent Shares, 1930–89

Year	Time-Lag Year[a]	Index of Absolute Data		Percent Shares	
		Economic	Social	Economic	Social
1930	1924	2	8	22.3	47.4
1935	1929	2	13	11.1	51.3
1940	1934	3	16	14.1	47.9
1945	1939	7	31	20.5	57.1
1950	1944	8	38	20.3	60.8
1955	1949	20	65	26.2	56.0
1960	1954	29	31	41.8	29.0
1965	1959	55	75	39.2	34.9
1970	1964	100	100	47.1	25.9
1975	1969	222	252	47.5	27.6
1980	1974	342	639	39.2	39.5
1985	1979	575	781	44.1	32.2
1989	1983	328	899	48.2	29.9

PART II: Sexenial Data, Time-Lagged Six Years, 1923–82

Time-Lag Sexenio	Econ. Fields	Social Fields
1923–28	15.4	52.8
1929–34	14.1	50.6
1935–40	20.3	54.5
1941–46	23.5	52.5
1947–52	28.9	49.5
1953–58	40.8	33.3
1959–64	42.7	30.1
1965–70	48.4	27.7
1971–76	40.9	37.5
1977–82	46.0	30.7

SOURCE: Adapted from Lorey, *Rise of the Professions*, Tables 11 and 12.

NOTE: Economic fields refer to BUS and ENG categories; social fields to HEALTH and TEACH categories.

[a] This column shows the estimated year of career-field decision of university degree recipients or egresados (for use in comparison with data on historical patterns in government policy priorities; see Chapter Three).

TABLE 5

The Mexican Economy's Demand for Professionals

PART I: Percent of Professionals and Technicians in Economically Active Population (EAP) and University Graduates, by Economic Sector, 1950–90

Year	EAP[a]			Year	Degrees granted			Egresados[b]		
	Primary	Secondary	Tertiary		Primary	Secondary	Tertiary	Primary	Secondary	Tertiary
1950	0.6	13.6	83.8	1950	4.5	4.0	91.5	–	–	–
1960	3.9	19.7	75.7	1961[c]	4.2	15.6	80.2	–	–	–
1970	2.6	18.5	76.3	1970	6.5	13.0	80.5	5.2	17.9	76.9
1980	1.8	27.2	66.1	1980	–	–	–	7.6	11.0	81.4
1990	2.4	19.4	74.1	1989	–	–	–	7.5	8.6	83.9

SOURCE: Derived from Mexican census data and the data in Tables 1, 2, and 3 above; see also Lorey, *Rise of the Professions*, Tables 24, 25.
[a]Sums do not equal 100 owing to insufficiently specified economic sector in the census.
[b]Sums do not equal 100 owing to rounding.
[c]Data for 1960 do not fit the secular trend.

TABLE 5 (cont'd)

PART II: Percent of Professional Employment and Degrees Granted, 1950, and Professional Employment and Egresados, 1980

	Employment				Degrees granted, 1950				Egresados, 1980			
	ENG	HEALTH	Law	TEACH	ENG	HEALTH	Law	TEACH	ENG	HEALTH	Law	TEACH
1950	11.2%	16.3%	10.9%	3.1%	13.5%	45.5%	12.5%	15.3%	–	–	–	–
1980	18.7	20.1	–	12.8	–	–	–	–	25.1%	21.8%	–	17.1%

SOURCE: Lorey, *Rise of the Professions*, Table 30.

TABLE 5 (cont'd)

PART III: Professionals and Technicians in EAP and University Graduates, 1950, 1980, and 1990

| | Professionals and technicians as pct. of EAP | | | Pct. change 1950–80 | Implicit annual rates of change[b] | |
	1950	1980	1990		1950–80	1980–90
Professionals[a]						
Wide definition	1.8%	3.3%	5.0%	384.3%	5.4%	4.8%
Narrow definition	1.3	2.5	3.7	417.8	5.6	4.6
Technicians[a]						
Wide definition	2.5	8.9	12.8	848.7	7.8	4.3
Narrow definition	1.6	6.7	9.5	1,055.3	8.5	4.1

SOURCE: Lorey, *Rise of the Professions*, Tables 30 and 31.

[a]Narrow and wide definitions are developed in Lorey, *Rise of the Professions*, Table 30.

[b]Compound rates of change are calculated with the following formula: annual rate equals antilog of {log[P_n/P_o]/n}, minus 1, where P_o equals the original population and P_n equals the population after n years. A 100 percent change over ten years equals 7.18 percent change per year.

TABLE 5 (cont'd)

PART IV: Implicit Annual Rates of Change by Decade, 1930–89

Decade	Degrees granted	Egresados	Degrees registered
1930–40	7.2%	–	–
1940–50	6.1	–	–
1950–60	5.8	–	–
1960–70[a]	12.4	14.0%	–
1970–80[b]	–	13.9	10.7%
1980–89	–	5.4	–

SOURCE: Same as for Part III.
[a]Egresados data are for 1967–70.
[b]Degrees registered data are for 1971–80.

TABLE 5 (cont'd)

PART V: Professional-Job Creation and University Egresados, 1950–90[a]

Period	Positions for professionals	University egresados
1950–60	70,000	50,000
1960–70	100,000	120,000
1970–80	270,000	452,257
1980–90	311,452	1,162,352

SOURCE: David Lorey and Aída Mostkoff, "Mexico's 'Lost Decade': Evidence on Class Structure and Professional Employment from the 1990 Census," *Statistical Abstract of Latin America*, 30:2.
[a]Data are partially estimated.

TABLE 6

Measuring the Quality of Mexican Higher Education:
All Universities

Year	Estimated pesos of 1970 per student	Average students per faculty	Percent full-time faculty
1930	1,013	15.3	–
1935	2,535	9.3	–
1940	1,830	7.3[a]	–
1945	1,754	–	–
1950	1,815	4.9	–
1955	1,614	7.8	–
1958	4,641	7.3	–
1965	2,161	10.3	6.9%
1970	1,628	9.8	8.2
1975	1,993	11.4	8.6[b]
1980	2,084	11.6	17.2
1985	–	10.1	20.9
1990	–	10.3	25.1

SOURCE: Adapted from Lorey, *Rise of the Professions*, Tables 32, 34, and 35.
[a]1939.
[b]1976.

TABLE 7

Quality Measures at Sample Public and Private Universities,
1970, 1980, and 1990

	Percent of full-time faculty	Ratio of students to all faculty	Ratio of students to full-time faculty
Public[a]			
1970	8.5%	10	205
1980	21.7	16	90
1990	28.9	13	52
Private[b]			
1970	18.0	8	85
1980	33.5	11	31
1990	25.6	10	67

SOURCE: Adapted from Lorey, *Rise of the Professions*, Table 40.
NOTE: The data represent unweighted averages.
[a]Public universities in the 1970 sample are UNAM; IPN; Universidad Autónoma de Baja California; Universidad Autónoma de Coahuila; Universidad Autónoma de Chihuahua; Universidad de Guanajuato; Universidad de Guadalajara; Universidad Autónoma de Estado de México; Universidad Autónoma de Nuevo León; Universidad Autónoma de Puebla; Universidad Autónoma de San Luis Potosí; Universidad Autónoma de Sinaloa; Universidad Autónoma de Tamaulipas; Universidad de Guadalajara; Universidad Michoacana de San Nicolás; and the Universidad Veracruzana. In 1980 and 1990, Universidad Autónoma Metropolitana was added.
[b]Private universities in the sample for 1970 are the Universidad Iberoaméricana; the Instituto Tecnológico Autónoma de México; the Instituto Tecnológico y de Estudios Superiores de Monterrey; Universidad Anáhuac; and the Universidad Autónoma de Guadalajara. In 1980 and 1990 the Universidad de las Américas-Puebla was added.

TABLE 8

Deconcentration of the Mexican University System, 1967–89:
Egresados of Public and Private Universities

PART I. *UNAM, IPN, and Public and Private Shares[a]*

Year	Egresados of UNAM and IPN as percent of egresados of all universities	Egresados of private universities as percent of egresados of all universities[b]	Egresados of public universities as percent of egresados of all universities[b]
1967	44.7%	11.6%	88.4%
1970	45.8	11.2	88.8
1975	37.6	14.2	85.8
1980	29.3	15.1	84.9
1985	21.1	19.8	80.2
1989	19.6	19.3	80.7

PART II. *Fourteen-University Sample[b]*

Year	Egresados of sample universities as percent of egresados of all universities	Egresados of private universities in sample as percent of egresados of all private universities	Egresados of public universities in sample as percent of egresados of all public universities
1967	78.0%	61.7%	95.1%
1970	78.5	56.9	91.5
1975	70.1	48.9	85.5
1980	71.0	36.7	77.2
1985	61.9	30.0	69.8
1989	57.0	23.7	65.0

SOURCE: Lorey, *Rise of the Professions*, Tables 46, 47, and 48.
[a]Private and public shares are estimated 1967–75.
[b]The sample includes 11 public and three private universities. Public: Universidad Autónoma de Coahuila; Universidad Autónoma de Chihuahua; Universidad Autónoma de Estado de México; Universidad Autónoma de Nuevo León; Universidad Autónoma de Puebla; Universidad Autónoma de San Luis Potosí; Universidad Autónoma de Sinaloa; Universidad Autónoma de Tamaulipas; Universidad Autónoma de Guadalajara; Universidad Michoacana de San Nicolás; and Universidad Veracruzana. Private: Instituto Tecnológico y de Estudios Superiores de Monterrey; Universidad Iberoamericana; and Universidad Autónoma de Guadalajara.

TABLE 9

Comparison of Growth Rates in University Degrees Granted,
Egresados, and Degrees Registered with Growth
of Social Classes, 1950–90
(Percent change per decade)

| Period | Professionals | | | Classes[a] | |
	Degrees granted	Egresados	Degrees registered	Stable middle	Semi-leisure
1950–60	75.1%	–	–	61.5%	141.2%
1960–70	232.1	–	–	73.6	95.7
1970–80	–	266.5	149.1	110.5	44.1
1980–90[b]	–	69.6	–	20.5	14.2

SOURCES: Calculated from Tables 1, 2, and 3 above and Lorey, *Rise of the Professions*, Table 54.

[a]Data are for growth of absolute number of places in class strata defined by income and occupation. See Lorey, *Rise of the Professions*, Tables 51 and 54. Also see Lorey and Aída Mostkoff, "Mexico's 'Lost Decade': Evidence on Class Structure and Professional Employment from the 1990 Census," *Statistical Abstract of Latin America*, 30:2.

[b]Egresados data are for 1980–89.

TABLE 10

Social Mobility in the Mexican University

PART I: Highest Level of Schooling Attained by Fathers of UNAM
Students, 1949, 1963, 1970, and 1980 (percent)

	Professional	Preparatory/ Vocational	Technical	Secondary	Primary	Total
1949	23.6%	–	–	–	9.5%	–
1963	20.8	–	–	–	14.3	
1970[a]	19.0	4.0	3.0	7.0	19.0	52.0
1980	17.4	4.4	2.1	10.4	27.3	61.6

PART II: Class Background (by Family Income)
of UNAM Students, 1963, 1970, and 1980 (percent)

Class	1963	1970	1980
Lower	4.6%	4.3%	7.1%
Middle	29.5	29.5	57.2
Upper	66.4	62.5	33.6
No response	–	3.7	2.1
Lower+transitional middle	14.2	13.3	37.3

SOURCE: Lorey, *Rise of the Professions*, Tables 55 and 57.
[a]Rounded figures are given in source.

TABLE II

Women Enrolled in Selected Fields as a Percent of
Total Enrollment in Those Fields, *1969, 1980, and 1990*

	1969	1980	1990
Accounting	17.8%	37.2%	50.2%
Architecture	9.5	20.7	35.0
Bus. Admin.	10.7	33.7	48.8
Communications	33.3	50.2	65.5
Dentistry	44.9	54.7	64.8
Economics	12.7	26.3	37.1
ENG	2.8	9.0	21.6
HUM	61.5	57.2	55.0
Law	14.3	27.8	39.1
Medicine	20.6	33.0	43.9
Nursing	88.3	88.0	92.4
Pharm. Chem.	76.6	64.6	68.3
Psych./SW	70.5	73.5	76.0
SCI	60.1	37.0	39.8
TEACH	76.9	64.7	63.4

SOURCES: Calculated from ANUIES (Asociación Nacional de Universidades e Institutos de Educación Superior), *Anuario estadístico, Enseñanza superior en México,* and *Educación superior en México,* various years.

Notes

Notes to Chapter One

1. I use the term "university system" to refer to all public and private institutions of higher education.

2. A brief review of university autonomy is found in Raúl Moreno Wonchee, "La autonomía y el desarrollo histórico de la universidad," *El Día*, Oct. 31, 1976, pp. 6–8. See also John F. Dulles, *Yesterday in Mexico: A Chronicle of the Revolution, 1919–1936* (Austin: University of Texas Press, 1961), pp. 464–68.

3. For description and analysis of the law, see Silva Herzog, *Una historia de la Universidad de México y sus problemas* (Mexico City: Siglo XXI, 1986), pp. 32–60. For a comparison of passages from three university laws, see Carlos Pascual Ruiz Fernández, "Los fines de la educación superior en México," *El Día*, July 3, 1989, p. 18. For a review of the events leading up to the granting of autonomy in 1929, see Renate Mariske, "El movimiento estudiantil de 1929 y la autonomía de la Universidad Nacional de México," *Revista de Educación Superior*, n.s. 44 (Oct.–Dec. 1982), pp. 5–30.

4. The term "economic development" has been adopted here as the most appropriate single term for paraphrasing Mexican goals for change. For an idea of what economic development has meant to Mexican leaders over time, see Secretaría de Programación y Presupuesto (SPP), *Antología de la planeación en México*, esp. vol. 1, pp. 15–134. The terms

"progress," much used in the late nineteenth century, and "modernization," in vogue until the 1960s, are subsumed here within the more general notion of economic development. Historians long used the idea of Mexico's desire to "modernize" as a basic backdrop for their analyses. See Charles C. Cumberland's *Mexico: The Struggle for Modernity* (Oxford, Eng.: Oxford University Press, 1968) and Roger D. Hansen's *The Politics of Mexican Development* (Baltimore: Johns Hopkins University Press, 1971). "Modernization" was reintroduced in the late 1980s by President Carlos Salinas de Gortari (1989–92). See Cindy Anders, "Informe: Salinas Prepares the Nation for Less Government," *Mexico Journal*, Nov. 13, 1989, p. 16. Anders notes that Salinas used the word "modernization" fourteen times in his first *informe* (state-of-the-union address) compared to once by de la Madrid in his six annual *informes*; Salinas did not use the word "development" at all, whereas previous presidents had used it on average five times in their *informes*.

5. Howard F. Cline, *Mexico: Revolution to Evolution, 1940–1960* (New York: Oxford University Press, 1963), p. 244; Jorge I. Domínguez in Domínguez, ed., *The Political Economy of Mexico* (Beverly Hills: Sage, 1982), p. 12.

6. Brandenburg, *The Making of Modern Mexico* (Englewood Cliffs: Prentice-Hall, 1964), p. 138. See also Roberto Newell G. and Luis Rubio F., *Mexico's Dilemma: The Political Origins of Economic Crisis* (Boulder, Colo.: Westview Press, 1984), pp. 74–75. Newell and Rubio see a political consensus based more squarely on economic growth, industrialization, and employment creation than on general goals of economic development and social betterment. Jorge I. Domínguez shares this view: see Domínguez, ed., *Political Economy of Mexico*, p. 11.

7. Tannenbaum, *Mexico: The Struggle for Peace and Bread* (Englewood Cliffs: Prentice-Hall, 1950), p. 174; and Clark Reynolds, *The Mexican Economy: Twentieth-Century Structure and Growth* (New Haven: Yale University Press, 1970), p. 42.

8. The Mexican president takes office on December 1 but gains control of the budget the following year. Throughout this study the president's term is considered the six year period during which he controls the budget.

9. Pablo González Casanova, "México: El ciclo de una revolución agraria," *Cuadernos Americanos*, 120, no. 1 (Jan.–Feb. 1962). Cf. González's later comments on social mobility in *Democracia en México* (Mexico City: Ediciones Era, 1965).

10. For a comprehensive review of the literature on the Mexican university, see Lorey, *The Rise of the Professions in Twentieth-Century Mexico: University Graduates and Occupational Change*

since 1929 (Los Angeles: UCLA Latin American Center Publications, 1992).

11. Iván Jaksic, "The Politics of Higher Education in Latin America." *Latin American Research Review*, 20, no. 1 (1985), p. 210.

12. For the classic statements of human-capital theory, see Schultz, *The Economic Value of Education* (New York: Columbia University Press, 1963); and G. S. Becker, *Human Capital: A Theoretical and Empirical Analysis, with Special Reference to Education* (Princeton, N.J.: Princeton University Press, 1964).

13. Frederick Harbison and Charles A. Myers, *Education, Manpower, and Economic Growth: Strategies of Human Resource Development* (New York: McGraw–Hill, 1964), p. ix.

14. See, for example, Leopoldo Solís M., *Controversias sobre el crecimiento y la distribución* (Mexico City: Fondo de Cultura Económica, 1972), pp. 203–4.

15. Charles N. Myers, *Education and National Development* (Princeton: Industrial Relations Section, Princeton University, 1965). Myers's volume is typical of the genre in most respects, but stands out for its analysis of regional differences in human resource development. See also Myers's article on estimating demand for health professionals: "Proyección de la Demanda de Médicos," pp. 77–103.

16. For the classic formulation of this critique of the human-capital concept, see Kenneth Arrow, *Higher Education as a Filter* (Stanford, Calif.: Stanford University Press, 1972). The debate has settled at a middle ground. Most scholars see education as being important to economic growth, but not as crucial as the original human-capital proponents thought. See discussion in Martin Carnoy et al., *Economía política del financiamiento educativo en países en vías de desarrollo* (Mexico City: Ediciones Gérnika, 1986), pp. 25–36.

17. In a series of articles published beginning in the 1970s, Carlos Muñoz Izquierdo applied the newer economics-of-education theories to different quantitative data sets with very enlightening results. See the following articles for more detailed development of Muñoz's arguments: "Educación, estado, y sociedad en México (1930–1976)," *Revista de Educación Superior*, n.s., 34 (1980); Muñoz Izquierdo and Lobo, "Expansión escolar, mercado de trabajo, y distribución de ingreso en México: Un análisis longitudinal, 1960–1970," *Revista del Centro de Estudios Educativos*, 4, no. 1 (1974), 9–30; Muñoz Izquierdo et al., "Educación y mercado de trabajo," *Revista del Centro de Estudios Educativos*, 8, no. 2 (1978), 1–90. See also Víctor Gómez Campo, "Relaciones entre educación y estructura económica: Dos grandes marcos de interpretación," *Revista de Educación Superior*, n.s. 41 (Jan.–Mar. 1982), pp. 5–43.

Notes to Chapter Two

1. This discussion of the colonial period focuses on civil professionals. For discussion of clerics as professionals, see Kicza, "Business and Society in Late Colonial Mexico City," Ph.D. Diss. University of California, Los Angeles, 1979.

2. On the early development of the medical profession in Mexico, see Leslie Byrd Simpson, *Many Mexicos* (Berkeley: University of California Press, 1952), pp. 159–61.

3. Kicza, "Business and Society," p. 293.

4. Ibid., pp. 291, 294.

5. Simpson, *Many Mexicos*, pp. 158–59.

6. See Simpson, *Many Mexicos*, p. 158. On general issues of race and class in the early period, see John K. Chance, *Race and Class in Colonial Oaxaca* (Stanford, Calif.: Stanford University Press, 1978).

7. Lockhart and Schwartz, *Early Latin America* (Cambridge, Eng.: Cambridge University Press, 1983), p. 422.

8. Ibid., p. 334.

9. Peter Bakewell, "Zacatecas: An Economic and Social Outline of a Silver Mining District, 1547–1700," in *Provinces of Early Mexico*, ed. James Lockhart and Ida Altman (Los Angeles: UCLA Latin American Center Publications, 1976), p. 205.

10. Ibid., p. 210.

11. Dorothy Tanck de Estrada, "La Colonia," in *Historia de las profesiones en México*, ed. Josefina Z. Vásquez (Mexico City: El Colegio de México, 1982), p. 68.

12. See Linda Arnold, *Bureaucracy and Bureaucrats in Mexico City, 1742–1835* (Tucson: University of Arizona Press, 1988).

13. On the role of merchants and moneylenders in the development of a national economy in the nineteenth century, see Barbara Tennenbaum, *The Politics of Penury: Debts and Taxes in Mexico, 1821–1856* (Albuquerque: University of New Mexico Press, 1986), pp. 84, 116–17.

14. For the financial crisis, see John TePaske, "The Financial Disintegration of the Royal Government of Mexico During the Epoch of Independence"; on taxes and finance, see Barbara A. Tennenbaum, "Taxation and Tyranny: Public Finance During the Iturbide Period, 1821–1823"; on mining, see de Gortari Rabiela, "La minería durante la guerra de independencia y los primeros años de México independiente, 1810–1824"; all in *The Independence of Mexico and the Creation of the New Nation*, ed. Jaime E. Rodriguez (Los Angeles: UCLA Latin American Center Publications, 1989).

15. Rosalío Wences Reza, *La universidad en la historia de México* (Mexico City: Editorial Línea, 1984), p. 49. This attitude had ante-

cedents in the eighteenth century. See Frank Safford, "Politics, Ideology, and Society," in *Spanish America After Independence*, ed. Leslie Bethell (Cambridge, Eng.: Cambridge University Press, 1987), pp. 85–86.

16. Conservatives may have shared some of the Liberals' complaints about the university, but they tended to soften their criticism because of the university's ties to the Church. The Church, of course, became the central point of contention between Liberals and Conservatives, who had more common attitudes toward other basic questions such as Mexico's need to develop its economy and industrialize. See Safford, "Politics, Ideology, and Society," pp. 86, 89. For a study of all levels of education and society during the late nineteenth century, see Mary Kay Vaughan, *The State, Education, and Social Class in Mexico, 1880–1928* (DeKalb: Northern Illinois University Press, 1980). On the relationship between Church and state during the Porfiriato, and on the late-nineteenth-century social scene, see Jean-Pierre Bastian, "La estructura social en México a fines del siglo XIX y principios del XX," *Revista Mexicana de Sociología*, 51, no. 2 (1989), pp. 413–29.

17. While both Liberals and Conservatives had supported a double role for education—an instrument for material betterment and a force in modeling a loyal citizenry—after independence it was the Liberals who incorporated educational reform into a national project for economic development. See de Gortari Rabiela, "Educación y conciencia nacional: Los ingenieros después de la revolución mexicana," *Revista Mexicana de Sociología*, 49, no. 3 p. 123; and Josefina Vásquez, *Nacionalismo y educación en México* (Mexico City: El Colegio de México, 1970).

18. Ramón Eduardo Ruíz, *The Great Rebellion* (New York: W. W. Norton, 1980), p. 20.

19. For analyses of the positive and negative aspects of foreign involvement in Mexican development in the late nineteenth century, see Ruíz, *Great Rebellion*, chap. 7 ("Foreigners: The Blessing and the Bane"); and John Mason Hart, *Revolutionary Mexico: The Coming and Process of the Mexican Revolution* (Berkeley: University of California Press, 1987).

20. See René Villareal, "The Policy of Import-Substituting Industrialization, 1929–1975," in *Authoritarianism in Mexico*, ed. José Luis Reyna and Richard S. Weinert (Philadelphia: Institute for the Study of Human Issues, 1977), p. 68. See also John Mason Hart, *Revolutionary Mexico* (Berkeley: University of California Press, 1987), pp. 142, 134; and Fernando Rosenzweig Hernández, *El desarrollo económico de México, 1800–1910* (Mexico City: El Colegio Mexiquense, A.C./ITAM, 1989), p. 228. The influence of foreign capital in Mexican economic development was not significantly reduced until after 1930; see Tannenbaum,

Mexico, p. 229; and Leopoldo Solís, *La realidad económica mexicana: Retrovisión y perspectivas* (Mexico City: Siglo XXI, 1987), pp. 93–94.

21. See Stephen Haber, *Industry and Underdevelopment: The Industrialization of Mexico, 1890–1940* (Stanford, Calif.: Stanford University Press, 1989), pp. 37 and 62. For the earlier nineteenth century, see Robert A. Potash, *Mexican Government and Industrial Development in the Early Republic: The Banco de Avío* (Amherst: University of Massachusetts Press, 1983), p. 153.

22. Potash, *Mexican Government and Industrial Development,* p. 175. The complaint forms one of the leitmotifs of Ramón Eduardo Ruiz's *Labor and the Ambivalent Revolutionaries: Mexico, 1911–1923* (Baltimore: Johns Hopkins University Press, 1976).

23. Marvin D. Bernstein, *The Mexican Mining Industry, 1890–1950* (Albany: State University of New York Press, 1965), p. 84.

24. Bernstein, *Mexican Mining Industry,* p. 50.

25. Mílada Bazant, "La República Restaurada y El Porfiriato," in *Historia de las Profesiones,* p. 172.

26. See Ruíz, *Great Rebellion,* pp. 14–19.

27. de Gortari Rabiela, "Educación y conciencia nacional," pp. 134–36.

28. Models for reform that involved designs for an education system responsive to government policy had been developed before, of course. Important earlier influences of such models, the Bourbon Reforms of the late eighteenth century and the Physiocrat and Enlightenment creeds, for example, are not discussed here because they were not plans for national economic development. For interpretations of the role of the state in economic planning in the early nineteenth century, see Tennenbaum, *Politics of Penury;* Potash, *Mexican Government and Industrial Development;* and David W. Walker, *Kinship, Business, and Politics: The Martínez del Río Family in Mexico, 1823–1867* (Austin: University of Texas Press, 1986).

29. On the científicos, see Rice, "Porfirian Elite," esp. pp. 11–26; and the comments of José Limantour (one of the leaders of the científico group) quoted in *Mexico: From Independence to Revolution, 1810–1910,* ed. W. Dirk Raat (Lincoln: University of Nebraska Press, 1982). See also James Cockcroft, *Intellectual Precursors of the Mexican Revolution, 1900–1913* (Austin: University of Texas Press, 1968) for a brief but insightful survey of the científico group and their positivism, and Leopoldo Zea, *El positivismo en México: Nacimiento, apogeo, y decadencia* (Mexico City: Fondo de Cultura Económica, 1968), esp. pp. 397–421.

30. Alan Knight, *The Mexican Revolution. Vol. I: Porfirians, Liberals, and Peasants* (Cambridge: Cambridge University Press, 1986), p. 22.

31. John Coatsworth paraphrased in de Gortari Rabiela, "Educación y conciencia nacional," pp. 134–35.

32. Knight, *Mexican Revolution*, p. 23.

33. See Ruíz, *Great Rebellion*, pp. 19–21.

34. Knight, *Mexican Revolution*, pp. 23, 24. Also see Arnaldo Córdova, *La ideología de la revolución mexicana: La formación del nuevo régimen* (Mexico City: UNAM, 1973).

35. Safford, "Politics, Ideology, and Society," pp. 85–86.

36. Wences Reza, *Universidad*, p. 90.

37. See data and analysis in Kicza, "Business and Society."

38. See Mílada Bazant, "La república restaurada y el porfiriato," in *Historia de las profesiones*, pp. 207–22, for sample data from the period. Also see Rosenzweig, *El desarrollo económico de México*, pp. 236, 237, and 245; and Ciro F. S. Cardoso, Francisco G. Hermosillo, and Salvador Hernández, *La clase obrera en la historia de México: De la dictadura porfirista a los tiempos libertarios* (Mexico City: Siglo XXI, 1980), pp. 46–47.

39. Rice, "Porfirian Elite," and "Beyond the Científicos: The Educational Background of the Porfirian Political Elite," *Aztlán*, 14, no. 2, pp. 289–306. For another, broader sample of the Porfirian elite, see François-Xavier Guerra, *Le Mexique: de l'Ancien Regime a la Revolution* (Paris: l'Harmattan, 1985). The formation of Mexico's nineteenth-century elite is the subject of *Formación y desarrollo de la burguesía en México. siglo XIX* (Mexico City: Siglo XXI, 1978).

40. On Vasconcelos's life and thought, see Jérez Jiménez, *Vasconcelos y la educación nacionalista*; and Tannenbaum, *Mexico*, p. 155. Vasconcelos was also a practical politician who saw that the university would have to take on an active social role if it was to survive in revolutionary Mexico. See Arce Gurza, "El inicio de una nueva era, 1910–1945," in Vásquez, ed., *Historia de las profesiones en México*, pp. 235–36.

41. For discussions of the interaction of Vasconcelos, Caso, and Lombardo, see Enrique Krauze, *Caudillos culturales en la revolución mexicana* (Mexico City: SEP-Siglo XXI, 1985) and Gilberto Guevara Niebla, *La democracia en la calle: Crónica del movimiento estudiantil mexicano* (Mexico City: Siglo XXI, 1988).

42. For some of the subtleties of these currents in the 1930s and of the debate between Lombardo and Caso, see Martha Robles, *Educación y sociedad en la historia de México* (Mexico City: Siglo XXI Editores, 1977), pp. 137–46; and Michael E. Burke, "The University of Mexico and the Revolution, 1910–1940," *Americas*, 34, no. 2 (1977), 252–273.

43. The history of Lombardo's relationship with the university is complex and replete with reversals. See Donald J. Mabry, *The Mexican University and the State: Student Conflicts, 1910–1971* (College Station:

Texas A & M Press, 1982), for a detailed account of Lombardo's involvement with the politics of students and the state.

44. Raymond Vernon saw it as a difference between presidential styles and the substance of policy: see his *The Dilemma of Mexico's Development: The Roles of the Private and Public Sectors* (Cambridge, MA: Harvard University Press, 1963), p. 124. See also my analysis in Chapter Three.

45. John Gunther, *Inside Latin America* (New York: Harper, 1940), p. 77.

46. Technical professions also provide a greater number of "lateral exits," that is, an engineering student can leave the university at a pre-degree level with skills that will enable him or her to find work. For discussion of the links between engineering and technical education and the social revolutionary aims of the Cárdenas administration, see Arce Gurza, "El inicio de una nueva era," pp. 257–60.

47. Robles, *Educación y Sociedad*, p. 159.

48. See Brandenburg, *Making of Modern Mexico*, pp. 104, 108.

49. Mabry, *Mexican University and the State*, pp. 189–213. Silva Herzog terms the 1948–66 period the "Paz Cuasi Octaviana" in his *Historia de la Universidad*.

50. Brandenburg, *Making of Modern Mexico*, p. 114.

51. For a scholarly expression of this perception, see Robert E. Quirk, *Mexico* (Englewood Cliffs, N.J.: Prentice-Hall, 1971), p. 121.

52. For an analysis of the role of the Left in forcing open-door admission policies and lax achievement standards at Mexican universities, see Olac Fuentes Molinar, "Universidad y democracia: La mirada hacia la izquierda," *Cuadernos Políticos*, 53 (Jan.-Apr. 1981), pp. 4–18.

53. For a narrative account of these student-state conflicts, see Mabry, *Mexican University and the State*. For a more concise review, see Arthur Liebman, Kenneth N. Walker, and Myron Glazer, *Latin American University Students: A Six Nation Study* (Cambridge, MA: Harvard University Press, 1972), pp.179–200.

54. Quoted in Raúl Domínguez, *El proyecto universitario del rector Barros Sierra (estudio histórico)* (Mexico City: UNAM, CESU (Centro de Estudios sobre la Universidad), 1986), p. 118.

55. Echeverría also greatly expanded press freedom (until 1976), giving intellectuals a greater voice, and released many political prisoners jailed during the railway strike of 1958 and the student movement unrest of 1968. In a direct move to curry favor with students and their sympathizers, Echeverría intervened on the side of students in a dispute at the Autonomous University of Nuevo León (June 1970).

56. James Cypher, *State and Capital in Mexico: Development Policy since 1940* (Boulder, CO: Westview Press, 1990), p. 90; and Robert E.

Looney, *Economic Policymaking in Mexico: Factors Underlying the 1982 Crisis* (Durham, NC: Duke University Press, 1985), pp. 57–68.

57. In this connection, see "El progreso del país requiere que todos los técnicos tengan trabajo: Echeverría," *El Día*, July 23, 1971.

58. Luis Echeverría, quoted in Nigel Brooke, John Oxenham, and Angela Little, *Qualifications and Employment in Mexico* (International Development Studies Research Report. Sussex: University of Sussex, 1978), p. 9.

59. Ibid., p. 10.

60. On de la Madrid's educational policies, see Daniel Morales-Gómez and Carlos Alberto Torres, *The State, Corporatist Politics, and Educational Policy Making in Mexico* (New York: Praeger, 1990), pp. 70–74.

61. Nathaniel and Sylvia Weyl, *The Reconquest of Mexico: The Years of Lázaro Cárdenas* (London: Oxford University Press, 1939), p. 328.

62. Ironically, the IPN also became a center of government opposition, striking in 1942 to gain the same status for their degrees as those granted graduates of UNAM.

63. Mabry, *Mexican University and the State*, p. 154.

64. One observer characterizes a similar three-part chronology as "the divorce," the conciliations," and "the rupture"; see Salvador Martínez Della Rocca, *Estado y universidad en México 1920–1968: Historia de los movimientos estudiantiles en la UNAM* (Mexico City: Joan Boldó i Climent Editores, 1986).

Notes to Chapter Three

1. The Mexican licentiate degree is roughly equivalent to the U.S. Bachelor of Arts or Bachelor of Science degree, and yet is more vocationally oriented; see Lorey, *Rise of the Professions*.

2. For further definition and discussion of these three indicators, see Lorey, *Rise of the Professions*. The data set on registered degrees is the only one of the three sets to include any number of foreign degrees. Degrees granted to Mexicans by foreign universities are very few compared to degrees granted by Mexican universities, regardless of the fact that the political importance of their holders is sometimes great.

3. See Lorey, *Rise of the Professions*, for discussion of this time lag in Mexico.

4. A common approach was to take graduates and deflate for mortality to deduce human-capital supply: these results could then be compared with projected human-capital needs. For an example, see the case of Argentina as developed by Morris A. Horowitz, "High-Level Manpower in the Economic Development of Argentina," in Harbison and Myers,

Manpower and Education. In Mexico it was more common to use the easier-to-obtain enrollment data, but they lead to inflated results. See discussion of enrollment data and their use in Lorey, *Rise of the Professions.*

5. See, for example, data on university enrollment in 1878, 1900, 1907, and 1910, presented in Francois-Xavier Guerra, *Le Mexique,* p. 385.

6. See Lorey, *Rise of the Professions,* table 6 for a comparison of the rates of growth of the three indicators used in this chapter.

7. For the first year of the Salinas administration, from 1988 to 1989, the number of eggresados increased by 1.0 percent.

8. Throughout this study, when referring to annual rates of change, I use implicit compound rates calculated with the following formula: annual rate equals antilog of $(\log(Pn/Po)/n)$, minus 1, where Po equals the original population, and Pn equals the population after n years. For example, a 100 percent change over ten years equals 7.18 percent annual change.

9. Comparative data are drawn from *Statistical Abstract of Latin America,* 25, table 911, p. 159. Data on egresados from this study yield 0.8 percent in humanities (which includes fine arts) and 1.5 percent in social sciences. The United States makes a convenient comparison; I do not mean to imply that the United States should be the model for Mexico's development. Figures for the social sciences represent a more broadly defined category than the one employed in this study, and include economics and business administration.

10. Data on degrees granted in the humanities and social sciences are not disaggregated in the sources by these areas; the 1.8 percent figure is a rough estimate. It was arrived at by dividing in half the percent share of the "other" category in the 1964–71 period, because although some part of the other category is made up of licentiate degrees in such fields as political science and philosophy, the exact share cannot be ascertained.

11. For the situation of the sciences in the late 1940s, see Sanford Mosk, *Industrial Revolution in Mexico* (Berkeley: University of California Press, 1950), p. 268 .

12. Roderic Camp suggests that graduate study became important among the Mexican political elite as the Mexican political system "modernized;" see his "Political Technocrat in Mexico," p. 99. See also Alfonso Galindo, "Higher Educational Backgrounds of Mexican Government Officials," *Statistical Abstract of Latin America,* 30: 1 (forthcoming 1992), 72–89.

13. These figures can be compared with 30.1 percent in the United States in 1981. See *Statistical Abstract of Latin America,* 25, table 912, p. 160.

14. About a third of all graduate egresados in Mexico in the mid-1980s were in health fields, one-quarter in business, one-fifth in law, and one-eighth in technical and engineering fields. See, for example, ANUIES-AE (Posgrado), 1986. This distribution itself is sometimes blamed for problems in Mexico's economic development: see, for example, José Martínez, "La investigación, divorciada de las necesidades del país," *El Financiero*, June 18, 1987, p. 36. As in the case of licentiate-level studies, it is more likely that trends in graduate study and research follow from the historical pattern and growth of Mexico's economy. See "Implications for Economic Development" below.

15. Many observers suggest that universities have not fulfilled the government's desires or expectations. See, for example, Daniel C. Levy, *Higher Education and the State in Latin America: Private Challenges to Public Dominance* (Chicago: University of Chicago Press, 1986), p. 158, and ANUIES, Programa Integral para el Desarrollo de la Educación Superior," in *Revista de Educación Superior*, 15, no. 60 (Oct.–Dec. 1986), p. 87.

16. See Wilkie, *La revolución mexicana: Gasto federal y cambio social, 1910–1970* (Mexico City: Fondo de Cultura Económica, 1978); and "The Six Ideological Phases of Mexico's 'Permanent Revolution' since 1910," in *Society and Economy in Mexico*, ed. James W. Wilkie (Los Angeles: UCLA Latin American Center Publications, 1990). The basic outlines of Wilkie's phases are apparent also in trends in government investment in different economic sectors; see Howard F. Cline, *Mexico: Revolution to Evolution, 1940–1960* (New York: Oxford University Press, 1963), p. 246. See also Wilkie's critics, particularly Enrique A. Baloyra, "Oil Policies and Budgets in Venezuela, 1938–1968," *Latin American Research Review*, 9, no. 2 (Summer, 1974), 28–72; and Thomas E.Skidmore and Peter H. Smith, "Notes on Quantitative History: Federal Expenditure and Social Change in Mexico since 1910," *Latin American Research Review*, 5, no. 1 (Spring, 1970), 71–85. Wilkie replies in "On Methodology and the Use of Historical Statistics," *Latin American Research Review*, 5, no. 1 (1970), pp. 87–91. See also Kenneth M.Coleman and John Wanat, "On Measuring Presidential Ideology through Budgets: A Reappraisal of the Wilkie Approach," *Latin American Research Review*, 10, no. 1 (Spring, 1975), 77–88; and James A. Hanson, "Federal Expenditures and 'Personalism' in the Mexican 'Institutional' Revolution," in *Money and Politics in Latin America*, ed. James W. Wilkie (Los Angeles: UCLA Latin American Center Publications, 1977).

17. Administrative professions are not considered separately here. Law was the primary profession associated with government administration into the 1950s, and its historical development is discussed

below. The administrative category in the federal budget is eclipsed by economic and social emphases after the 1930s, and thus economic and social fields are the most important areas for gauging shifts in policy priorities.

18. Clearly, the sample economic and social professional groups cannot reflect many complex interconnections between economic and social reality. The healthier population produced by doctors (social professionals here), for example, contributes to the economic productivity of workers in ways that will not register here.

19. An index is used for the absolute numbers because historical trends in the data, rather than the absolute data for any given year, constitute the centerpiece of analysis here. For disaggregated series, see Lorey, *Rise of the Professions*, tables 10 and 11.

20. Percent-change figures are calculated from the indexes. All references are to the time-lag year (calendar year minus six years).

21. Percentage data for the three series were averaged in overlapping years. For disaggregated series, see Lorey, *Rise of the Professions*, tables 10 and 11.

22. Tests of correlation between expenditure and data on professional fields without the time lag yield no significant positive correlation. Additional results of statistical tests on the relationship between expenditure and fields of study are found in Lorey, *Rise of the Professions*, table 12.

23. See, for example, Tannenbaum, *Mexico*; the El Colegio series on the Mexican Revolution; Judith Hellman, *Crisis in Mexico* (New York: Holmes and Meier, 1978); and Sanford Mosk, *Industrial Revolution in Mexico* (Berkeley and Los Angeles: University of California Press, 1950).

24. See Stanley R. Ross, *Is the Mexican Revolution Dead?* (New York: Knopf, 1966) for the views of Mexican and U.S. scholars on the periodization of the Revolution and the significance of changes in or around 1940. Stephen Haber, in his *Industry and Underdevelopment: The Industrialization of Mexico, 1890–1940* (Stanford, Calif.: Stanford University Press, 1989), points out that one reason for the perceived shift lies in the nature of the collection and publication of statistics on economic and social aspects of Mexican life, which became organized on an aggregate national basis for the most part beginning in 1940.

25. William P. Glade, "Revolution and Economic Development: A Mexican Reprise," in Glade and Anderson, *The Political Economy of Mexico* (Madison: University of Wisconsin Press, 1963), p. 82.

26. For discussion of efforts at reconstruction after the revolutionary upheaval and the attempts to complete the work begun during the late Porfiriato, see de Gortari Rabiela, "Educación y Conciencia Nacional"; and Enrique Krauze, Jean Meyer, and Cayetano Reyes, *La Reconstrucción Económica* (México, D. F.: El Colegio de México, 1977).

27. See my "Development of Engineering Expertise," pp. 71–102.

28. See Roderic A. Camp, *Mexico's Leaders: Their Education and Recruitment* (Tucson: University of Arizona Press, 1980).

29. See Peter S. Cleaves, *Las profesiones y el estado: El caso de México* (Mexico City: El Colegio de México, 1985), pp. 69–75.

30. We will have to wait until the twenty-first century to fully assess the effect on university education of professionals of Miguel de la Madrid's "industrial reconversion" policies and Salinas's opening of the Mexican economy.

Notes to Chapter Four

1. See, for example, Howard F. Cline, Mexico, p. 204; Pablo Latapí, *Análisis de un sexenio de educación en México, 1970–1976* (Mexico City: Editorial Nueva Imagen, 1980), pp. 207–8; José Angel Pescador Osuna, "El balance de la educación superior en el sexenio 1976–1982," in UAP, *Perspectivas de la educación superior* (Puebla: UAP, 1984), pp. 41–87; María Esther Ibarra, "Decide la SEP que se encojan las universidades," *Proceso*, Sept. 29, 1986, p. 19; and Noel F. McGinn and Susan L. Street, *Higher Education Policies in Mexico* (Austin: Institute of Latin American Studies, University of Texas at Austin, 1980), p. 1. The Mexican press is full of articles claiming alternately that the university produces "too many" and "too few" professionals in certain fields: see, for example, Deirdre Fretz, "Wanted: Engineers," *Mexico Journal*, Nov. 13, 1989, pp. 25–26; Isabel Llinas Zárate, "La universidad ha cumplido con creces después de la revolución: Luis E. Todd," *Uno Mas Uno*, Jan. 28, 1990, p. 2; "México necesita 300 mil profesionistas por año, para asegurar su crecimiento," *Ocho Columnas* (Guadalajara), Oct. 15, 1989; "Mexican Higher Education Degrees," translation of article from *La Jornada*, Oct. 6, 1989, in *U.S.-Mexico Report*, 8, no. 11 (Nov. 1989), p. 12; and Mario García Sordo, "Desempleados o subempleados, más de 90 mil agrónomos," *El Financiero*, Oct. 5, 1988, p. 39.

2. See, for example, "El sector educativo debe preparar cuadros técnicos acorde con las necesidades del país: CANACINTRA," *Uno Mas Uno*, June 26, 1987, p. 14.

3. Robert E. Looney, *Mexico's Economy: A Policy Analysis with Forecasts to 1990* (Boulder, Colo.: Westview, 1978), p. 63.

4. The comparison can be oversimplified. See Latapí, *Análisis de un sexenio de educación*, pp. 207–8.

5. Only in 1950, 1980, and 1990 is it possible to separate professionals from technicians. In other census years, census informants classifying themselves as either professionals or technicians were placed in a single category. See discussion of the historical relationship between professionals and technicians below; see also Lorey, *Rise of the Professions*.

6. The correspondence would be closer if a portion of business professionals had been placed in the secondary sector; for simplicity's sake, I did not subdivide any of the basic categories here. I have adjusted data on EAP by sector for 1980 to make them comparable to data for other years. See Lorey, *Rise of the Professions* and Lorey and Aída Mostkoff, "Mexico's 'Lost Decade': Evidence on Class Structure and Professional Employment from the 1990 Census," *Statistical Abstract of Latin America*, 30, part 2.

7. See, for example, Alfonso Rangel Guerra, *Systems of Higher Education: Mexico* (New York: International Council for Educational Development, 1978), p. 58.

8. Want ads in newspapers and journals, a commonly mentioned source for measuring demand, are not useful because the vast majority of professional-level jobs in Mexico are never announced in this manner.

9. The data are for samples of employed professionals, and some of the data are more comprehensive than others. All series, however, represent enough employed professionals so that general trends and patterns can be ascertained. See UANL and Cámera de la Industria de Transformación de Nuevo León, *La demanda de técnicos y profesionistas en el estado de Nuevo León* (Monterrey: UANL, 1981).

10. Teaching was not among the fields considered by the UANL project.

11. Data are for employed graduates of the UANL. See UANL, *Demanda de técnicos y profesionistas*.

12. Richard G. King found, for example, that an average of 61.4 percent of university professors in nine states taught in the same region where they had received their university training in 1970. The fact that an additional 27 percent received their training in the Federal District implies that professionals migrate within Mexico from the capital to the provinces. See Richard G. King, Alfonso Rangel Guerra, David Kline, and Noel F. McGinn, *Nueve universidades mexicanas: Un análisis de su crecimiento y desarrollo* (Mexico City: ANUIES, 1972).

13. To get a sense of how Nuevo León fits into the Mexican mosaic, see David Lorey, *United States-Mexico Border Statistics Since 1900* (Los Angeles: UCLA Latin American Center Publications, 1990).

14. It is not clear how widely available the results of the project's survey are. Wide availability might have some effect on the career decisions of students in professional fields.

15. For discussion of the sample and methodology, see Raúl Pérez, et al., *Características de la ocupación de los profesionales en las empresas de la península de Yucatán* (N.p. [Mérida]: Centro de Desarrollo Universitario, Universidad Autónoma de Yucatán, 1983). Data have

been rounded to the nearest 5 percent to avoid giving a sense of greater accuracy than is possible. It must be noted that there may be distortions between data on employed university graduates and field distribution of egresados due to four factors: (1) there are year-to-year variations in the field distribution of egresados, (2) there are significant differences among the states of the Yucatán peninsula, both in employment of professionals and professional field distribution of egresados, (3) there is some time lag between changes in employment opportunities and changes in the pattern of egresados, and (4) in the survey data, some persons will be missed and some sectors are probably better represented than others. For example, although the Nuevo León survey sample gives a fairly representative view of the different economic sectors, the Yucatán study does not supply such information.

16. Data on employer demands for professionals in the Federal District provide circumstantial evidence for similar patterns of demand in highly developed regions. The American Chamber of Commerce of Mexico publishes an annual booklet of job opportunities for Mexican professionals. Among these opportunities are the best positions for professionals in Mexico—prestigious and well-paying posts with important firms, half of which are subsidiaries of U.S. firms or in which U.S. investment plays an important part. In 1987, almost half of positions advertised were in the engineering and applied sciences fields, another third were in business fields. The sample is of 193 companies in all of Mexico, most of them located in the Federal District. The primacy of two career areas in the Federal District—engineering and business—mirrors the reality in Nuevo León.

17. Gómez Campo and Víctor Manuel, "Educación superior, mercado de trabajo, y práctica profesional: Un análisis comparativa de diversos estudios en México," *Revista de Educación Superior*, n.s. 45, p. 5.

18. Arthur D. Little's 1963 study of Mexico cited in Davis, *Scientific, Engineering and Technical Education.*

19. Brooke, Oxenham, and Little, *Qualifications and Employment*, p. 21. See also UAM, *Quince años de estadística* (Mexico City: UAM, 1989), p. 86; data show that 85.4 percent of UAM egresados work in their field of study.

20. Here as elsewhere in this study, capital letters indicate an aggregate career field, while small letters indicate a single-degree category.

21. The percent share of Health in the data for both egresados and registered degrees is greater than that in public-sector employment. This is because the Health category for registered degrees and egresados includes doctors, dentists, optometrists, and licentiate nurses, whereas the public-sector data refer only to medical doctors.

22. Pescador and Torres, *Poder político y educación*, p. 95.

23. Beatriz Medina Lara, et al., *Oferta y demanda de profesionales, 1980–82* (Mérida: Centro de Desarrollo Universitario, Universidad Autónoma de Yucatán, 1983).

24. The UANL survey data were tabulated by economic sector rather than by the public/private nature of employers.

25. Mario García Sordo reports in "Desempleados o subempleados, más de 90 mil agrónomos," *El Financiero*, Oct. 5, 1988, p. 39, that the 90,000 un- or sub-employed agronomists of the article's title tended to stabilize the job market and "drastically" reduce the number of entering students at agronomy schools.

26. For a detailed discussion of professionals and technicians in Mexico's changing occupational structure, see Lorey, *Rise of the Professions*, chap. 2. The definition of professional and technician here is broader than that employed in the Mexican census. Professionals include upper-level teachers and professors, upper-level functionaries in the public sector, and artists and writers; technicians include upper-level office workers. See definitions in Lorey, *Rise of the Professions*, chap. 3.

27. See, for example, Brandenburg, *Making of Modern Mexico*, pp. 240–41; Keesing, "Structural Change Early in Development: Mexico's Changing Industrial and Occupational Structure from 1895 to 1950," *Journal of Economic History*, 29, no. 4 (December, 1969), 716–38; Clark Reynolds, *The Mexican Economy*; and Peter Gregory, *The Myth of Market Failure: Employment and the Labor Market in Mexico*. (Baltimore: Johns Hopkins University Press, 1986).

28. Many analysts equate sectoral distribution and occupational structure: see, for example, A. J. Jaffe, *People, Jobs, and Economic Development: A Case History of Puerto Rico Supplemented by Recent Mexican Experiences* (Glencoe, Ill.: Free Press, 1959), p. 109; and Jorge A. Padua, "Movilidad social y universidad," in Gilberto Guevara Niebla, *La crisis de la educación superior en México* (Mexico City: Nueva Imagen, 1981), pp. 131–32.

29. For an early analysis, see Tannenbaum, *Mexico*, pp. 195–96 (analysis of 1940 census data). The category that has attracted most attention is services, which appears in census data after 1950. For an analysis of shifts in the services sector and what they mean, see Gregory, *Myth of Market Failure*, app. to chap. 1.

30. If we use a broader definition of professionals and technicians, the rates are 384.3 percent for professionals and 848.7 percent for technicians. See Lorey, *Rise of the Professions*, table 30. For analysis of the period from 1980 to 1990 see Lorey and Aída Mostkoff, "Mexico's 'Lost Decade'": Evidence on Class Structure and Professional Employment from the 1990 Census," *Statistical Abstract of Latin America*, 30:2.

31. The relationship between these two factors is probably impos-

sible to ascertain in the case of Mexico, given available data. It is not easy to ascertain even for the United States, with the availability of highly developed statistical resources. For a brief sketch of the U.S. case, see John K. Folger and Charles B. Nam, *Education of the American Population* (Washington: Government Printing Office, 1967), discussed in Ivar Berg, *Education and Jobs: The Great Training Robbery* (Boston: Beacon Press, 1971), pp. 66–68. Ideally, of course, numerous technicians *should* be educated to support each professional. But the ratio in Mexico by 1980 seems unusually large. The ratio in the United States in 1985 was 1.5 technicians for each professional, whereas that for Mexico was 2.7 to 1 in 1980. See the *Statistical Abstract of the United States*, 1987, 385–86.

32. For data, see Lorey, *Rise of the Professions*, table 9.

33. See, for example, Sanford Mosk, *Industrial Revolution in Mexico*, pp. 265–66 and 271–72.

34. Myers, *Education and National Development*, p. 123.

35. Data from Banco de México cited in Ibid., pp. 123–24ff.

36. This shift is implied by Reynolds, *The Mexican Economy*, pp. 236–38.

37. Padua, "Movilidad Social y Universidad," p. 144.

38. Cited in Myers, *Education and National Development*, p. 123.

39. See Jesús Reyes Heroles González Garza, *Política macroeconómica y bienestar en México* (Mexico City: Fondo de Cultura Económica, 1983), pp. 95, 102; and Gregory's discussion of Reyes Heroles in *The Myth of Market Failure*, pp. 255–56. Neither author specifically compares professional wages to technician wages.

40. The census data do not allow for calculation of annual growth rates of professional and technician EAP by decade.

41. It is necessary to restrict consideration of registrations to the 1975–80 period because changes in regulations caused a major surge in degrees registered between 1974 and 1975.

42. See Brandenburg, *Making of Modern Mexico*, pp. 232–33 and Reynolds, *Mexican Economy*, pp. 236–38.

43. William P. Glade, "Revolution and Economic Development: A Mexican Reprise," in Glade and Anderson, *Political Economy*, pp. 87–88.

44. Ibid., pp. 87–88.

45. For a discussion of the banking institutions established during these years, see Ibid., pp. 71–72.

46. In general, Mexico's economic development after the late 1950s took place in a context of relatively abundant labor even as employment expanded. See Reyes Heroles González Garza, *Política macroeconómica y bienestar*, p. 106 and Gregory, *Myth of Market Failure*, p. 268.

47. This basic trend in employment opportunities for professionals is partially related to the Mexican economy's general inability by the

1960s to create jobs at the rate of population growth. Unemployment at all levels rose, although it is difficult to ascertain rates of unemployment by occupation due to the nature of census and other official data. See Looney, *Mexico's Economy*, p. 61.

48. Tannenbaum recognized early this relationship in Mexico. See his *Mexico*, p. 198.

49. Robert Looney, *Economic Policymaking in Mexico*, p. 35.

50. Ibid., p. 32.

51. Daniel Reséndiz Nuñez, "Science and Technology in Mexico: Looking Forward," p. 39. The author of "La investigación tecnológica, en crisis," *Uno Más Uno*, Jan. 29, 1990, p. 3, claims that 92 percent of Mexican businesses, both public and private, possess obsolete machinery.

52. For data on imports of capital goods as a share of all imports, see Miguel D. Ramírez, *Mexico's Economic Crisis* (New York: Praeger, 1989), p. 57. Between 1955 and 1970, capital-goods imports hovered at an average of 47.7 percent of all imports. See also René Villareal, "El desarrollo industrial de México: Una perspectiva histórica," in *México: 75 años de revolución. Desarrollo económico I* (Mexico City: Fondo de Cultura Económica, 1988), pp. 297 and 307–8; and Cypher, *State and Capital in Mexico*, pp. 7, 65, 75, 76, 162.

53. Laura Randall, *The Political Economy of Mexican Oil* (New York: Praeger, 1989), p. 71.

54. See Olga Pellicer de Brody and Esteban L. Mancilla, *El entendimiento con los Estados Unidos y la gestación del desarrollo estabilizador* (Mexico City: El Colegio de México, 1978), pp. 210–211, and 263–67; Timothy King, *Mexico: Industrialization and Trade Policies Since 1940* (London: Oxford University Press, 1970), p. 72 (table 4.3)and p. 140 (table 6.11); Looney, *Economic Policymaking in Mexico*, pp. 62–63; and Cypher, *State and Capital in Mexico*, pp. 76–77 (table 3.3).

55. Cypher, *State and Capital in Mexico*, p. 66.

56. See Looney, *Economic Policymaking in Mexico*, pp. 36 and 41; and Cypher, *State and Capital in Mexico*, p. 56.

57. Cypher, *State and Capital in Mexico*, pp. 115–116. The period is 1977 through 1981.

58. For an interesting analysis of the relationship between historical technological development and economic growth in Mexico in the context of the Mexican political economy of the 1980s and 1990s, see IBAFIN/CIDAC, *Tecnología e industria en el futuro de México: Posibles vinculaciones estratégicas* (Mexico City: Editorial Diana, 1989). The authors suggest that it is not necessary for a country like Mexico to be on the cutting edge of technological development, but rather more efficient to become adept (like Japan) at adapting technology to domestic and international markets; see pp. 27, 31.

59. Bennett and Sharpe, *Transnational Corporations Versus the State*, p. 36.

60. Ibid., pp. 54–55 and 115–16.

61. See Randall, *Political Economy of Mexican Oil*, pp. 71–73; and George Philip, "Mexican Politics Under Stress: Austerity and After," in *Politics in Mexico*, ed. George Philip (London: Croom Helm, 1985), esp. p. 58. The author of "La Investigación Tecnológica, en Crisis" claims that ten times as much is invested to import capital goods than is invested in research. Little work has been done on the relationship between the production of capital goods and demands for professional expertise in Mexico; the best study for Latin America is that of Nathaniel H. Leff, *The Brazilian Capital Goods Industry, 1929–1964* (Cambridge, Mass.: Harvard University Press, 1968), especially pp. 41–87.

62. Cypher, *State and Capital in Mexico*, p. 65.

63. Protection of the textile industry has a long history in Mexico. For its development during the early years after Independence, see Potash, *Mexican Government and Industrial Development*.

64. Lack of investment and reinvestment was also due to a lack of investor confidence during the violent phase of the Revolution and during the depressed 1925–32 period. Lack of new investment or reinvestment was common in many industries besides textile manufacturing. See Haber, *Industry and Underdevelopment*.

65. Ibid., p. 193.

66. Data from 76 firms with operations in the U.S. and Latin America indicate that only about half of the disparities in worker productivity between Latin American workers and workers in the developed world can be attributed to differences in workers' education. Latin American workers are about 77 percent as productive as their North American counterparts, despite much lower median education per worker in Latin America. See Leff, *Brazilian Capital Goods Industry*, pp. 46–47.

67. See Cypher, *State and Capital in Mexico*, p. 7.

68. Philip, "Public Enterprise in Mexico," in *Public Enterprise and the Development World*, ed. V. V. Ramanadham (London and Sydney: Croom Helm, 1984), p. 36; and Héctor Aguilar Camín, *Despues del milagro* (Mexico City: Cal y Arena, 1990), pp. 66–77.

69. Instituto Nacional de Estadística, Geografía, e Informática (INEGI), *Participación del sector público en el producto interno bruto de México, 1975-1983* (Mexico City: Secretaría de Programación y Presupuesto (SPP), 1984), pp. 5, 7.

70. See Tannenbaum, *Mexico*, pp. 218–19 and J. Richard Powell, *The Mexican Petroleum Industry, 1938–1950* (Berkeley: University of California Press, 1956), p. 130. For statistics on oil production, see James

Wilkie, "From Economic Growth to Economic Stagnation in Mexico," *Statistical Abstract of Latin America*, vol. 27, pp. 913–36.

71. Edward J. Williams, "Petroleum and Political Change," in Domínguez, *Political Economy of Mexico*, pp. 54–55. See also Grayson, *Politics of Mexican Oil*; Randall, *Political Economy of Mexican Oil*, pp. 87–93; and George Philip, *Oil and Politics in Latin America* (Cambridge, Eng.: Cambridge University Press, 1982).

72. INEGI, *Participación del Sector Público en el Producto Interno Bruto*, p. 7.

73. Cypher, *State and Capital in Mexico*, p. 112.

74. Haber traces the failure to develop a self-sustaining and competitive Mexican industry to the dynamic of the first wave of industrialization in Mexico, 1890–1940, suggesting that constraints such as low rates of capacity utilization, low productivity of labor, and difficulties in mobilizing capital led to a manufacturing sector that needed a great deal of protection and relied heavily on imported capital goods. See Haber, *Industry and Underdevelopment*.

75. It is all too common to assert the opposite without evidence from the historical record: see, for example, José de Jesús Guadarrama H., "México Necesita Multiplicar 20 Veces su Número de Ingenieros Antes de 25 Años," *El Financiero*, April 19, 1988, p. 53 (Guadarrama reports on comments of Daniel Reséndiz, director of the UNAM's engineering faculty).

76. Looney, *Mexico's Economy*, p. 19. The connection between the sluggish growth of sciences in Mexico and the weaknesses of Mexican industrial growth was noted early on in the industrial revolution by Mendieta y Nuñez and Gómez Robleda in their *Problemas de la universidad*, pp. 81–82. For an analysis of how scientists and graduate engineers played a determinant role in forcing changes in the structure of production, and the development of technology, in Brazil, see Erick D. Langer, "Generations of Scientists and Engineers: Origins of the Computer Industry in Brazil," *Latin American Research Review*, 24, no. 2 (1989), pp. 95–111.

77. Daniel Reséndiz Nuñez, "Science and Technology in Mexico: Looking Forward," *Voices*, 6 (1989), p. 38.

78. Links between Mexico's economic development and the development of scientific research have not been recognized by most observers. Instead, myriad theories have been forwarded to explain the sluggish development of science in Mexico. See, for example, "La centralización de la investigación es una de las causas de nuestro subdesarrollo científico," *El Día*, June 24, 1971; and José de Jesús Guadarrama H., "Políticas heterodoxas y sexenales mantienen a México al margen de la revolución científica," *El Financiero*, Mar. 14, 1988, p. 85, and "Los recortes presupuestales en el campo de la ciencia amenazan con conver-

tir a México en un país maquilador," *El Día*, Jan. 16, 1988, p. 19.

79. Reynolds, *Mexican Economy*; and A. J. Jaffe, *People, Jobs, and Economic Development: A Case History of Puerto Rico Supplemented by Recent Mexican Experiences* (Glencoe, Il: The Free Press of Glencoe Illinois, 1959), p. 269. See also *The Economist*, Jan. 4, 1992, pp. 15–18.

80. It is this relationship between Mexico's economic development and opportunities for professionals that make most arguments that a brain drain of professionals has slowed Mexico's development untenable (for this argument, see Matt Moffett, "Brain Drain Slows Mexico's Development: Researchers, Professionals, Skilled Workers Are Lured Abroad," *Wall Street Journal*, May 5, 1989, p. A10). Ironically, it is Mexico's historical economic development, with its restricted opportunities for betterment at the professional level, that has caused the flight of professionals toward opportunities abroad. See David Lorey, "Mexican Professional Education in the United States and the Myth of "Brain Drain'," Ensayos (Revista del Departamento de Relaciones Internacionales, Universidad de las Américas-Puebla), 4, no. 9 (1988), pp. 56–59.

81. For discussion of interpreting Mexico's changing trade patterns, see Reynolds, *Mexican Economy*, pp. 301–2.

82. See Brooke, Oxenham, and Little, *Qualifications and Employment*, p. 11; and Muñoz Izquierdo, "El desempleo en México," p. 688, table 1.

83. See Daniel Levy, "Pugna política sobre quién paga la educación superior en México," *Revista Latinoamericana de Estudios Educativos*, 9, no. 2 (1979), pp. 1–38 for a discussion of all the arguments for and against government support of university fees, particularly on how support or lack of support affects the political autonomy of the university. Levy suggests that the government has wanted to extricate itself from this responsibility since the 1930s but has been unable to due to the political strength of public-university students. See also Chapter Six.

84. Myers, *Education and National Development*, p. 125.

85. There is some evidence that the demand for middle-level expertise is also over-supplied in Mexico. For an analysis of the links between secondary education and the structure of the Mexican economy, see Muñoz Izquierdo and Gerardo Rodríguez, "La enseñanza técnica: ¿Canal de movilidad social para los trabajadores?" *Revista de Educación e Investigación Técnica*, no. 6–7 (double issue) (July–August–September, 1980), 70–86.

86. For a discussion of how fee and quota policies shape demand, see Martin Carnoy, *Education and Employment: A Critical Appraisal* (Paris: UNESCO, International Institute for Educational Planning, 1977); and George Psacharopoulos and Bikas C. Sanyal, *Higher Education and Employment: The IIEP Experience in Five Less Developed Countries* (Paris: UNESCO, 1981).

87. See for example, Mosk, *Industrial Revolution*, pp. 268–72.

88. Brandenburg, *Making of Modern Mexico*, p. 162.

89. This expensive substitution is explained and its social implications discussed at length in Chapter Six.

Notes to Chapter Five

1. See for example María Esther Ibarra, "Decide la SEP que se encojan las universidades"; and UNAM, *Fortaleza y debilidad de la UNAM: Respuesta de la comunidad universitaria: Propuestas y alternativas,* Suplemento Extraordinario, no. 16 (Ciudad Universitaria: UNAM, 1986).

2. See, for example, McGinn and Street, *Higher Education Policies,* p. 1.

3. For a discussion of quality at Latin American universities and its measurement, see Liebman, Walker, and Glazer, *Latin American University Students,* pp. 68–78. The authors emphasize the importance of teachers and the quality of instruction received by students (pp. 74–78).

4. Available data on expenditure per student at Mexican universities refer almost entirely to government expenditure for public-university education. The government provides almost no funds to private universities and few universities in Mexico receive any financial assistance from alumni or investment. See Thomas Noel Osborn, *Higher Education in Mexico: History, Growth, and Problems in a Dichotomized Industry* (El Paso: Texas Western Press, 1976). I deflate data on government expenditure for higher education with James W. Wilkie's macro price index to take account of inflation. Some analysts have used undeflated, current peso figures in their analyses, yielding a view of growing funds that hides a reality of growing inflation: see for example Carlos Muñoz Izquierdo, "Educación, estado, y sociedad en México (1930–1976)"; Gilberto Guevara Niebla, *La rosa de los cambios: Breve historia de la UNAM* (Mexico City: Cal y Arena, 1990) pp. 102–3; and Isidoro del Camino, "Gasto educativo nacional, desperdicio escolar y económico, pirámide escolar en México," *Revista del Centro de Estudios Educativos,* 1, no. 4 (1971), 1–34. The bulk of expenditure for university education in Mexico goes for salaries for teaching staff. See UNESCO-Statistical Yearbook.

5. For UNESCO data, see Lorey, *Rise of the Professions,* table 33. There are important differences among universities in terms of expenditure per student, ranging in 1981 from 10,759 pesos of 1970 at the Universidad Autónoma Metropolitana (UAM) to 1,491 at the Universidad de Guadalajara. See Wences Reza, *Universidad,* p. 149.

6. Data on the number of teachers must be considered in the context of the number of students. There is little point in stressing the rapid

growth in absolute numbers of teachers if the rate of growth of the student body has been of an equal or greater magnitude. For an example of an analysis of "undeflated" figures on teachers, see Miguel A. Casillas, "Académicos: Lenta transición hacia la modernidad," *El Cotidiano*, 28 (Mar.-Apr. 1989), pp. 44–51.

7. The lack of full-time-equivalent (FTE) statistics on teachers makes calculation of student/teacher ratios complex. There is no reliable data on class size or attendance, both of which make a great deal of difference in the effectiveness of teaching staff. Sources for data do not always indicate whether data pertain solely to the licentiate level. The relatively low (positive) ratio of students to teachers is due primarily to the large number of teachers hired on an hourly basis: see discussion. Non-teaching faculty are generally included in the data for faculty.

8. It should be noted that full-time faculty are not necessarily "better" teachers than those hired on an hourly basis. But professors generally begin their teaching careers as hourly employees and move up to full-time status on the basis of seniority. Faculty hired on an hourly basis frequently must split their time between their teaching duties and other employment. Full-time teachers, on the other hand, devote themselves for the most part solely to their teaching and research. For this reason, a higher quality of education is to be expected when students have frequent and meaningful contact with full-time faculty.

9. Professors can be hired on more than one basis, holding various appointments at different universities or even in different departments. See Manuel Gil Antón, "Los académicos y la reforma universitaria: Tres propuestas a discusión," *El Cotidiano*, 29 (May-June 1989), debate, ii–vi.

10. Comparison of expenditure data from the UNAM and from all universities suggests that the UNAM has historically been treated rather well in this respect. It has not experienced the same ups and downs as the average university, and it continued to do well even in the midst of economic crisis in the mid-1980s.

11. For a slightly different set of figures for the period from 1931 to 1943, see Lucio Mendieta y Nuñez and José Gómez Robledo, *Problemas de la universidad* (Mexico City: UNAM, 1948), p. 170. The authors cite no exact sources for their series.

12. See Lorey, *Rise of the Professions*, table 34, for budget data from 1968 to 1988. Arturo González Cosío, *Historia estadística de la Universidad, 1910–1967* (Mexico City: UNAM, 1968), pp. 66–68, gives data for the percent share in the UNAM budget of a combined teaching and research category for the years 1929–67. The UNAM has periodically published data on its faculty, their training, their experience, their pay, and their qualifications. Unfortunately, the data are not consistent from year to year and cover only short periods of time; they are therefore not

very useful for analysis of long-term change. See UNAM, *Diagnóstico de personel académico* (Mexico City: UNAM, 1984) and *Censo de personel académico* (Mexico City: UNAM, 1986).

13. The sample public universities were chosen by a minimum number of teachers; thus the largest universities are represented. The private universities were chosen to represent both older, larger institutions (Instituto Tecnológico y de Estudios Superiores de Monterrey—ITESM; Universidad Autónoma de Guadalajara—UAG) and smaller institutions (the Universidad Iberoaméricana and the Universidad de las Américas).

14. The average of all Mexican universities, public and private, was 8.2 percent full-time in 1970 and 17.2 percent full-time in 1980. The lower averages for all universities than for the sample universities is due to the presence of many small universities in the total data, both public and private, that are able to maintain only a few full-time faculty.

15. In a reversal of the usual naming pattern, the Universidad Autónoma de Guadalajara is private, while the Universidad de Guadalajara is public.

16. In 1970, UANL and Universidad Autónoma de Sinaloa were subtracted from the sample; in 1980, UANL, UASIN, and UAM were subtracted from the sample. See Table 8, Statistical Appendix.

17. Slow growth in quality at the UNAM is apparent in the data analyzed by Nava Díaz, "Perspectiva de complemento al financiamiento," pp. 64, 66.

18. See Rangel Guerra, *Systems of Higher Education*, p. 59; and María Esther Ibarra, "Decide la SEP que se encojan las universidades," p. 21.

19. Such teachers, like the number of teachers who are hired by professors subletting their positions, cannot be extracted from the data.

20. These ratios are rough estimates. There is a great deal of variation among both public and private universities and among faculties. On the marked decline of professor's salaries at the UNAM following the economic crisis of 1982, see Wilkie, "Six Ideological Phases," introduction and table 9.

21. Conversations with Gustavo Chapela (General Rector of UAM system) and Silvia Ortega (Rectora, UAM-A), Jan. 1991. For a study of salaries at the UAM, see Ernesto Soto Reyes Garmendia, " Modernización educativa y salarios en la educación superior," *El Cotidiano*, 36 (July–Aug. 1990), pp. 9–18.

22. The UNAM and the IPN are exceptional cases in this regard, because they invest heavily in the latest technology for research.

23. Robert W. Quirk, *Mexico* (Englewood Cliffs, N.J.: Prentice-Hall, 1971), p. 121. The idea is an old one; see, for example, Tannenbaum, *Mexico*, p. 171.

24. See, for example, Cleaves's flow chart of causes of "decline" in quality. Cleaves, *Profesiones y el estado,* p. 118; Muñoz Izquierdo, "Educación, estado, y sociedad," p. 33; and Rangel Guerra, *Systems of Higher Education,* p. 59. Rangel Guerra introduces the idea that it has not been possible to train teachers at the rate of growth in university enrollment, an assessment not borne out by the data analyzed above.

25. Nor is it reasonable to argue that a weakness in secondary preparation is to blame for low university quality. It is more plausible, particularly given the evidence of Chapter Four, that the secondary system (much of which is controlled by the public universities) produces what the universities demand. The experience of private universities in this regard would appear instructive. Private universities have found that secondary schools (public as well as private in some cases) adapt their curricula to the entrance requirements and general academic level of nearby private universities.

26. See, for example, Jorge A. Padua, "Movilidad social y universidad," in Gilberto Guevara Niebla, *La crisis de la educación superior en México* (Mexico City: Nueva Imagen, 1981), p. 145.

27. See Cleaves, *Profesiones y el estado,* pp. 122–30; also Levy, "Serving Private Enterprise and the State," p. 98.

28. See Liebman, Walker, and Glazer, *Latin American University Students,* p. 57.

29. See, for example, Howard Cline, *Mexico: Revolution to Evolution,* p. 207, on ITESM. See also the section "Implications of Historical Deconcentration" in this chapter.

30. This link is clear in impressionistic data. Compare, for example, the jobs bulletin of the American Chamber of Congress in Mexico with the catalogs of private universities.

31. Institutos Mexicanos de Educación Superior Privada (IMESP), *La educación privada en México, 1980–81: Su aportación al desarrollo de la nación (Anteproyecto)* ([Mexico City: N.p., n.d. [1979]). See also Levy, *Higher Education,* pp. 148–57.

32. See Chapter Four.

33. See Lorey, *Rise of the Professions,* table 41, for data on enrollment by field at public and private universities during the period 1959–64.

34. See also IMESP, *Educación privada.* The twenty private universities that make up the Association of Institutes of Private Higher Education boasted a full-time staff to student ratio that in 1981 was 1 to 36 and improving rapidly, a figure close to that derived from sample private universities above. The twenty universities in IMESP account for 63 percent of enrollment at private institutions.

35. Ibid.

36. For a discussion of the different patterns of socialization of public-

and private-university students, see Pescador and Torres, *Poder político y educación*, pp. 85–117 and table 12 (pp. 109–11).

37. For a discussion of the differences in curricula and values at public and private universities, see Levy, *Higher Education*. Also see the statistics and discussion in Patricia de Leonardo Ramírez, "Los cuadros de la derecha," El Cotidiano, 24 (July–August, 1988), pp. 92–94, which focuses on the UAG, the ISTESM, and the Universidad Iberoamericana.

38. For a review of ideas on the the relationship between institutions for higher education and dual and segmented labor markets, see Muñoz Izquierdo, "Observaciones críticas a una previsión de recursos humanos basada en el enfoque de Herbert Parnes," *Revista de Educación e Investigación Técnica*, no. 10 (1981), 66–73.

39. A difference in ideological perspective has also made difficult links between the private sector and public-university research. See "Poco valora la investigación universitaria por IP y estado," *La Jornada*, May 25, 1988, p. 7, which reports the comments of Oscar González Cuevas, rector of the UAM.

40. Camp, "Political Technocrat in Mexico," p. 107. See also Camp's *Entrepreneurs and Politics in Twentieth-Century Mexico* (Oxford, Eng.: Oxford University Press, 1989), pp. 92–93; José Antonio Crespo, "Niveles de información política en los universitarios mexicanos," *Foro Internacional*, 114, no. 2 (Oct.-Dec. 1988), pp. 319–37 (Crespo employs a very small and possibly biased sample); and Pescador and Alberto Torres, *Poder Político y Educación*, pp. 85–117.

41. See, for example, Camp, "The Political Technocrat in Mexico and the Survival of the Political System," *Latin American Research Review*, 20, no. 1 (1985), p. 107; Oscar Hinojosa, "La universidad privada escala posiciones como proveedora de funcionarios," *Proceso*, March 31, 1986, pp. 6–11; de Leonardo Ramírez, "Cuadros de la Derecha"; and Pescador and Torres, *Poder Político y Educación*, p. 96.

42. For example, Levy, *Higher Education*.

43. Author's conversations with the dean of the economics faculty.

44. The private-university boom is seen by many analysts as beginning in the late 1970s. See, for example, Camp, "Political Technocrat in Mexico," which states in 1985 that the previous decade has seen a shift from public to private universities (p. 106).

45. Analysis of trends in the 1928–66 period must rely on data for enrollment, because little reliable data exist for graduates or egresados of universities by specific institution until 1967.

46. See Lorey, *Rise of the Professions*, table 48.

47. Eyler N. Simpson, *The Ejido: Mexico's Way Out* (Chapel Hill: University of North Carolina Press, 1937), pp. 579–80.

48. See Tannenbaum, *Mexico*, p. 171.

49. See Guevara Niebla, *Democracia en la calle*, p. 72. Throughout this discussion I refer to Mexico's well-established private universities rather than to the dozens of private institutions offering only a few career areas that rose to prominence in the 1980s. Enrollment at these latter schools expanded rapidly after 1982 to satisfy demand for places that could not be met by the major public universities.

50. Levy, *Higher Education*, p. 121. See also Cline, *Mexico: Revolution to Evolution*, p. 207; Sanford Mosk, *Industrial Revolution in Mexico*, p. 269; Guevara Niebla, *Crisis de la educación superior*, p. 141; and Francisco Ortiz Pinchetti, "El Grupo Monterrey crea sus propias fábricas de hombres," *Proceso*, June 23, 1980, pp. 10–13. On the involvement of Monterrey's first families in the foundation of the ITESM, see José Fuentes Mares, *Monterrey: Una ciudad creadora y sus capitanes* (Mexico City: Editorial JUS, 1976), pp. 153–80.

51. When the economics faculty of the UNAM debated academic changes in 1989, they asserted that they were not "ITAM-izing" the UNAM: see Saúl Vázquez Granados, "Inicia la facultad de economía de la UNAM cambios académicos: Mejora su preparación," *El Financiero*, Sept. 11, 1989, p. 63.

52. For a discussion of ties between private universities and private-sector business interests, see Levy, *Higher Education*, pp. 126–31. The private sector has also tried to influence the function of the universities by participating in lower levels of education. See, for example, "Mayor participación en la educación, piden empresarios," *La Jornada*, Aug. 26, 1987, p. 9.

53. The government has lent financial support to some of the most innovative programs for improving quality at private universities. See Gómez Junco, "Presente y futuro de cinco innovaciones," pp. 32–46.

54. Central and decentralized sectors of the government have had different demands for professionals, with the decentralized sector apparently demanding professionals in newer fields and perhaps more professionals with private-university backgrounds. See Chapter Four and Comisión de Recursos Humanos del Sector Público del Gobierno Federal, *Censo de recursos humanos del sector público federal: Administración central 1975* (Mexico City: Comisión de Recursos Humanos del Sector Público del Gobierno Federal, 1976) and *Administración descentralizada y de participación estatal mayoritaria 1975* (Mexico City: Comisión de Recursos Humanos del Sector Público del Gobierno Federal, 1976).

55. Data for private universities between 1967 and 1976 have been partially estimated.

56. For an analysis of the relationship between quality of higher education, social-class origin of students, and social mobility, see Olac

Fuentes Molinar, "Universidad y democracia: La mirada hacia la izquierda." Clearly, I do not see the different roles of public and private universities in Mexico as indicative of a strict "dichotomy" in the higher education system; compare with Osborn, *Higher Education in Mexico.*

57. On the function of the state universities within the system, see also Fuentes Molinar, "Universidad y democracia," p. 7.

Notes to Chapter Six

1. It is clear that in Mexico, as in most other parts of the world there is a strong correlation between earnings and educational attainment. For analysis of the Mexican case in the Latin American context, see Martin Carnoy, "Rates of Return to Schooling in Latin America," *Journal of Human Resources,* 2, no. 3 (Summer 1967), pp. 359–74. See also Carnoy's "The Costs and Returns to Schooling in Mexico," Ph.D. Diss. University of Chicago, 1964 and "Earnings and Schooling in Mexico," *Economic Development and Cultural Change,* 15, no. 4 (July 1967), pp. 408–19; also Wouter van Ginneken, *Socioeconomic Groups and Income Distribution in Mexico* (New York: St. Martin's Press, 1980). Whether the relationship between earnings and attainment is due to productivity increases associated by some analysts with education or with the socializing function of education emphasized by others is far from clear. For reviews of the issues involved in this debate, see Blaug, *Economics of Education;* and Muñoz Izquierdo and Lobo, "Expansión escolar." Data on salaries in areas of professional employment indicate that professional fields continue to offer the hope of a higher salary: for data on income and expenditure by level of academic achievement, see BANAMEX, *Como es México,* (Mexico City: BANAMEX, 1983).

2. Years before the appearance of literature on dual and segmented labor markets, for example, Mexican students and their families recognized that different sectors of the economy, and particularly different areas within the public sector, had created relatively autonomous internal labor markets. Students used both lore and concrete information about the characteristics of these labor markets to shape their career decisions.

3. See Leopoldo Solís M., *Controversias sobre el crecimiento y la distribución* (Mexico City: Fondo de Cultura Económica, 1972), p. 207.

4. *La UNAM hoy y su proyección al futuro: Una biografía de la ideas de Jorge Carpizo Rector* (Mexico City: UNAM, 1987), p. 17.

5. Leslie B. Simpson, *Many Mexicos,* pp. 158–59.

6. William P. Glade, "Revolution and Economic Development: A Mexican Reprise," p. 31. See also Rodríguez, "National University of

Mexico," Ph.D. diss., University of Texas, Austin, 1958, pp. 240, 323, and 326.

7. Rangel Guerra, *Systems of Higher Education*, pp. 59–60. See also p. 53.

8. See, for example, Jorge Padua, "Movilidad social y universidad," p. 128. Also see Roderic Camp, *Entrepreneurs and Politics in Twentieth-Century Mexico* (Oxford, Eng.: Oxford University Press, 1989), p. 90.

9. The term "social mobility" is used here to mean both inter-generational and intra-generational structural mobility, because both are reflected in time-series data derived from the Mexican census.

10. For the most sophisticated recent study of income distribution on Mexico, see van Ginneken, *Socioeconomic Groups and Income Distribution*. Also see the early analyses of Leopoldo Solís, *La realidad económica mexicana: Retrovisión y perspectivas*, chap. 7; Pablo González Casanova, *Democracy in Mexico* (London: Oxford University Press, 1970), chap. 6; and Arturo González Cosío, "Clases y estratos sociales," in *México: Cincuenta años de revolución, Tomo II*, (Mexico City: Fondo de Cultura Económica, 1961). For regional analyses, see José Luis Reyna, Manuel Vill, and Kirsten Albrechtsen, "Dinámica de la estratificación social en algunas ciudades pequeñas y medianas de México," in *Revista de Demografía y Economía*, 1, no. 3 (1967); and Enrique Contreras Suárez, *Estratificación y movilidad social en la ciudad de México* (Mexico City: UNAM, 1978).

11. See Howard F. Cline, *Mexico: Revolution to Evolution, 1940–1960* (New York: Oxford University Press, 1963), p. 124; and Aída Mostkoff and Stephanie Granato, "The Class Structure of Mexico, 1895–1980," in Wilkie, ed., *Society and Economy*. I have not reworked the categories used by Mostkoff and Granato in line with my definitions of professional and technician in order to test my general argument about employment for professionals and social mobility against an independent set of data. For discussion of the period from 1980 to 1990 see Lorey and Mostkoff, "Mexico's 'Lost Decade'." At least one author has used educational attainment itself as a gauge of social class; see Joseph A. Kahl, *Comparative Perspectives on Stratification: Mexico, Great Britain, Japan* (Boston: Little, Brown, 1968).

12. The terms "upper" and "middle" are adopted from Mostkoff and Granato for the sake of consistency. I substitute "working" for "lower." An alternate terminology for measuring class structure in Latin America is presented by Alejandro Portes, "Latin American Class Structures: Their Composition and Change During the Last Decades," *Latin American Research Review*, 20, no. 3 (1985), pp. 7–39. The analysis is highly aggregate and most of the data employed go back only to 1970. For his class categories, Portes uses the terms "Dominant," "Bureaucratic-

Technical," "Formal Proletariat," "Informal Petty Bourgeoisie," and "Informal Proletariat." Although the time-period considered is very brief, some social mobility is apparent for Latin America as a whole, although not for Mexico, for which Portes does not present time-series data.

13. Rosario Enríquez, "The Rise and Collapse of Stabilising Development," in Philip, *Mexican Economy*, p. 15.

14. The terms "stable" and "semi-leisure" are adopted from the original sources. The stable middle class is an average of (1) persons reporting a monthly income of 300 to 1,000 pesos of 1950, and (2) two-thirds of persons reporting professional occupations, one-half of those respondents classifying themselves as office workers, and one-third of persons who considered themselves tradespeople. The semi-leisure upper class is an average of persons who reported monthly incomes of between 1,001 and 3,000 pesos of 1950 and one-third of persons who reported professional occupations.

15. Data for "combined" income and occupation represent an average of data in the two categories.

16. The following discussion focuses on the period since 1950 because data on income and occupation are comparable only for the censuses since that date.

17. The number of university graduates grew at a rate of 19.3 percent annually between 1929 and 1949 and 29.6 percent between 1950 and 1971. Data obtained by calculation from data in Lorey, *Rise of the Professions*.

18. It will be remembered that in the case of job opportunities presented in Chapter Five, data were only available for 1950 and 1980. In this case data exist for 1950, 1960, 1970, and 1980.

19. Mark Szuchman's work on nineteenth-century Argentina shows that income and occupation are separate although frequently related phenomena. Szuchman found that in Argentine cities, upward occupational mobility was not accompanied by higher income. See Mark D. Zsuchman, *Mobility and Integration in Urban Argentina: Córdoba in the Liberal Era* (Austin: University of Texas Press, 1980).

20. See Contreras Suárez, *Estratificación y movilidad social*, p. 213.

21. Not all analysts agree with this assessment. For example, Guevara Niebla, in his *Democracia en la calle*, concludes that there was a considerable increase in students from working-class backgrounds at UNAM after 1968.

22. Consistent reliable data on students' backgrounds and how they may have changed over time exist for no other Mexican university.

23. Data for these paragraphs are derived from several sources that were not created for analysis of long-term trends. The data were modi-

fied and partially estimated in an attempt to make the historical series used here. The reader is advised to consult the original sources.

24. Ten of the respondents were older professionals.

25. Cleaves, *Profesiones y el estado*, p. 130 [emphasis mine].

26. There are fine gradations within regions. In Puebla, for example, the private Universidad de las Américas is widely recognized as the school of Puebla's elite, the UPAEP (Universidad Popular Autónoma del Estado de Puebla, also private) is considered a relatively distant second, and the UAP is at the bottom, serving a much larger proportion of the working and transitional middle classes of the city and state.

27. Reliable data for female titulados are not available after 1971. For a comparison of female enrollment and degrees granted to women, see Lorey, *Rise of the Professions*, table 61. Women made up 18.3 percent of enrolled students, 18.6 percent of egresados, and 14.6 percent of degree recipients.

28. Liebman, Walker, and Glazer, *Latin American University Students*, pp. 56–58.

29. See Ramírez, *Mexico's Economic Crisis*, pp. 74–75.

30. Hla Myint, "Education and Economic Development," in ECLA, *Education, Human Resources, and Development in Latin America* (New York: United Nations, 1968), p. 65.

31. Even with recent restriction on the size of the entering classes at Mexico's largest public universities, the admission standards cannot be said to be high.

32. Rangel Guerra, *Systems of Higher Education*, pp. 54–55.

33. See Muñoz Izquierdo, "Evaluación del desarrollo educativo." Daniel Levy, "Pugna política sobre quién paga la educación superior en México," suggests that a government-supported university is inherently retrograde, because the Mexican tax structure is regressive and the primary- and secondary-education system selects better-off Mexicans for university education. See also Wences Reza, *Universidad*, p. 162.

34. For an analysis of the impact of low fees, see Quintero H., "Metas de Igualdad," pp. 59–92. Quintero concludes that government-subsidized fees neither promote greater equality of access to the university nor contribute to a positive redistribution of income (p. 84). See also Jean Pierre Jallade, "Financiamiento de la educación y distribución del ingreso," *Revista del Centro de Estudios Educativos*, 6, no. 4 (1976); and Olac Fuentes Molinar, "Universidad y democracia: La mirada hacia la izquierda." The heat of the debate over fees is captured in Hugo Morales Galván, "Se sumará la UNAM a planteles elitistas," *Quehacer Político*, 4, no. 192 (May 27, 1985), pp. 26–29.

35. While scarce, the available evidence suggests that egresados tend to be predominantly working-class Mexicans, while those students who achieve degrees (titulados) tend to be from the middle and upper

classes. See Muñoz Izquierdo and Gerardo Rodríguez, "Enseñanza técnica," p. 26. Padua, in "Movilidad social y universidad," estimates that between 75 and 80 percent of graduating students are from the middle class (p. 148).

36. For a discussion of the general effects of such implicit selection schemes, see ECLA, *Education, Human Resources, and Development,* p. 124.

37. *Uno Mas Uno,* June 11, 1988, p. 3, quotes a study by the UNAM's Dirección General de Planeación and a paper given by Rafael Vidal Uribe y Pío Alcántara, "Trayectoría Escolar en el Nivel Licenciatura."

38. Cleaves, *Profesiones y el Estado,* pp. 129–30.

39. It is sometimes argued that any amount of time spent by students at a university is beneficial to society. But there are also social costs involved in supporting students who do not complete their studies. See ECLA, *Education, Human Resources, and Development,* p. 116.

40. Ibid., p. 127.

41. Quoted in Roderic Camp, *Entrepreneurs and Politics,* p. 96.

42. There is some recognition of a professional employment problem, although the larger historical realities are generally only dimly understood: see, for example, Rosa Elvira Vargas, "Destruiría a la UNAM imitar la estructura del poder público," *El Financiero,* Nov. 7, 1989, p. 45; and Mario García Sordo, "Desempleados o subempleados, más de 90 mil agrónomos". Qualitatively underemployed means that graduates work below the level of their degree qualifications. See Davis, *Science, Engineering, and Technical Education in Mexico.* (New York: Education and World Affairs, 1967), pp. 13–19, for a discussion of the definition and differentiation of different employment levels.

43. Liebman, Walker, and Glazer, *Latin American University Students,* pp. 52–53. These latter numbers are pretty close to one direct study of intergenerational mobility of secondary technical students: 42 percent felt they had moved up, 34 percent moved down, and 24 percent thought they had remained at the same level. See Muñoz Izquierdo and Gerardo Rodríguez, "Enseñanza técnica," pp. 70–86.

44. For a note on the relationship between adopted ideology and employment in Argentina, see Charles Bergquist, *Labor in Latin America: Comparative Essays on Chile, Argentina, Venezuela, and Colombia* (Stanford, Calif.: Stanford University Press, 1986), p. 108.

Notes to Chapter Seven

1. See Cleaves, *Profesiones y el estado,* p. 109.

2. See Mabry, *Mexican University and the State,* pp. 209–10. See also the review of Mabry in Iván Jaksic's "Politics of Higher Education," pp. 217–18.

3. Morales-Gómez and Alberto Torres, *State, Corporatist Politics, and Educational Policy Making*, p. 31; and Paul Luke, "Debt and Oil-Led Development: The Economy Under López Portillo (1977–1982)," in Philip, *Mexican Economy*, p. 43.

4. Wilkie, "Six Ideological Phases," p. 44.

5. Estimates from conversations with the Director General of the ABC Hospital in Mexico City, 1990.

6. Liebman, Walker, and Glazer, *Latin American University Students*, p. 185.

7. For the classic discussion of the events of 1968, see Zermeño, *México*.

8. Liebman, Walker, and Glazer, *Latin American University Students*, p. 182, suggests that physical proximity of schools may play a role in student activism.

9. *Uno Mas Uno*, Aug. 5, 1988.

10. Dirección de Planeación Universitaria, *Universidad en cifras* (Monterrey: UANL, various years).

11. At least one analyst affiliated with the government recognized the probable negative effect of the renewed reliance on foreign investment to spur economic growth and professional employment. See Samaniego, "El desafío del empleo," pp. 156–57.

12. See María Amparo Casar, "La reestructuración de la participación del estado en la industria nacional," *El Cotidiano*, 23 (1988), pp. 28–38.

Notes to Statistical Appendix

1. In assigning professional fields to categories, I have relied on sources outlining degree programs and employment opportunities of various professional programs, particularly ANUIES, *Catálogo de carreras 1986*; and SEP, *Información profesional y subprofesional*.

2. Basic field definitions for titulados are adopted from Dirección General de Estadística, *Anuario estadístico* and *Compendio estadístico*; no indication is generally given in these sources about changing the specific makeup of these fields.

3. Electrical, mechanical, and mechanical-electrical engineering are combined here for several reasons. Much older data on engineering degrees granted combine the three groups under one heading and separate fields cannot be disaggregated. This aggregation does not cause a large problem, because these three involve similar training and because in modern practice in Mexico the fields are closely tied.

4. Military and rural doctors are included. Specialists in homeopathic medicine, who work primarily with herbal cures, have also been included. Pharmaceutical chemists have been included.

5. Psychology is tabulated separately only for the years 1964–71 in data sources and so is placed in the "other" category for all years. In

the egresados and degrees-registered series, psychology and social work have been placed together in a separate category.

6. The "other" category in sources apparently includes only secondary-level degrees and diplomas and so has not been included in my tabulations. After 1963, the "other" category becomes more specific, and I have included other university-level degrees when it was possible to discern differences in levels of degrees. Such degrees include licenciate degrees in social sciences, political science, public administration, tourism, optometry, and library sciences.

7. An egresado has finished course work for a degree but has yet to complete the written thesis or other requirements for the degree. Degree-program names vary from university to university; I have used the most common designations.

8. The public-administration degree granted in business programs has been included here; degrees granted as "Social Science and Public Administration" or "Political Science and Public Administration" have been placed in the social-sciences category.

9. The sciences category includes only professionals who have simple titles. Complex degree fields have been included in fields of similar occupational orientation. Industrial chemistry, for example, has been tabulated with chemical engineering.

10. Data for the registered-degrees category represent only the most numerous specialties in each discipline, and thus are not comprehensive. For this reason, an index has been used to show the changing relative importance and growth rates of the different professional fields and to contrast data presented in the two other series.

Selected Bibliography

The body of scholarly work on higher education in Mexico is large. This bibliography lists sources that have directly influenced the arguments of the present study. Works referred to on peripheral issues are given full citations in the notes and are not included here.

Primary Statistical Sources

Asociación Nacional de Universidades e Institutos de Enseñanza Superior (ANUIES). *Anuario estadístico.* Various years.
———. *La enseñanza superior en México* and *La educación superior en México.*
———. *Programa integral para el desarrollo de la educación superior.* Mexico City: 1986.
Attolini, José. *Las finanzas de la universidad a través del tiempo.* Mexico City: Escuela Nacional de Economía (UNAM), 1951.
Dirección General de Estadística. Anuario estadístico. Various years.
———. *Compendio estadístico.* Various years.
———. *Estadísticas para el sistema de educación nacional.* Various years.
Dirección General de Profesiones. Unpublished data.
Estrada Campo, Humberto. *Historia de los cursos de postgrado de la UNAM.* Mexico City: UNAM, 1983.

González Cosío, Arturo. *Historia estadística de la universidad, 1910–1967.* Mexico City: UNAM, 1968.

Instituto de Estadística, Geografía, e Informática (INEGI). *Estadísticas históricas de México.* Mexico City: INEGI, 1985.

Mostkoff, Aída, and Stephanie Granato. "Quantifying Mexico's Class Structure." In *Society and Economy in Mexico.* James W. Wilkie, ed. Los Angeles: UCLA Latin American Center Publications, 1989.

Nacional Financiera, S. A. (NAFINSA). *La economía mexicana en cifras.*

Obra educativa de López Mateos. N.p.: N.p. [ANUIES], n.d. [1965].

Secretaría de Educación Pública (SEP). *La educación pública en México 1964/1970.* Mexico City: SEP, 1970.

———. *Estadística básica del sistema educativo nacional, 1971–1972.* Mexico City: SEP, 1972.

———. *Obra Educativa, 1970–1976.* Mexico City: SEP, n.d. [1976].

Secretaría de la Presidencia. *50 años de revolución mexicana en cifras.* Mexico City: NAFINSA, 1963.

UNAM. *Anuario estadístico.* Various years.

———. Dirección General de Administración, Departamento de Estadística. *Cuadernos estadísticos año lectivo 1979–1980.* Mexico City: UNAM, n.d. [1980].

———. *Primer censo universitario.* Mexico City: UNAM, 1953.

———. Dirección General de Administración. *Estadísticas del aspecto escolar, 1970.* México D.F.: UNAM, 1970.

———. *Exámenes profesionales practicados de 1841–1975.* Mexico City: n.d. [1975].

———. Dirección General de Asuntos del Personal Académico. *Diagnóstico del personal académico de la UNAM* (1984) and *Censo del personal académico* (1986). Mexico City: UNAM, 1984 and 1986.

———. *Presupuesto por programas.* Various years.

Secondary Sources

Almond, Gabriel A. "The Development of Political Development." In *Understanding Political Development.* Ed. Samuel P. Huntington and Myron Weiner. Boston: Little, Brown and Company, 1987.

American Chamber of Commerce of Mexico, A. C. *Mexico: Oportunidades de empleo 1987.* Mexico City: American Chamber of Commerce of Mexico, 1987.

Amparo Casar, María. "La reestructuración de la participación del estado en la industria nacional." *El Cotidiano,* 23 (1988), 28-38.

Arce Gurza, Francisco. "El inicio de una nueva era, 1910–1945." In *Historia de las profesiones en México.* Mexico City: El Colegio de México, 1982.

Asociación Nacional de Universidades e Institutos de Enseñanza Superior (ANUIES). *Carreras del área de la química en México: Planes de estudio.* Mexico City: ANUIES, 1980.

———. *Catálogo de carreras 1986.* Mexico City: ANUIES, 1986.

———. *La enseñanza de la ingeniería en México: Estudio preliminar.* Mexico City: ANUIES, 1962.

———. *Aspectos normativos de la educación superior.* México. D.F.: ANUIES, 1982.

———. *Planeación de la educación en México.* Mexico City: ANUIES, 1979.

———. *Programa integral para el desarrollo de la educación superior (PROIDES).* Mexico City: ANUIES, n.d. [1986].

Arizmendi Rodríguez, Roberto. *La decentralización de la educación superior.* Mexico City: SEP/ANUIES, 1982.

Arrow, K. *Higher Education as a Filter.* Stanford: Stanford University Press, 1972.

Aspe, Pedro, and Paul E. Sigmund, eds. *The Political Economy of Income Distribution in Mexico.* New York: Holmes and Meier Publishers, 1984.

Ayala, Gustavo. "Ingeniería civil: Importancia y consecuencias." In *Ciencia y desarrollo, número especial: Los estudios de posgrado en México. Naturaleza, funciones, diagnóstico.* Mexico City: CONACYT, 1987.

Baloyra, Enrique A. "Oil Policies and Budgets in Venezuela, 1938–1968." *Latin American Research Review,* 9, no. 2 (Summer, 1974), 28–72.

Banco de México. Departamento de Investigaciones Industriales. *El empleo de personal técnico en la industria de transformación.* Mexico City: Banco de México, 1959.

———. *Programas de becas y datos profesionales de los becarios.* Mexico City: Banco de México, 1964.

Barkin, David. "La educación: ¿Una barrera al desarrollo económico?" *El Trimestre Económico,* 33, no. 4 (October–December, 1971), 951–993.

Barrios, Maritza, and Russel G. Davis. "The Rate-of-Return Approach to Educational Planning." In *Planning Education for Development: Volume I, Issues and Problems in the Planning of Education in Developing Countries, USAID/Harvard.* Ed. Russell G. Davis. Cambridge, MA: Center for Education and Development, Harvard University, 1980.

Bartolucci, Jorge. "Demanda de los sectores medios." *Revista Mexicana de Ciencias Políticas y Sociales,* n.s. 29 (Nueva Epoca), 129–142.

Beck, Robert E. "The Liberal Arts Major in the Bell System Management: Project Quill Report." Washington, D.C.: Association of American Colleges, 1981.

Becker, G. S. *Human Capital: A Theoretical and Empirical Analysis, with Special Reference to Education.* Princeton: Princeton University Press, 1964.

Behrman, Jere R. "Schooling in Latin America: What Are the Patterns and What Is the Impact?" *Journal of Interamerican Studies and World Affairs*, 27, no. 4 (Winter, 1985–1986).

Bennett, Douglas C., and Kenneth E. Sharpe. *Transnational Corporations versus the State: The Political Economy of the Mexican Auto Industry.* Princeton: Princeton University Press, 1985.

Benveniste, Guy. *Bureaucracy and National Planning: A Sociological Case Study of Mexico.* New York: Praeger, 1970.

Berg, Ivar. *Education and Jobs: The Great Training Robbery.* Boston: Beacon Press, 1971.

Bialostozky, Clara J. de. *Recursos humanos: Tabulaciones con base en una muestra del censo de población de 1960.* Mexico City: El Colegio de México, 1970.

Blaug, Mark. *The Economics of Education: An Annotated Bibliography.* Oxford: Pergamon Press, 1978.

———. *Education and the Employment Problem in Developing Countries.* Geneva: International Labor Office, 1974.

———. *An Introduction to the Economics of Education.* London: Penguin, 1970.

Bortz, Jeffrey. "The Development of Quantitative History in Mexico since 1940: Socioeconomic Change, Income Distribution, and Wages." In *Statistical Abstract of Latin America*, vol. 27, pp. 1107–1127.

Brandenburg, Frank. *The Making of Modern Mexico.* Englewood Cliffs: Prentice-Hall, 1964.

Bravo Ahuja, Víctor. *Obra educativa, 1970–1976.* Mexico City: SEP, 1976.

Bravo Ugarte, José. *La educación en México.* Mexico City: Editorial Jus, 1966.

Brooke, Nigel. "Actitudes de los empleadores mexicanos respeto a la educación: Un test de la teoría de capital humano?" *Revista del Centro de Estudios Educativos*, 8, no. 4 (1978), 109–32.

Brooke, Nigel, John Oxenham, and Angela Little. *Qualifications and Employment in Mexico.* International Development Studies Research Report. Sussex: University of Sussex, 1978.

Burke, Michael E. "The University of Mexico and the Revolution, 1910–1940." *Americas*, 34, no. 2 (1977), 252–273.

Camp, Roderic A. "The Cabinet and the Técnico in Mexico and the United States." *Journal of Comparative Administration*, no. 3 (August, 1971), 200–1.

———"Intellectuals: Agents of Change in Mexico?" *Journal of Interamerican Studies and World Affairs*, 23, no. 3 (August, 1981).

——. *Intellectuals and the State in Twentieth–Century Mexico.* Austin: University of Texas Press, 1985.

——. "Mexican Governors since Cárdenas: Education and Career Contacts." *Journal of Interamerican Studies and World Affairs*, 16, no. 4 (November, 1974).

——. *Mexico's Leaders: Their Education and Recruitment.* Tucson: University of Arizona Press, 1980.

——. *Mexican Political Biographies, 1935–75.* Tucson: University of Arizona Press, 1976.

——. "The Middle–Level Technocrat in Mexico." *Journal of Developing Areas*, 6, no. 4 (July, 1972), 571–582.

——. "The Political Technocrat in Mexico and the Survival of the Political System." *Latin American Research Review*, 20, no. 1 (1985), 97–118.

——. *The Role of Economists in Policy–Making: A Comparative Case Study of Mexico and the United States.* Tucson: University of Arizona Press, 1977.

Carmino Ruiz, Gilardo, et al. *Estudio comparativo de la oferta y demanda actual para profesores con nivel de postgrado para las instituciones de educación agropecuaria superior en México (1983–1985).* Chapingo: Colegio de Postgrado, 1986.

Carnoy, Martin. "The Costs and Returns to Schooling in Mexico." Ph.D. Diss. University of Chicago, 1964.

——. "Earnings and Schooling in Mexico." *Economic Development and Cultural Change*, 15, no. 4 (July 1967), pp. 408–19.

——. *Education and Employment: A Critical Appraisal.* Paris: UNESCO, International Institute for Educational Planning, 1977.

——. *Education and Employment: A Method for Local Policy Research.* Studies Series 71. Paris: UNESCO, Division of Educational Policy and Planning, 1979.

——. "Education in Latin America: An Empirical Approach." In *Viewpoints on Education and Social Change in Latin America.* Center for Latin American Studies. Occasional Publications no. 5. Lawrence: University of Kansas Press, 1965, pp. 41–54.

——, Henry Levin, et al. *Economía política del financiamiento educativo en países en vías de desarrollo.* Mexico City: Ediciones Gérnika, 1986.

Castillo, Isidro. *México: Sus revoluciones sociales y la educación.* Volumes 2 and 4. N.p.: Gobierno del Estado de Michoacán, 1976.

Castillo Miranda, Wilfrido. *Asi nació la carrera de administración de empresas.* Mexico City: Colegio de Licenciados en Administración de Empresas, 1970.

Castrejón Diez, Jaime. *La educación superior en ocho países de América Latina y el Caribe.* Mexico City: ANUIES, 1978.

——. *La educación superior en México.* Mexico City: Editorial Edicol, S.A., 1979.

—— y Marisol Pérez Lizaur. *Historia de las universidades estatales.* 2 vols. Mexico City: SEP, 1976.

Center for Latin American Studies. *Viewpoints on Education and Social Change in Latin America.* Occasional Publications No. 5. Lawrence: University of Kansas Press, 1965.

Centro de Investigación para el Desarrollo, A. C. (CIDAC). *Tecnología e industria en el futuro de México: Posibles vinculaciones estratégicas.* Mexico City: Editorial Diana, 1989.

Clark, Burton R., ed. *The Academic Profession: Nations, Disciplines, and Institutional Settings.* Berkeley and Los Angeles: University of California Press, 1987.

Cleaves, Peter S. *Las profesiones y el estado: El caso de México.* Mexico City: El Colegio de México, 1985.

——. *Professions and the State: The Mexican Case.* Tucson: University of Arizona Press, 1987.

Cline, Howard F. *Mexico: Revolution to Evolution, 1940–1960.* New York: Oxford University Press, 1963.

Cochrane, James D. "Mexico's New Científicos: The Díaz Ordaz Cabinet." *Interamerican Economic Affairs,* no. 21 (Summer, 1967), 61–72.

Cockcroft, James. *Intellectual Precursors of the Mexican Revolution, 1900–1913.* Austin: University of Texas Press, 1968.

Coleman, Kenneth M., and John Wanat. "On Measuring Presidential Ideology through Budgets: A Reappraisal of the Wilkie Approach." *Latin American Research Review,* 10, no. 1 (Spring, 1975), 77–88.

Comisión de Recursos Humanos del Sector Público del Gobierno Federal. *Censo de recursos humanos del sector público federal: Administración central 1975.* México, D. F.: Comisión de Recursos Humanos del Sector Público del Gobierno Federal, 1976.

——. *Administración decentralizada y de participación estatal mayoritaria 1975.* Mexico City: Comisión de Recursos Humanos del Sector Público del Gobierno Federal, 1976.

CONACYT. *La ciencia y la tecnología en el sector medicina y salud: Diagnóstico y política.* Mexico City: CONACYT, 1976.

——. *Programa nacional de ciencia y tecnología, 1978–1982.* México, D. F.: CONACYT, 1978.

Consejo Interamericano para Educación, Ciencia y Cultura (CIECC). "Exodo de profesionales y técnicos en los países latinoamericanos" *Revista del Centro de Estudios Educativos,* 2, no. 2 (1972), 61–83.

COPLAMAR. *Necesidades esenciales en México.* Mexico City: Siglo XXI, 1982, Vol. 2 (La Educación).

Correa, Hector, and Ana María Chávez. *Planificación de recursos hu-*

manos para la industria siderúrgica. Mexico City: n.p., 1976.

Covo, Milena. "Apuntes para el análisis de la trayectoría de una generación universitaria." In *Educación y realidad socioeconómica.* Mexico City: Centro de Estudios Educativos, 1979.

Cravalta Franco, María Aparecida, and Claudia de Moura Castro. "La contribución de educación técnica a la movilidad social." *Revista Latinoamericana de Estudios Educativos,* 11, no. 1, 1–42.

Cruz Valverde, Aurelio. "Economía y educación: Una panorama." *Revista de Educación Superior,* n.s. 30, 32.

Cypher, James M. *State and Capital in Mexico: Development Policy since 1940.* Boulder, CO: Westview Press, 1990.

Davis, Russell G. "The Manpower Requirements Approach to Educational Planning." In *Planning Education for Development: Volume I, Issues and Problems in the Planning of Education in Developing Countries, USAID/Harvard.* Ed. Russell G. Davis. Cambridge, MA: Center for Education and Development, Harvard University, 1980.

———.*Science, Engineering, and Technical Education in Mexico.* New York: Education and World Affairs, 1967.

———, ed. *Planning Education for Development: Volume I, Issues and Problems in the Planning of Education in Developing Countries.* Cambridge, MA: Center for Education and Development, Harvard University, 1980.

de Ibarrola, María. "El crecimiento de la escolaridad superior en México como expresión de los proyectos socioeducativos del estado y la burguesía." *Cuadernos de Investigación Educativa,* 9.

———. "Estudio de producción, mercado de trabajo, y escolaridad en México." *Cuadernos de Investigación Educativa* 14.

———. "La formación de profesores y la producción nacional." *Revista de Educación e Investigación Técnica,* no. 14 (Autumn, 1984), 22–31.

del Camino, Isidoro. "Gasto educativo nacional, desperdicio escolar y económico, pirámide escolar en México." *Revista del Centro de Estudios Educativos,* 1, no. 4 (1971), 1–34.

de Leonardo Ramírez, Patricia. "Los cuadros de la derecha." *El Cotidiano,* 24 (July–August, 1988), 89–94.

Derossi, Flavia. *The Mexican Entrepreneur.* Paris: Development Centre of the Organisation for Economic Co–operation and Development, 1971.

Dirección de Enfermería de la Secretaría de Salud y Asistencia. *Estudio de recursos de enfermería y obstétricia en México.* Mexico City: Dirección de Enfermería de la Secretaría de Salud y Asistencia, 1979.

Domínguez, Jorge I. *The Political Economy of Mexico: Challenges at Home and Abroad.* Beverly Hills: Sage, 1982.

Domínguez, Raúl. *El proyecto universitario del rector Barros Sierra (estudio histórico)*. Mexico City: UNAM, CESU (Centro de Estudios sobre la Universidad), 1986.

Dore, Ronald. *The Diploma Disease: Education, Qualification, and Development*. London: George Allen and Unwin, 1976.

ECLA. *Education, Human Resources, and Development in Latin America*. New York: United Nations, 1968.

"El progreso del país requiere que todos los técnicos tengan trabajo: Echeverría." *El Día*, July 23, 1971.

Espinosa, Evan D. "La explosión demográfica en México: Análisis y implicaciones educativas." *Revista de Educación Superior*, n.s. 25, 16–48.

Figueroa, Rodolfo. *Prioridades nacionales y reclutamiento de funcionarios públicos*. Mexico City: El Colegio de México, 1981.

Folger, John K., and Charles B. Nam. "Education of the American Population." In *Education and Jobs: The Great Training Robbery*. Ed. Ivar Berg. Boston: Beacon Press, 1971.

Foster, Edward, and Jack Rodgers. "Quality of Education and Student Earnings." *Higher Education*, no. 8 (1979), 21–37.

Fretz, Deirdre. "Wanted: Engineers." *Mexico Journal*, November 13, 1989, pp. 25–26.

Fuentes Molinar, Olac. *Educación y política en México*. Mexico City: Nueva Imagen, 1983.

———. "Universidad y democracia: La mirada hacia la izquierda." *Cuadernos Políticos*, 53 (January/April, 1981), 4–18.

Gallo, María. *Las políticas educativas en México como indicadores de una situación nacional (1958–1976)*. Mexico City: CIESAS (Centro de Investigación y Estudios Superiores en Antropología Social), 1987.

García Esquivel, Alfonso, et al. *Los recursos humanos en la fabricación de productos metálicos*. Mexico City: Servicio Nacional de Adiestramiento Rápido de la Mano de Obra en la Industria, 1976.

García Sancho, Francisco, and Leoncio Hernández. *Educación superior, ciencia y tecnología en México, 1945–1975: Un diagnóstico de la educación superior y de la investigación científica y tecnológica en México*. Mexico City: SEP, 1977.

García Sordo, Mario. "Desempleados o subempleados, más de 90 mil agrónomos." *El Financiero*, October 5, 1988, p. 39.

Garza, Graciela. *La titulación en la UNAM*. Mexico City: UNAM, CESU (Centro de Estudios sobre la Universidad), 1986.

Gil, Clark C. *Education in a Changing Mexico*. Washington, D.C.: Office of Education, U.S. Department of Health, Education, and Welfare, 1969.

Ginneken, Wouter van. *Socioeconomic Groups and Income Distribution in Mexico*. New York: St. Martin's Press, 1980.

Glade, William P., Jr., and Charles W. Anderson. *The Political Economy of Mexico*. Madison: University of Wisconsin Press, 1963.

——. "Revolution and Economic Development: A Mexican Reprise." In William P. Glade and Charles W. Anderson, *The Political Economy of Mexico*. Madison: University of Wisconsin Press, 1963, pp. 87–88.

Gleason Galicia, Rubén. *Las estadísticas y censos de México: Su organización y estado actual*. Mexico City: UNAM, IIS (Instituto de Investigaciones Sociales), 1968.

Goldblatt, Phyllis. "The Geography of Youth Employment and School Enrollment Rates in Mexico." In *Education and Development: Latin America and the Caribbean*. Ed. Thomas J. LaBelle. Los Angeles: UCLA Latin American Center, 1972.

Gómez Campo, Víctor Manuel. "Educación superior, mercado de trabajo, y práctica profesional: Un análisis comparativo de diversos estudios en México." *Revista de Educación Superior*, n.s. 45, 5–48.

——. "Relaciones entre educación y estructura económica: Dos grandes marcos de interpretación." *Revista de Educación Superior*, n.s. 41 (January–March, 1982), 5–43.

Gómez Junco, Horacio. "Presente y futuro de cinco innovaciones en el Tecnológica de Monterrey." *Revista de Educación Superior*, o.s. 4, no. 1 (1975), 32–46.

——. "Teaching and Research in the Social Sciences." *Voices of Mexico* (June–August, 1987), 20–22.

González Casanova, Pablo. *Democracia en México*. Mexico City: Ediciones Era, 1965.

——. "México: El ciclo de una revolución agraria," *Cuadernos Americanos*, 120, no. 1 (January–February, 1962).

Gortari Rabiela, Rebeca de. "Educación y conciencia nacional: Los ingenieros después de la revolución mexicana." *Revista Mexicana de Sociología*, 49, no. 3.

González Salazar, Gloria. *Subocupación y estructura de clases sociales en México*. Mexico City: UNAM, 1972.

Grayson, George. *The Politics of Mexican Oil*. Pittsburgh: University of Pittsburgh Press, 1980.

Greenberg, Martin H. *Bureaucracy and Development: A Mexican Case Study*. Lexington: D.C. Heath, 1970.

Gregory, Peter. *The Myth of Market Failure: Employment and the Labor Market in Mexico*. Baltimore: Johns Hopkins University Press, 1986.

Grindle, Merilee. "Power, Expertise and the 'Técnico': Suggestions from a Mexican Case Study." *Journal of Politics*, 39, no. 2 (May, 1977), 399–426.

Gruber, W. "Career Patterns of Mexican Political Elites." *Western Political Quarterly*, 24, no. 3 (September, 1971).

Guardarrama H., José de Jesús. "México necesita multiplicar 20 veces su número de ingenieros antes de 25 años." *El Financiero*, April 19, 1988, p. 53.

Guevara Niebla, Gilberto. *La democracia en la calle: Crónica del movimiento estudiantil mexicano*. Mexico City: Siglo XXI, 1988.

———, ed. *Las luchas estudiantiles en México*. 2 vols. Mexico City: Editorial Línea, 1983.

———. *La rosa de los cambios: Breve historia de la UNAM*. Mexico City: Cal y Arena, 1990.

Haber, Stephen H. *Industry and Underdevelopment: The Industrialization of Mexico, 1890-1940*. Stanford: Stanford University Press, 1989.

Hanson, James A. "Federal Expenditures and 'Personalism' in the Mexican 'Institutional' Revolution." In *Money and Politics in Latin America*. Ed. James W. Wilkie. Los Angeles: UCLA Latin American Center Publications, 1977.

Harbison, Frederick, and Charles A. Myers. *Education, Manpower, and Economic Growth: Strategies of Human Resource Development*. New York: McGraw–Hill, 1964.

———. *Manpower and Education: Country Studies in Economic Development*. New York: McGraw–Hill, 1965.

Harris, Rivera, and Yolanda Aguirre. *Características socioacadémicas de las escuelas de trabajo social en la república mexicana*. Mexico City: UNAM, 1984.

Heyduk, Daniel, ed. *Education and Work: A Symposium*. New York: Institute of International Education (IIE), Council on Higher Education in the American Republics (CHEAR), 1979.

Hinojosa, Oscar. "La universidad privada escala posiciones como proveedora de funcionarios." *Proceso*, March 31, 1986, pp. 6–11.

Hirsch Adler, Ana. "Panorama de la formación de profesores universitarios en México." *Revista de Educación Superior*, n.s. 46 (1983), 16–44.

Historia de las profesiones en México. Mexico City: El Colegio de México, 1982.

Huntington, Samuel P. "The Goals of Development." In *Understanding Political Development*. Eds. Samuel P. Huntington and Myron Weiner. Boston: Little, Brown and Company, 1987.

Ibarra, María Esther. "Decide la SEP que se encojan las universidades," *Proceso*, September 29, 1986, p. 1.

Institute of International Education (IIE). *Profile of Foreign Students in the United States*. New York: IIE, 1981.

————. *Profiles: Detailed Analyses of the Foreign Student Population 1983/84.* New York: IIE, 1985.

————. Council on Higher Education in the American Republics (CHEAR). *La agricultura y la universidad.* Buenos Aires: N.p., 1966.

Institutos Mexicanos de Educación Superior Privada (IMESP). *La educación privada en México, 1980–81: Su aportación al desarrollo de la nación (Anteproyecto).* [Mexico City: N.p., n.d. [1979].

Instituto Nacional de Estadística, Geografía, e Informática (INEGI). *Participación del sector público en el producto interno bruto de México, 1975-1983.* Mexico City: Secretaría de Programación y Presupuesto (SPP), 1984.

Instituto Tecnológico Regional de Ciudad Juárez. *Estudio de la demanda social de carreras profesionales de nivel técnico y de licenciatura.* Juárez: Instituto Tecnológico Regional de Ciudad Juárez, 1977.

"La investigación tecnológica, en crisis." *Unomásuno,* January 29, 1990, p. 3.

Jaffe, A. J. *People, Jobs, and Economic Development: A Case History of Puerto Rico Supplemented by Recent Mexican Experiences.* Glencoc, Il: The Free Press of Glencoe Illinois, 1959.

Jaksic, Iván. "The Politics of Higher Education in Latin America." *Latin American Research Review,* 20, no. 1 (1985), 209–221.

Jérez Jiménez, Cuauhtémoc. *Vasconcelos y la educación nacionalista.* Mexico City: SEP, 1986.

Jiménez Mier y Terán, Fernando. *El autoritarismo en el gobierno de la UNAM.* Mexico City: Foro Universitario, 1982.

Keesing, Donald, B. "Employment and Lack of Employment in Mexico, 1900–70." In *Quantitative Latin American Studies: Methods and findings.* Eds. James W. Wilkie and Kenneth Ruddle. Los Angeles: UCLA Latin American Center Publications, 1977.

————. "Structural Change Early in Development: Mexico's Changing Industrial and Occupational Structure from 1895 to 1950." *Journal of Economic History,* 29, no. 4 (December, 1969), 716–738.

Kelly, Guillermo. *Politics and Administration in Mexico: Recruitment and Promotion of the Politico–Administrative Class.* Technical Paper Series (33). Austin: Institute of Latin American Studies, University of Texas, 1981.

Kicza, John E. "Business and Society in Late Colonial Mexico City." Ph.D. Diss. University of California, Los Angeles, 1979.

————. *Colonial Entrepreneurs: Families and Business in Bourbon Mexico City.* Albuquerque: University of New Mexico Press, 1983.

King, Richard G., Alfonso Rangel Guerra, David Kline, and Noel F. McGinn. *Nueve universidades mexicanas: Un análisis de su crecimiento y desarrollo.* Mexico City: ANUIES, 1972.

King, Richard G., et al. *The Provincial Universities of Mexico: An Analysis of Growth and Development.* New York: Praeger, 1971.

Knight, Alan. *The Mexican Revolution. Vol. I: Porfirians, Liberals, and Peasants.* Cambridge: Cambridge University Press, 1986.

Krauze, Enrique. *Caudillos culturales en la revolución mexicana.* Mexico City: SEP; Siglo XXI Editores, 1985.

Labastida, Horacio. *Banco de datos censales para el desarrollo social.* Mexico City: UNAM, 1972.

LaBelle, Thomas J. *Nonformal Education and Social Change in Latin America.* Los Angeles: UCLA Latin American Center, University of California, Los Angeles, 1976.

Lajous, Alejandro. *Los orígenes del partido único en México.* Mexico City: El Colegio de México, 1981.

Lajous Vargas, Adrián. "Aspectos de la educación superior y el empleo de profesionistas en México 1959–1967." Licenciate Thesis, UNAM, Escuela Nacional de Economía, 1967.

Latapí, Pablo. *Análisis de un sexenio de educación en México, 1970–1976.* Mexico City: Editorial Nueva Imagen, 1980.

———. *Diagnóstico educativo nacional: Balanza y progreso escolar de México durante los últimos seis años.* Mexico City: Centro de Estudios Educativos, 1964.

———. *Mitos y verdades de la educación mexicana/1971–1972 (Una opinión independiente).* Mexico City: Centro de Estudios Educativos, 1973.

———. *Temas de la política educativa (1976–1978).* Mexico City: SEP, Fondo de Cultura Económica, 1982.

Leff, Nathaniel H. *The Brazilian Capital Goods Industry, 1929–1964.* Cambridge, MA: Harvard University Press, 1968.

León López, Enrique G. "La educación técnica superior." In *El perfil de México en 1980.* Mexico City: Siglo XXI Editores, 1970.

———. *La ingeniería en México.* Mexico City: SEP/Setentas, 1974.

Leonardo R., Patricia de. *La educación superior privada en México: Bosquejo histórico.* Mexico City: Editorial Línea, 1983.

Lerner, Victoria. *La educación socialista.* Mexico City: El Colegio de México, 1979.

Levy, Daniel C. *Higher Education and the State in Latin America: Private Challenges to Public Dominance.* Chicago: University of Chicago Press, 1986.

———. "Serving Private Enterprise and the State: A Comparison of Mexico's Private and Public Universities." Paper presented at XI Congreso Internacional de LASA (Mexico City, September 29–October 1, 1983) cited in José Angel Pescador and Carlos Alberto Torres, *Poder político y educación en México* (Mexico City: Unión Tipográfica Editorial Hispano Americano, 1985).

———. *University and Government in Mexico: Autonomy in an Authoritarian System.* New York: Praeger, 1980.

———. "University Autonomy versus Government Control: The Mexican Case." Ph.D. Diss. University of North Carolina, 1977.

Liebman, Arthur, Kenneth N. Walker, and Myron Glazer. *Latin American University Students: A Six Nation Study.* Cambridge, MA: Harvard University Press, 1972.

Lipset, Martin. "Values, Education, and Entrepreneurship." In *Elites in Latin America.* Eds. Martin Lipset and Aldo Solari. New York: Oxford University Press, 1967.

Llinas Zárate, Isabel. "La universidad ha cumplido con creces después de la revolución: Luis E. Todd," *Unomásuno,* January 28, 1990, p. 2.

Lomnitz, Larissa. "Horizontal and Vertical Relations and the Social Structure of Urban Mexico." *Latin American Research Review,* 17, no. 2 (1982), 51–74.

———, Leticia Mayer, and Martha W. Rees. "Recruiting Technical Elites: Mexico's Veterinarians." *Human Organization,* 42, no. 1 (Spring, 1983), 23–29.

Looney, Robert E. *Economic Policymaking in Mexico: Factors Underlying the 1982 Crisis.* Durham, NC: Duke University Press, 1985.

———. *Mexico's Economy: A Policy Analysis with Forecasts to 1990.* Boulder, CO: Westview Press, 1978.

Lorentzen, Anne. *Capital Goods and Technological Development in Mexico.* Copenhagen: Centre for Development Research, 1986.

Lorey, David E. "The Development of Engineering Expertise for Economic and Social Modernization in Mexico since 1929." In *Society and Economy in Mexico.* Ed. James W. Wilkie. Los Angeles: UCLA Latin American Center Publications, 1989.

———. "Higher Education in Mexico: The Problems of Quality and Employment." In *Reciprocal Images: Education in U.S.–Mexican Relations.* Mexico City: ANUIES, 1990.

———. "Mexican Professional Education in the United States and the Myth of 'Brain Drain'," *Ensayos* (Revista del Departamento de Relaciones Internacionales, Universidad de las Américas-Puebla), 4, no. 9 (1988), 56-59.

———. "Professional Expertise and Mexican Modernization: Sources, Methods, and Preliminary Findings." In *Statistical Abstract of Latin America,* vol. 26, pp. 899-912.

———. *The Rise of the Professions in Twentieth-Century Mexico: University Graduates and Occupational Change since 1929.* Los Angeles: UCLA Latin American Center Publications, 1992.

———. *United States-Mexico Border Statistics since 1900.* Los Angeles: UCLA Latin American Center Publications, 1990.

——— and Aída Mostkoff, "Mexico's 'Lost Decade': Evidence on Class

Structure and Professional Employment from the 1990 Census." *Statistical Abstract of Latin America*, 30, part 2.

Mabry, Donald J. *The Mexican University and the State: Student Conflicts, 1910–1971.* College Station: Texas A & M Press, 1982.

———. "Changing Models of Mexican Politics, a Review Essay." *The New Scholar*, 5, no. 1 (1975), 31–37.

———, and Roderic A. Camp. "Mexican Political Elites 1935–1973: A Comparative Study." *The Americas*, no. 31 (April, 1975), 456–467.

Malo, Salvador, Jonathan Garst, and Graciela Garza. *El egresado del postgrado de la UNAM. Mexico City: UNAM*, 1981.

———, R. G. Davis, and Richard King. *The Technology of Instruction in Mexican Universities.* New York: Education and World Affairs, 1968.

Marquis, Carlos. "Sobre los egresados de la UAM–Azcapotzalco." *Revista Latinoamericana de Estudios Educativos*, 14, no. 4 (1984), 87–108.

Martínez Della Rocca, Salvador. *Estado y universidad en México 1920–1968: Historia de los movimientos estudiantiles en la UNAM.* Mexico City: Joan Boldó i Climent Editores, 1986.

———, and Imano Ordorika Sacristán. "*UNAM*: Espejo del mejor México posible: La universidad en el contexto educativo nacional." Manuscript of November 1991.

McGinn, Noel F., and Susan L. Street. *Higher Education Policies in Mexico.* Austin: Institute of Latin American Studies, University of Texas at Austin, 1980.

Medin, Tzvi. "La mexicanidad política y filosófica en el sexenio de Miguel Alemán, 1946–1952." *Estudios Interdisciplinarios de América Latina y el Caribe*, 1, no. 1 (January-June, 1990), 5–22.

Medina, Alberto Hernández, and Alfredo Rentería Agraz. "El perfil de personal docente en las universidades de provincia." *Revista Latinoamericana de Estudios Educativos*, 14, no. 3, 13–65.

Medina Lara, Beatriz, et al. *Oferta y demanda de profesionales, 1980–82.* Mérida: Centro de Desarrollo Universitario, Universidad Autónoma de Yucatán, 1983.

Mendieta y Nuñez, Lucio, and José Gómez Robledo. *Problemas de la universidad.* Mexico City: UNAM, 1948.

Mendoza Avila, Eusebio. *La educación tecnológica en México.* Mexico City: IPN, 1980.

Mendoza Rojas, Javier. "Política del estado hacia la educación superior, 1983–1988." *Pensamiento Universitario*, 68 (Nueva Epoca).

Menéndez Guzmán, Alberto. *Tendencias del presupuesto universitario (1967–1976).* Mexico City: UNAM, Dirección General de Presupuesto por Programación, n.d.

Meneses, Ernesto. *La Iberoamericana en el contexto de la educación superior contemporánea*. Mexico City: Universidad Iberoamericana, 1979.

"Mexican Higher Education Degrees." Translation of article from *La Jornada*, October 6, 1989, in *U.S.-Mexico Report*, 8, no. 11 (November, 1989), p. 12.

"México necesita 300 mil profesionistas por año, para asegurar su crecimiento," *Ocho Columnas* (Guadalajara, Jalisco), October 15, 1989.

Meyer, Lorenzo, Rafael Segovia, and Alejandra Lajous. *Los inicios de la institucionalización: La política del maximato*. México D.F.: El Colegio de México, 1978.

Moffett, Matt. "Brain Drain Slows Mexico's Development: Researchers, Professionals, Skilled Workers Are Lured Abroad." *Wall Street Journal*, May 5, 1989, p. A1.

Mohar B., Oscar. *Crisis y contradicciones en la educación técnica de México*. Mexico City: Editorial Gaceta, 1984.

Montavon, Paul. "Some Questions on Education and Economic Development." In *Viewpoints on Education and Social Change in Latin America*. Occasional Publications no. 5. Lawrence: University of Kansas Press, 1965.

Morales–Gómez, Daniel, and Carlos Alberto Torres. *The State, Corporatist Politics, and Educational Policy Making in Mexico*. New York: Praeger, 1990.

Mosk, Sanford. *Industrial Revolution in Mexico*. Berkeley and Los Angeles: University of California Press, 1950.

———. Muñoz Izquierdo, Carlos "El desempleo en México: Características generales." *El Trimestre Económica*, 62, no. 167 (1975).

———. "Evaluación del desarrollo educativo en México (1958–1970) y factores que lo han determinado." *Revista del Centro de Estudios Educativos*, 3, no. 3 (1973).

———."Observaciones críticas a una previsión de recursos humanos basada en el enfoque de Herbert Parnes." *Revista de Educación e Investigación Técnica*, no. 10 (1981), 66–73.

———, and José Lobo. "Expansión escolar, mercado de trabajo, y distribución de ingreso en México: Un análisis longitudinal, 1960–1970." *Revista del Centro de Estudios Educativos*, 4, no. 1 (1974), 9–30.

———, José Lobo, Alberto Hernández Medina, and Pedro Gerardo Rodríguez. "Educación y mercado de trabajo." *Revista del Centro de Estudios Educativos*, 8, no. 2 (1978), 1–90.

———, and Pedro Gerardo Rodríguez. *Costos, financiamiento y eficiencia de la educación formal en México*. Mexico City: Centro de Estudios Educativos, 1977.

———. "La eseñanza técnica: ¿Canal de movilidad social para los trabajadores?" *Revista de Educación e Investigación Técnica*, no. 6–7 (double issue) (July–August–September, 1980), 70–86.

Myers, Charles Nash. *Education and National Development.* Princeton: Industrial Relations Section, Princeton University, 1965.

———. *U.S. University Activity Abroad: The Mexican Case.* New York: Education and World Affairs, 1968.

Myers, Charles Nash. "Proyección de la demanda de médicos en México: 1965–1980." *Revista de Educación Superior*, 1, no. 3 (1972), 77–103.

———. *Education and Emigration: Study Abroad and the Migration of Human Resources.* New York: David McKay, 1972.

Nava Díaz, Eduardo. "Perspectiva de complemento al financiamiento del sector público en materia de educación superior: El caso de México, 1967–1980." *Revista de Educación Superior*, n.s. 17 (1976), 48–86.

Oliver H., Rogelio. *Elección de carrera.* Mexico City: Editorial LIMUSA, 1981.

Organization for Economic Cooperation and Development (OECD). *Industry and University.* Paris: OECD, 1984.

Osborn, Thomas Noel. *Higher Education in Mexico: History, Growth, and Problems in a Dichotomized Industry.* El Paso: Texas Western Press, 1976.

———. "A Survey of Developments and Current Trends in Higher Education in Mexico." Boulder: University of Colorado International Economic Studies Center, n.d.

Oxenham, John. "The University and High-Level Manpower." *Higher Education*, no. 9 (1980), 643–655.

Padilla, Jorge Díaz. "El impacto de los planes de desarrollo económico en la demanda de servicios de ingenieros industriales." *Revista de Educación e Investigación Técnica*, no. 4 (January–February–March, 1980), 60–68.

Padua, Jorge. *Educación, industrialización y progreso técnico en México.* Mexico City: El Colegio de México, 1984.

———. "Movilidad social y universidad." In *La crisis de la educación superior en México.* Ed. Gilberto Guevara Niebla. Mexico City: Nueva Imagen, 1981.

Pan American Health Organization. *Migration of Health Personnel, Scientists, and Engineers from Latin America.* Washington, D. C.: World Health Organization, 1966.

Pantoja Morán, David. *Notas y reflexiones acerca de la historia del bachillerato.* Mexico City: Colegio de Ciencias y Humanidades, UNAM, 1983.

Pellicer de Brody, Olga, and Esteban L. Mancilla. *El entendimiento con los Estados Unidos y la gestacíon del desarrollo estabilizador.* Mexico City: El Colegio de México, 1978.

Peña de la Mora, Eduardo. "Evaluación de las actitudes de compromiso social en institutos de educación técnica superior." *Revista de Educación e Investigación Técnica,* no. 13 (March, 1982), 9–17.

Pérez, Raúl, et al. *Características de la ocupación de los profesionales en las empresas de la península de Yucatán.* N.p. [Mérida]: Centro de Desarrollo Universitario, Universidad Autónoma de Yucatán, 1983.

Pérez Lizaur, Marisal. *Historia de las universidades estatales,* 2 vols. Mexico City: SEP, 1976.

Pérez Roche, Manuel. "Algunos aspectos de la restructuración académica de la enseñanza superior: Cursos semestrales, salidas laterales, y sistemas de titulación." *Revista de Educación Superior,* 1, no. 4 (1972), 9–16.

Pescador Osuna, José Angel. "El balance de la educación superior en el sexenio 1976–1982." In UAP, *Perspectivas de la educación superior en México.* Puebla: UAP, 1984.

———, and Carlos Alberto Torres. "Educación superior, cultural, política y socialización del personal del estado: El papel político contradictorio de la universidad pública y privada en México." In *Poder político y educación en México.* Ed. José Angel Pescador and Carlos Alberto Torres. Mexico City: Unión Tipográfica Editorial Hispano Americano, 1985.

———, and Carlos Alberto Torres. *Poder político y educación en México.* Mexico City: Unión Tipográfica Editorial Hispano Americana, 1985.

Philip, George. *The Mexican Economy.* New York: Routledge, 1988.

———. *Oil and Politics in Latin America.* Cambridge: Cambridge University Press, 1982.

———. "Mexican Politics Under Stress: Austerity and After." In *Politics in Mexico.* Ed. George Philip. London: Croom Helm, 1985.

———. "Public Enterprise in Mexico." In *Public Enterprise and the Development World.* Ed. V. V. Ramanadham. London and Sydney: Croom Helm, 1984.

Portas Cabrera, Eduardo. "La demanda, el personal docente, y el financiamiento de la educación superior en México." Social Service Project for ANUIES, n.d.

Potash, Robert A. *Mexican Government and Industrial Development in the Early Republic: The Banco de Avío.* Amherst: University of Massachusetts Press, 1983.

Programa de Seguimiento de Egresados UANL. *Estudio sobre el egresado al titularse en la Universidad Autónoma de Nuevo León 1980/81.* Monterrey: N.p. [UANL], n.d.[1981].

Proyecto para la Planeación de Recursos Humanos. *La estructura ocupacional de México 1930–80.* Mexico City: Comisión Consultiva del Empleo y la Productividad, Subcomisión de Recursos Humanos, 1982.

———. *La estructura ocupacional de México 1930–80: Anexo metodológico, anexo estadístico.* Mexico City: Comisión Consultiva del Empleo y la Productividad, Subcomisión de Recursos Humanos, 1982.

———. *Necesidades de recursos humanos de México, 1980–2000.* Mexico City: Comisión Consultiva del Empleo y la Productividad, Subcomisión de Recursos Humanas, n.d.

Prysor–Jones, Susanne. "Education and Equality in Developing Countries." In *Planning Education for Development: Volume I, Issues and Problems in the Planning of Education in Developing Countries, USAID/Harvard.* Ed. Russell G. Davis. Cambridge, MA: Center for Education and Development, Harvard University, 1980.

Psacharopoulos, George, and Bikas C. Sanyal. *Higher Education and Employment: The IIEP Experience in Five Less Developed Countries.* Paris: UNESCO, 1981.

Quintero H., José Luis. "Metas de igualdad y efectos de subsidio de la educación superior mexicana." *Revista del Centro de Estudios Educativos,* 8, no. 3 (1978), 59–92.

Quirk, Robert E. *Mexico.* Englewood Cliffs: Prentice-Hall, 1971.

Ramírez, Celia. *La formación profesional en la UNAM.* Pensamiento Universitario 67 (Nueva Epoca). Mexico City: Centro de Estudios sobre la Universidad, 1986.

Ramírez, Miguel D. *Mexico's Economic Crisis.* New York: Praeger, 1989.

Ramírez, Ramón. *El movimiento estudiantíl de México: Julio–diciembre 1968.* Mexico City: Ediciones Era, 1969.

Randall, Laura. *The Political Economy of Mexican Oil.* New York: Praeger Press, 1989.

Rangel Guerra, Alfonso. "La decentralización de la educación superior." *Revista de Educación Superior,* n.s. 19 (1976), 42–48.

———. *La educación superior en México.* Mexico City: El Colegio de México, 1979.

———. "Higher Education and Employment." In *Education and Work: A Symposium.* Ed. Daniel Heyduk. New York: Institute of International Education (IIE), Council on Higher Education in the American Republics (CHEAR), 1979.

———. "Objetivos de la enseñanza superior frente a los requerimientos del desarrollo y el avance técnico." *Revista de Educación Superior,* o.s. 1, no. 1 (1972), 33–38.

———. *Systems of Higher Education: Mexico.* New York: International Council for Educational Development, 1978.

————, and Alma Chapoy Bonifaz. *Estructura de la Universidad Nacional Autónoma de México: Ensayo socioeconómico.* México, D. F.: Fondo de Cultura Popular, 1970.

"Reflecciones sobre planeación, 1917–1985." In *Antología de la planeación en México (1917–1985).* Vol. 1. Mexico City: Fondo de Cultura Económica, 1985.

Requelme, Marcial Antonio, et al. "Educación y empleo en el municipio de Naucalpan, Estado de México: Notas e indicadores para su estudio." *Revista de Educación e Investigación Técnica,* no. 9 (1981), 43–70.

Reynolds, Clark. *The Mexican Economy: Twentieth-Century Structure and Growth.* New Haven and London: Yale University Press, 1970.

Reynolds, Clark W., and Blanca M. de Petricioli. *The Teaching of Economics in Mexico.* New York: Education and World Affairs, 1967.

Reyes Heroles González Garza, Jesús. *Política macroeconómica y bienestar en México.* Mexico City: Fondo de Cultura Económica, 1983.

Ribeiro, Darcy. "Universities and Social Development." In *Elites in Latin America.* Ed. Martin Lipset and Aldo Solari. New York: Oxford University Press, 1967.

Rice, Jaqueline Ann. "The Porfirian Political Elite: Life Patterns of the Delegates to the 1892 Unión Liberal Convention." Ph.D. Diss. University of California, Los Angeles, 1979.

Robles, Martha. *Educación y sociedad en la historia de México.* Mexico City: Siglo XXI Editores, 1977.

Ríos Ierrusca, Herculano. "El análisis de los recursos humanos en la medicina." *Revista de Educación Superior,* no. 6 (1980), 67–82.

Rivero, Martha. "La política económica durante la guerra." In *Entre la guerra y la estabilidad política: El México de los 40.* Ed. Rafael Loyola. Mexico City: Grijalbo, 1990.

Rodríguez, Valdemar. "National University of Mexico: Rebirth and Role of the Universitarios (1910–1957)." Ph.D. Diss. University of Texas at Austin, 1958.

Ruiz Massieu, Mario. *El cambio en la universidad.* Mexico City: UNAM, 1987.

Romero Bueno, Marcel, Manuel García Macías, and Francisco Reyes Araneo. "Historia de la educación secundaria técnica en México." *Revista de Educación e Investigación Técnica,* no. 12 (1982), 7–12.

Safford, Frank. "Politics, Ideology, and Society." In *Spanish America After Independence.* Ed. Leslie Bethell. Cambridge: Cambridge University Press, 1987.

Samaniego, Norma. "El desafío del empleo ante la modernización." In *Los profesionistas mexicanos y los desafíos de la modernidad.* Mexico City: Editorial Diana, 1989.

Sánchez, George. *Mexico: A Revolution by Education.* New York: Viking Press, 1936.

Schiefelbein, Ernesto. "Un modelo de simulación del sistema educativo mexicano." *Revista del Centro de Estudios Educativos*, 1, no. 4 (1971).

Schmelkes de Valle, Corina. "¿Por qué no se titulan graduados en México: Una investigación sobre pasantes como profesionales. Alternativas y recomendaciones para su titulación." *Revista de Educación e Investigación Técnica*, no. 10 (1981), 45–65.

———, et al. "La participación de la comunidad en el gasto educativo: Conclusiones de 24 casos de estudio en México." *Revista Latinoamericana de Estudios Educativos*, 13, no. 1, 9–47.

Schultz, Theodore. *The Economic Value of Education.* New York: Columbia University Press, 1963.

Schumacher, August. *Agricultural Development and Rural Employment: A Mexican Dilemma.* La Jolla: Program in United States–Mexican Studies, University of California, San Diego, 1981.

Scott, Robert E. "The Government Bureaucrat and Political Change in Latin America." *Journal of International Affairs*, no. 20 (1966), 294–95.

Secretaría de Educación Pública (SEP). *Aportaciones al estudio de los problemas de la educación.* Mexico City: N.p., n.d.

———. *Información profesional y subprofesional de México.* Mexico City: SEP, Dirección General de Enseñanza Superior e Investigación Científica, 1958.

———. *Manual de estadísticas básicas: IV, sector educativo.* Mexico City: SEP, n.d.[1979].

———. *Información profesional y subprofesional de México.* Mexico City: SEP, 1958.

———. Dirección General de Profesiones (DGP). *Análisis del mercado nacional de profesionistas y técnicos: Oferta 1967–1978, demanda 1967–1978, y proyecciones a 1990.* Mexico City: SEP, 1982.

Secretaría de Programación y Presupuesto (SPP). *Antología de la planeación en México (1917–1985).* Mexico City: Fondo de Cultura Económica, 1985.

"El sector educativo debe preparar cuadros técnicos acorde con las necesidades del país: CANACINTRA." *Unomásuno*, June 26, 1987, p. 14.

Shearer, J. C. *High–Level Manpower in Overseas Subsidiaries: Experience in Brazil and Mexico.* Princeton: Industrial Relations Section, Princeton University, 1960.

Silva Herzog, Jesús. *Una historia de la Universidad de México y sus problemas.* Mexico City: Siglo XXI Editores, 1986.

Skidmore, Thomas E., and Peter H. Smith. "Notes on Quantitative History: Federal Expenditure and Social Change in Mexico since 1910." *Latin American Research Review*, 5, no. 1 (Spring, 1970), 71–85.

Smith, Peter H. *Labyrinths of Power: Political Recruitment in Twentieth-Century Mexico*. Princeton: Princeton University Press, 1979.

———. "La movilidad política en el México contemporáneo." *Foro Internacional*, 15, no. 3 (1975), 399–427.

Snodgrass, Donald R. "The Distribution of Schooling and the Distribution of Income." In *Planning Education for Development: Volume I, Issues and Problems in the Planning of Education in Developing Countries, USAID/Harvard*. Ed. Russell G. Davis. Cambridge, MA: Center for Education and Development, Harvard University, 1980.

Solana, Fernando, et al. *Historia de la educación pública en México*. Mexico City: SEP and Fondo de Cultura Económica, 1981.

Solari, Aldo. "Secondary Education and the Development of Elites." In *Elites in Latin America*. Ed. Martin Lipset and Aldo Solari. New York: Oxford University Press, 1967.

Solís M., Leopoldo. *Controversias sobre el crecimiento y la distribución*. Mexico City: Fondo de Cultura Económica, 1972.

———. *La realidad económica mexicana: Retrovisión y perspectivas*. Mexico City: Siglo XXI, 1987.

Strassmann, Paul W. *Technological Change and Economic Development: The Manufacturing Experience in Mexico and Puerto Rico*. Ithaca, NY: Cornell University Press, 1968.

Stern, Claudio, and Joseph A. Kahl. "Stratification since the Revolution." In *Comparative Perspectives on Stratification: Mexico, Great Britain, and Japan*. Ed. Joseph A. Kahl. Boston: Little, Brown, and Company, 1968.

Tamayo, Jorge, ed. *Ley orgánica de la instrucción pública en el Distrito Federal de 1867*. Mexico City: UNAM, 1967.

Tannenbaum, Frank. *Mexico: The Struggle for Peace and Bread*. Englewood Cliffs: Prentice-Hall, 1950.

Thomas, Brinley. *Migration and Urban Development: A Reappraisal of British and American Long Cycles*. London: Methuen and Company, 1972.

Trujillo Cedillo, José Manuel. "Educación y capital humano." *Revista de Educación e Investigación Técnica*, no. 14 (Autumn, 1984), 32–57.

UAP. *Perspectivas de la educación superior en México*. Puebla: UAP, 1984.

UANL. *La demanda de profesionistas en el estado de Nuevo León*. Monterrey: UANL, n.d. [1977].

UANL and Cámera de la Industria de Transformación de Nuevo León. *La demanda de técnicos y profesionistas en el estado de Nuevo León*. Monterrey: UANL, 1981.

UNAM. *Bibliografía sobre educación superior en América Latina.* Mexico City: UNAM, 1983.

——. *Educación medio superior.* Mexico City: UNAM–SEP, 1984.

——. *Educación superior.* Mexico City: UNAM, 1983.

——. *Evaluación y marco de referencia para los cambios académicos administrativos.* Mexico City: UNAM, 1984.

——. *Fortaleza y debilidad de la UNAM: Respuesta de la comunidad universitaria: Propuestas y alternativa.* Suplemento Extraordinario No. 16. Ciudad Universitaria: UNAM, 1986.

——. *Modificaciones académicas en la Universidad Nacional Autónoma de México.* Mexico City: UNAM, 1986.

——. Instituto de Investigaciones Sociales (IIS). *Historia estadística de la universidad (1910–1967).* Mexico City: UNAM, 1968.

——. FCPS. *La questión de registro de los títulos y de las cédulas profesionales.* México, D. F.: UNAM, 1968.

——. Facultad de Ingeniería. *Visión histórica del posgrado en la facultad de ingeniería.* Mexico City: UNAM, 1984.

UNESCO. *Higher Education: International Trends, 1960–70.* New York: UNESCO, 1975.

——. *New Trends and New Responsibilities for Universities in Latin America.* Paris: UNESCO, 1980.

Urquidi, Víctor. "Technology Transfer between Mexico and the United States: Past Experience and Future Prospects." *Estudios Mexicanos,* 2, no. 2 (Summer, 1986), 179–193.

——, and Adrián Lajous Vargas. *Educación superior, ciencia y tecnología en el desarrollo económico de México.* Mexico City: El Colegio de México, 1967.

van Genneken, Wouter. *Socioeconomic Groups and Income Distribution in Mexico: A Study Prepared for the ILO World Employment Programme.* New York: St. Martin's Press, 1980.

Vaughan, Mary Kay. *The State, Education, and Social Class in Mexico, 1880–1928.* DeKalb: Northern Illinois University Press, 1982.

Vernon, Raymond. *The Dilemma of Mexico's Development: The Roles of the Private and Public Sectors.* Cambridge, MA: Harvard University Press, 1963.

——, ed. *Public Policy and Private Enterprise in Mexico.* Cambridge, MA: Harvard University Press, 1964.

Vielle, Jean–Pierre. "Planeación y reforma de la educación superior en México, 1970–1976." *Revista del Centro de Estudios Educativos,* 6, no. 4 (1976), 9–31.

Villa, Kitty. *Mexico: A Study of the Educational System of Mexico and a Guide to the Academic Placement of Students in Educational Institutions in the United States.* New York: World Education

Series, American Association of College Registrars and Admissions Officers, 1982.

Villagómez, Rafael, and Herculano Ríos. "Recursos humanos para la industria siderúrgica." *Revista de Educación Superior*, n.s. 18 (1976), 3–26.

Villareal, René. "El desarrollo industrial de México: Una perspectiva histórica." In *México: 75 años de revolución. Desarrollo económico I*. Mexico City: Fondo de Cultura Económica, 1988.

Villaseñor García, Guillermo. *Estado y universidad, 1976–1982*. Mexico City: UAM, 1988.

Villegas, Abelardo. *Positivismo y porfirismo*. Mexico City: SEP, 1972.

Waggoner, Barbara Ashton. "Latin American Universities in Transition." In *Viewpoints on Education and Social Change in Latin America*. Center for Latin American Studies. Occasional Publications no. 5. Lawrence: University of Kansas Press, 1965.

Wences Reza, Rosalío. *La universidad en la historia de México*. Mexico City: Editorial Línea, 1984.

Wichtrich, A. R. "Manpower Planning: A Business Perspective." In *Education and Work: A Symposium*. Ed. Daniel Heyduk. New York: Institute of International Education (IIE), Council on Higher Education in the American Republics (CHEAR), 1979.

Wilkie, James W. "From Economic Growth to Economic Stagnation in Mexico." In *Statistical Abstract of Latin America*, vol. 27, pp. 913–936.

———.*The Mexican Revolution: Federal Expendtiure and Social Change*. Berkeley and Los Angeles: University of California Press, 1967.

———. *La revolución mexicana: Gasto federal y cambio social, 1910–1970*. Mexico City: Fondo de Cultura Económica, 1978.

———. "The Six Ideological Phases of Mexico's 'Permanent Revolution' since 1910." In *Society and Economy in Mexico*. Ed. James W. Wilkie. Los Angeles: UCLA Latin American Center Publications, 1990.

Witker, Jorge V. *Universidad y dependencia científica y tecnológica en América Latina*. Mexico City: UNAM, 1979.

Zermeño, Sergio. *México: Una democracia utópica. El movimiento estudiantil del 68*. Mexico City: Siglo XXI Editores, 1985.

Index

In this index an "f" after a number indicates a separate reference on the next page, and an "ff" indicates separates references on the next two pages. A continuous discussion over two or more pages is indicated by a span of page numbers, e.g., "pp. 57–58." *Passim* is used for a cluster of references in close but not consecutive sequence.

Universidad Autónoma de Guadalajara (UAG), 116, 122, 130, 132

Universidad Autónoma de Puebla (UAP), 117, 131

Universidad Autónoma de Nuevo León (UANL), 79, 81, 85, 117, 133, 177

Universidad Autónoma Metropolitana (UAM), 34, 36, 116, 117, 129, 133

University City, 31

University crisis, 11, 40, 74, 107, 119, 136, 162, 166, 178

University politics, 176–77

University reform, 35, 173

Vasconcelos, José, 27–28

Wages of professionals, 81, 90

Women professionals, 150–56, 198

World War II, 4, 101

Yucatán peninsula, 83

Library of Congress Cataloging-in-Publication Data

Lorey, David E.
    The university system and economic development in Mexico since 1929 / David E. Lorey.
        p.   cm.
Includes bibliographical references and index.
ISBN 0-8047-2125-4
    1. Education, Higher—Mexico—History—20th century.
2. Education, Higher—Economic aspects—Mexico.   3. Economic development—Effect of education on.   4. Social mobility—Mexico.
5. College graduates—Mexico.   6. Educational surveys—Mexico.
I. Title.
LA427.L67   1993
378.72'09'043—dc20
93-20289   CIP

⊗This book is printed on acid-free paper.